Wiltshire Records Society

(formerly the Records Branch of the Wiltshire Archaeological and Natural History Society)

VOLUME XXV

FOR THE YEAR 1969

Impression of 400 copies

ABSTRACTS OF WILTSHIRE INCLOSURE AWARDS AND AGREEMENTS

EDITED BY

R. E. SANDELL

DEVIZES
1971

SBN: 901333 02 6

Set in Times New Roman 10/11 pt.

PRINTED IN GREAT BRITAIN BY
THE GLEVUM PRESS LTD.,
GLOUCESTER

CONTENTS

PREFACE

The idea of publishing abstracts of Wiltshire inclosure awards evolved in 1967 when Mr. Sandell was using the awards to compile information for the County Council in connexion with the registration of commons. The awards contain a great amount of varied material for the history and topography of Wiltshire, and it is thought that their publication in digested form will be useful for many sorts of historical inquiry. Most of the awards are in the custody of the Wiltshire County Council, to which the Society expresses its gratitude for help in the preparation of this volume—apart from its generous support of the Society year by year—and for permission to publish the documents. In the same way the Society thanks the owners of other Wiltshire documents not in the Wiltshire Record Office, namely the late Earl of Pembroke, Mr. Ambrose Hussey-Freke, the Gloucestershire County Council, the Somerset County Council, and the Mayor and Corporation of the City of New Sarum.

Mr. Sandell has asked me on his behalf to express his indebtedness and gratitude, to which are added those of the Society, to the County Archivist (Mr. M. G. Rathbone) and his staff for their help in providing access to the awards, to Mr. and Mrs. R. W. Willoughby for making the index, and to Mr. D. J. Bonney for computing the acreages of parishes for which figures were not otherwise available.

The Society is indebted to Mr. Sandell not only for his labour in editing the volume but also for his generosity in meeting the cost of producing the map.

November 1970 CHRISTOPHER ELRINGTON

ABBREVIATIONS

D.N.B.	*Dictionary of National Biography*
O.E.D.	*Oxford English Dictionary*
V.C.H.	*Victoria County History*
W.A.M.	*Wiltshire Archaeological Magazine*
W.R.O.	Wiltshire Record Office

INTRODUCTION

Inclosure is the process by which land that has formerly been owned and exploited collectively is divided into separate parcels, each owner exchanging his share of the common rights over the wider area for exclusive rights in part of it. It is not clear how far, in England, arable land was ever tilled, sown, or harvested in common. What was characteristic of a large part of England was the grazing in common, first, of land that for part of the year was owned, cultivated, and harvested (either of an arable crop or of hay) by individual owners and occupiers in severalty, and, secondly, of land that was essentially pasture land. The first sort of land is characteristically known as open and common fields and common meadow, the second as commons and wastes, more specifically and variously described as, for example, greens, pastures, leasows, marshes, moors, and downs.

The commoners' rights were not necessarily confined to grazing, and often included the right to collect fuel. It is perhaps necessary to emphasize that rights of common, of the sort referred to here, were not common to all, but were the property of a restricted and more or less precisely defined group of commoners: on cultivated land the 'common'—the right to pasture beasts in common, or 'common of pasture'—usually belonged to the owners and occupiers of land in the village or manor, while on uncultivated land in addition to those owners and occupiers the commoners usually included also the occupiers of a particular class of dwelling.

An essential physical feature of land that was subject to rights of common was that during the period of the year when it was commonable it should be undivided by fences, so that the grazing animals could wander over it unrestricted. Equally, so long as there were animals at large, it was necessary, if they were to be excluded from a piece of land in fact as well as in law, to surround the land with a fence. Although in a literal sense it was possible for land that was commonable to be inclosed by a fence and for land that lay open to be subject to no right of common, the extinction of common rights and the fencing of the land on which the rights were extinguished were normally so inextricably part of the same process that the word inclosure is taken to mean both the legal act of extinction and the practical act of fencing.

HISTORICAL AND LEGISLATIVE BACKGROUND

In that sense, inclosure in England presumably started early, and there is some documentary evidence of it, in the form of agreements between the parties concerned, as early as the 13th century. In the early 16th century in England as a whole the documentary evidence of inclosure becomes more plentiful as the result of the Crown's attempt to control inclosure by major landowners without the agreement of their tenants: the Crown was concerned to prevent the depopulation of the countryside, which was thought to be the direct result of inclosure for the sake of converting arable farms into sheep-runs. It is reasonable to assume that inclosure by private agreement continued at the same time, albeit less well documented. Some agreements took the form of a number of separate conveyances, by each of which one party to the agreement made over to another his rights of common in the land which was to become the exclusive property of the second party. From the early 17th century fuller records of inclosure by agreement become more frequent, partly because of better record keeping and partly because it became the practice to draw up a comprehensive agreement. An example of such an agreement in Wiltshire is that for Hannington in 1632, the earliest of the documents printed in abstract below **(101).**

The desire to give agreements greater authority led to the enrolment of some of them among the records of the central courts of justice, in the form of judgements in cases brought collusively before the courts. The same desire may have motivated the introduction of inclosure by Act of Parliament, which also had the advantage, for those who desired inclosure, of making it possible to constrain a minority of opponents. The first of all such Acts was in 1606; its successors were relatively few until the sixth decade of the 18th century.[1] Early Acts were various in form, some of them confirming agreements that were made before they were passed, but what became normal was for an Act to appoint inclosure commissioners who were authorized to make an award in accordance with the terms set out in the Act. The terms also varied considerably from one Act to another, though they usually provided for the enrolment of the award by the Clerk of the Peace.

Because each Act was independent and self-sufficient, the work in preparing it and securing its acceptance was long, the costs were high, and the results were not always predictable. After many years of agitation (some writers say 140) for legislation to reduce the costs, the Inclosure (Consolidation) Act, 1801 (41 G. III c.109) was passed. It was a 'Clauses Act' and was cited in almost every subsequent award, although commissioners covered themselves by adopting 'such provisions as are not repugnant'. The Act specified the duties of commissioners and the oaths that they should take. No commissioner was to buy lands in any parish to be inclosed within five years. Boundaries of parishes, manors, hamlets, and districts were to be determined. A plan was to be made and verified, public and private roads appointed, and herbage allotted to proprietors on either side. Small allotments could be depastured in common, and trees were to be the property of allottees who were to pay the former owners for them. Detailed instructions about fencing were included. Expenses could be deducted from allotments or raised on the security of allotments. Witnesses could be called but were not to travel more than eight

[1] F. Clifford, *Hist. of Private Bill Legislation* (1885), i. 13, 493. The Marden, Bodenham, Wellington, Sutton St. Michael, Murton, and Pipe Inclosure Act, 4 J. I c.11, confirming an earlier agreement, was a Public Act; the next inclosure Act, which did not concern open fields, was not until 1664, and, like most 18th-century inclosure Acts, was a Private Act, 16 C. II c.5; cf. *Trans. Royal Hist. Soc.* new ser. xix. 108.

miles. Rights of lords of manors were to be secured, and rectors and vicars could lease their allotments. Finally the award was to be enrolled in one of H.M. Courts of Record or with the Clerk of the Peace, and not more than 1*s*. was to be charged for its inspection.

The Inclosure Act, 1821 (1 & 2 G. IV c.23) enabled landlords to enter on allotments and distrain for rent. By the Inclosure Act, 1836 (6 & 7 W. IV c.115) open and common lands could be inclosed with the consent of two-thirds of the number of parties interested, and if seven-eighths agreed commissioners were not necessary. Otherwise one commissioner or more were to be appointed, and if any died or became incapable the majority of the interested parties were to appoint a new one. If they failed to do so within two months the remaining commissioner was to appoint. The commissioners were to appoint an umpire; their meeting place was to be within seven miles of the boundary of the place to be inclosed; they were to receive £3 3*s*. a day or a gross sum; and their decisions were subject to appeals to quarter sessions or assizes. They were to allot encroachments made within the last twenty years as part of the land to be inclosed, while older encroachments were to be treated as ancient inclosure, and they were to decide the course of husbandy to be followed until allotments were made. They were to settle who should pay for fencing, and could approve exchanges, the expenses of which were to be borne by those participating in them. The Inclosure Act, 1840 (3 & 4 Vic. c.31) was to be construed with that of 1836, which it extended to cover lands commonable during only part of the year.

The Inclosure Act, 1845 (8 & 9 Vic. c.118) started a new system. The principal Secretaries of State were empowered to appoint commissioners who were to act with the First Commissioner for Woods and Forests as Inclosure Commissioners for England and Wales. The commissioners were to report annually, their appointment was limited to five years, and regulations for their payment were made. The innovation ended the employment of local commissioners, and thenceforth the man who was the author of an award was known as the valuer.

From the same time the form of the awards altered, and the size of the documents became more regular. By that time tithes had been commuted in many places under the Tithe Act, and the new Inclosure Act allowed inclosure commissioners to make use of the tithe surveys. Among many other provisions were the following: no land within 15 miles of London, or 4 miles of a city of 100,000 people, or 2 miles of a city of 10,000 was to be inclosed without the authority of parliament; no village green was to be inclosed, though a green might be allotted to churchwardens or overseers for exercise and recreation; allotments for exercise and recreation could be made a condition of inclosure, on a scale relating to the size of the population; allotments were to be made for the labouring poor and for public purposes; encroachments made within the last twenty years were to be allotted, and rights not sustainable by law were to be allowed on proof of sixty years' use. Not all the awards subsequent to the Act of 1845 followed its provisions, since some which were completed afterwards had been initiated under earlier Acts.

THE DOCUMENTS

The collection of abstracts of Wiltshire Inclosure Awards that follows comprises 207 items representing 200 awards and agreements. The bulk of it is the 174 awards that were deposited with the Clerk of the Peace for Wiltshire and are now in the County Record Office at Trowbridge. In addition there are a further 25 documents from private collections in the Wiltshire Record Office (6 of them being duplicates of, or supplementary to, awards deposited with the Clerk of the Peace) and 5 awards of which the Wiltshire Record Office holds photocopies from other record offices, namely the Public Record Office (**147, 180, 200**), the Gloucestershire Record Office (**122**), and the Somerset Record Office (**112**). The collection is completed by the agreement for Hannington (**101**) from the archives of Mr. Ambrose Hussey-Freake and that for Fugglestone St. Peter (**97**) belonging to the earl of Pembroke. No attempt has been made to collect scattered evidence of inclosures which did not give rise to an extant formal agreement, or to search systematically for those that might be enrolled among the Public Records. Geographically the collection has been confined to the modern boundary of Wiltshire, and excludes Ashridge in Wokingham (transferred to Berkshire in 1844), Poulton (transferred to Gloucestershire in 1844), South Damerham and West Wellow (transferred to Hampshire in 1894), and Somerford Keynes and Shorncote (transferred to Gloucestershire in 1896), for all of which there are awards.[2] Chronologically, the earliest document is that of 1632 for Hannington (**101**), already referred to; the latest award for Wiltshire is that of 1883 for Seagry and Christian Malford (**164**), and the last award inclosing common arable fields is that of 1867 for Charlton Fields in Donhead St. Mary (**74**).

The collection does not include inclosure Acts for which no award is known. There was an Act of 1779 for Milston and Brigmerston, 19 G. III c.8 (Private Act), and it seems to have been followed by an award of some kind since the tithe award for Milston records that an inclosure award had commuted tithes on 776 a.; there are, however, references to sheep grazing in Milston as late as 1813,[3] so the inclosure award may not have dealt with all pasture rights for sheep. Of awards following Acts for Compton Bassett, 1725, Staunton, 1732, Orcheston St. George, 1809, Everleigh, 1816, and St. Paul's in Malmesbury, 1819, no sign has been found,[4] and the only indication of the award that was to follow the Act for Little Somerford, 1808, is a draft map dated 1815.[5]

2 Cf. W. E. Tate's list, still useful though open to revision, of Acts and awards in *W.A.M.* li. 127–73; cf. (for Poulton) *Trans. Bristol and Glos. Arch. Soc.* lxiv. 54.

3 *W.A.M.* xxxi. 2.

4 Respectively, 12 G.I c.2 (Private Act); 5 G.II c.32 (Private Act); 49 G.III c.11 (Local and Personal, not printed); 56 G.III c.68 (Private, not printed); 59 G.III c.5 (Private). There are Acts but apparently no awards for some places which have been transferred from Wilts. to, respectively, Glos. and Hants: Kemble and Poole Keynes, 1772, 12 G.III c.70 (Private Act); Whitsbury, 1798, 38 G.III c. 38 (Private and Personal, not printed).

5 See no. **171.**

WILTSHIRE INCLOSURE AWARDS

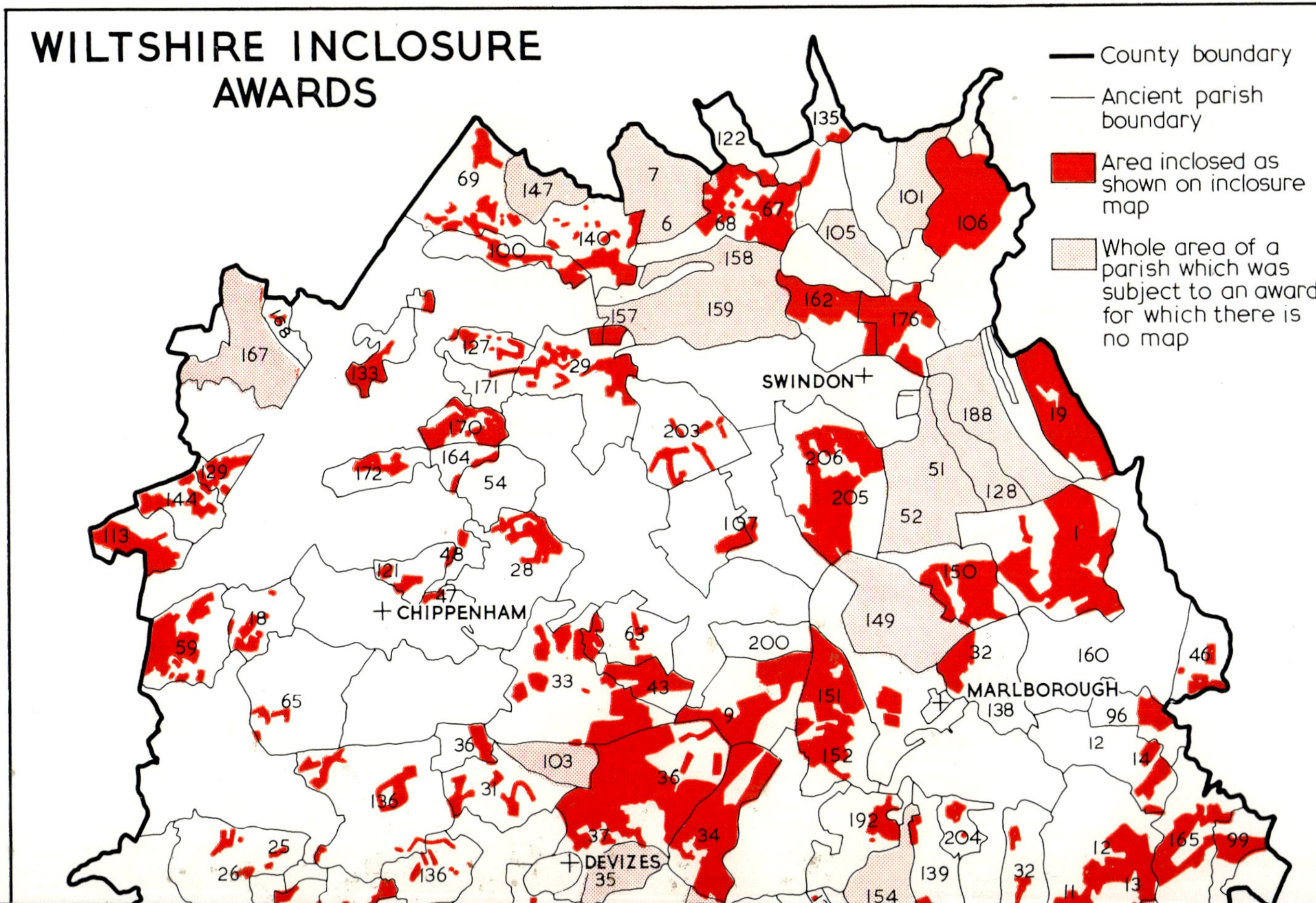

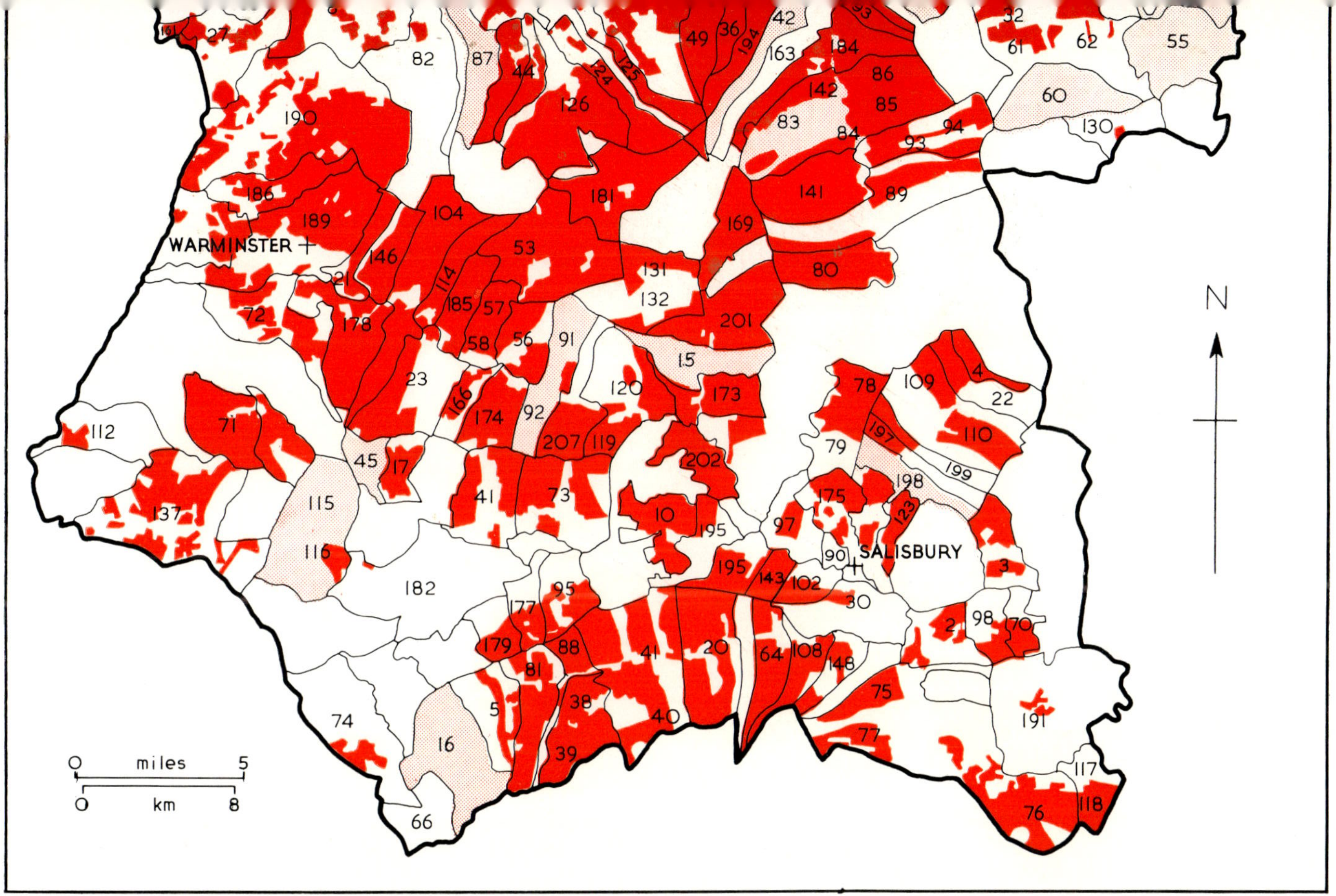

N
WARMINSTER
SALISBURY
miles
0
5
km
0
8

INCLOSURE BY PARLIAMENTARY AWARD IN WILTSHIRE

Parliamentary inclosure in Wiltshire is but one stage in the agricultural history of a village community, and not perhaps as decisive a stage as was at one time thought. One reason why it was not more decisive is that a considerable proportion of the open and commonable land had been inclosed before the era of parliamentary inclosure, by processes that have left relatively little record. Moreover there is plenty of evidence in the awards themselves that it was not found possible to change all at once from an open-field pattern to an inclosed one. In many awards it was laid down that certain fields were to continue to be fed in common, some allotments being not large enough to provide feed for their owners' beasts or to enable the owners to support themselves. In Fovant (**95**) in 1792 new common arable fields were established, but the new arrangement seems to have broken down by the time of the tithe award; in some similar instances a further inclosure award was necessary.

The period covered by the abstracts printed below is, as already stated, 1632–1883, but the earliest was under a private agreement, not an Act of Parliament, and the last did not concern common arable fields, so that the period of characteristic parliamentary inclosure is limited to 1732–1867. There were only eleven awards (including that of 1632) before 1770, and they continue decade by decade as follows:[6]

1770–9	9	1820–9	21
1780–9	21	1830–9	9
1790–9	30	1840–9	13
1800–9	31	1850–9	9
1810–19	31	1860–9	14

There is no evidence in Wiltshire for the rise in the number of awards in the period 1760–9 mentioned by writers on inclosure in general,[7] and indeed there are only three Wiltshire awards for that decade.

Nearly all of the early awards relate to the north and north-west part of the county, which lies on the Kimmeridge and Oxford Clays, the Corallian beds, and the lower slopes of the Jurassic. Much of the area was wooded, and was contained in the forests of Braydon, Chippenham, Melksham, and Selwood. The inclosures were of relatively restricted areas and among them were most of the inclosures of stretches of waste and common, notable ones being Brinkworth (**29**), Hankerton (**100**), and Wootton Bassett (**203**). Partly because the inclosures in the north and west tend to be early, few of them have surviving maps. The extensive chalk grasslands of the south and east, which supported vast sheep-runs, provide a contrast. The earliest award there was for Chicklade in 1781 (**45**), closely followed by those for Warminster and Corsley in 1783 (**189**) and Heytesbury in 1785 (**104**). The areas inclosed there were in general much larger than those in the north and west. Sometimes in the middle of such inclosed areas there can be seen on the map a piece of land not included in the award. In nearly every case it was where the lord of the

[6] One award (**26**) is not dated, and is not counted here.

[7] G. E. Mingay, *Enclosure and the Small Farmer in the Age of the Industrial Revolution*, 20.

manor had previously inclosed an area for his own use which was generally called 'The Farm'. The medieval deserted village of Middleton in Norton Bavant (**146**) shows very clearly in that way. A third, smaller geographical division of the county in the extreme south-east, represented among the inclosure awards by those for Landford Common (**118**) and Landford Wood (**117**) and for Whiteparish (**191**) lies on an extension of the Tertiaries of the New Forest.

A notable feature of the Wiltshire awards, further reflecting the geography of the county, is the importance of water-meadows in the agricultural economy. The value of water-meadows was clearly recognized by Davis as far back as 1794;[8] Aubrey mentions their introduction in Wiltshire in 1635,[9] while a modern writer takes them back elsewhere even further.[10] Their importance is shown in the shape of some of the parishes: there are areas in the valleys of the Bourne near the Winterbournes, of the Till near Winterbourne Stoke, of the Bristol Avon north-east of Chippenham, and at Pitmead on the Wylye south-west of Warminster where fragmented and detached parts of parishes are evidence of the need for the possession of water-meadows. Some awards, notably that for West Overton (**152**), set out detailed regulations for their use.[11] Other instances may be traced in the Index.

Since the organization and control of husbandry on the land to be inclosed were essentially manorial, not parochial, the date and scope of inclosure in particular places reflect the attitudes of the lords of manors. It is therefore relevant to consider the interest and influence of some of the major landowners. The inclosure by a single award of Alvediston, Bishopstone, Bower Chalke, Broad Chalke, Ebbesborne Wake, Fifield Bavant, Fovant, and Swallowcliffe was carried out in that way because all the manors except Fifield Bavant belonged to the earl of Pembroke, who evidently initiated the inclosure. For the Savernake district there are few inclosure awards, but some private agreements have survived in the archives of the marquess of Ailesbury and there is in addition a composite public award for Great and Little Bedwyn and Preshute (**12**). The earls of Radnor had interests in Little Somerford (**171**) and Stanton St. Quintin (**172**), apart from their estates nearer Longford Castle. The Hicks Beach estates in Chisenbury de la Folly (**142**), Fittleton (**93**), Idmiston (**109**), and Keevil (**111**) were all inclosed under one Act, though by separate awards, and all within two years. The importance of the church as a landowner is reflected partly by the allotment of totals, in the awards abstracted, of over 11,000 a. to the bishop of Salisbury, and over 8,000 a. to the dean and chapter of Salisbury, and of lesser amounts to the dean and chapter of Winchester, the dean and chapter of Gloucester, the dean and canons of Windsor, and the bishops of Winchester and Oxford. Appendix II provides a table of those who received large allotments by the inclosure awards. Much of the allotments to ecclesiastical dignitaries was in place of appropriated tithe, though where an award commuted or extinguished

8 Thomas Davis, *Gen. View of Agric. of Wilts.* 30 sqq.
9 John Aubrey, *Natural Hist. of Wilts.* (1847), 104.
10 E. Kerridge in *W.A.M.* lv. 105; cf. *V.C.H. Wilts.* iv. 56–7.
11 Cf. *W.A.M.* lv. 105; lviii. 403; *V.C.H. Wilts.* viii. 4.

tithes it did not necessarily cover all of the tithes. At Bremhill (**28**) the greater part of the lands allotted went to redeem tithes.

There is little evidence in the awards themselves about the degree of satisfaction with which they were received. Inevitably some people felt ill used. At Steeple Ashton (**8**) the award was delayed when Joshua Smith and five others claimed rights in the common fields there by virtue of their holdings elsewhere; the commissioners found against them; Smith and the others appealed to the King's Bench, and when the case was heard at Salisbury they were awarded 1*s.* damages and half of what they would have received if the commissioners had accepted their claim. There were similar claims at North Bradley (**27**). Other awards were delayed for different reasons: at Cricklade (**68**) one commissioner died and the other went mad; at Broad Chalke (**41**) a delay of 47 years resulted from failure to replace a commissioner who had died.

COMMISSIONERS, SURVEYORS, AND MAPMAKERS

The early awards were made by large groups of commissioners, which sometimes gave 'the appearance of a grand jury of umpires'.[12] Many of them were from the immediate locality. Purton in 1732 had thirteen (**157**) and in 1738 nine (**158**). There were six for Sherston Magna in 1743 (**167**), seven for Highworth (Broad Blunsdon) in 1749 (**105**), six for Chiseldon (Badbury) (**51**), and five for Heddington (**103**). The commissioners for the Heddington inclosure were nominated by the interested parties. In the last quarter of the 18th century the names of commissioners begin to be repeated in successive awards with the formation of a group of semi-professional commissioners. Richard Richardson figures in 63 awards; his address was in Devizes 1785–92, in Bath 1794–1800, and in London up to 1815; the Devizes directory for 1791 shows his occupation as commissioner.[13] Francis Webb of Stow-on-the-Wold and later of Salisbury was presumably related to Edward Webb of Stow, who also appears among the surveyors. William Smith, the geologist, was sent to learn his trade from Edward Webb at Stow in 1787.[14] Francis Webb figures 24 times as commissioner and 9 times as surveyor. He was described as surveyor in the Salisbury directory for 1791[15] and seems to have moved there from Stow between 1780 and 1787; he died in 1815. It is worth noting that the two surveyors for the inclosure of Highworth (Broad Blunsdon) in 1749 (**105**) were both schoolmasters. Many of the commissioners were stewards to local landowners, such as Thomas Davis of Longleat, John Charlton of Stourton, and John Seagrim of Wilton. Many of the mapmakers made their mark in other walks of life; Henry Weaver, whose designs can still be seen in many of the houses on the Bowood estate, was agent both to the marquess of Lansdowne and to the Poynder family of Hilmarton, and author of a book on

12 M. W. Beresford, *Essays in Agrarian Hist.* ii. 91.
13 *Universal British Directory*, ii. 780.
14 *D.N.B.*
15 *Univərsal British Directory*, iv. 562.

cottage architecture. Henry Augustus Biedermann, the maker of the Brinkworth map (**29**), was naturalized by an Act of 1804.[16]

The purposes and effects of parliamentary inclosure in Wiltshire have been discussed elsewhere,[17] and it would be out of place to discuss them in an introduction to documents which record not the results of change but the process that made change possible. It is clear from the awards themselves that the scope of parliamentary inclosure in Wiltshire was limited because it was merely the completion of a process that had started much earlier. Its object was to make total a breach with the past and its traditional restrictions. George Herbert, writing in the year when the earliest of the documents below was sealed, represented inclosure as characteristic of humanity's opposition to established authority.

If God had laid all common, certainly
Man would have been th' incloser: but since now
God hath impal'd us on the contrarie
Man breaks the fence and every ground will plough.[18]

ARRANGEMENT OF THE ABSTRACTS

The arrangement of the collection follows the principle that for each award there should be a single and separate abstract. In some instances an inclosure Act covered more than one place, but there was a separate award for each place: in such an instance there is a separate abstract below for each place. Alternatively one award may relate to two or more physically or legally distinct places, perhaps not even contiguous, in which case there is a single abstract below, though where possible the information relating to each place has been distinguished. Where a place has been affected by more than one award, each award is separately abstracted and there are cross-references from one abstract to another. An exception to the principle that each award is represented by a single abstract has been made with the award for Alvediston, Bishopstone, Bower Chalke, Broad Chalke, Ebbesborne Wake, Fifield Bavant, Fovant, and Swallowcliffe, since to have included so unusually large a number of places in one abstract would have been confusing.

An attempt has been made to discover the acreage of each parish at the time of inclosure, and the figure appears on the first line of an abstract or, where an abstract is sub-divided, on the first line of the sub-entry. (The figure is not repeated in successive abstracts for the same parish.) The acreage of a parish is to be distinguished from the acreage of the area subject to the inclosure award, which is given within each abstract against the word *Area* as mentioned below.

Each abstract has been made to follow, as nearly as possible, a standard arrangement. Against the word *Act* is given the regnal year of the parliament-

16 44 G.III c.8 (Private Act).
17 *V.C.H. Wilts.* iv. 65 sqq.
18 G. Herbert, *The Church Porch*, 4.

ary session and the chapter number; the chapter number is invariably given in arabic type, regardless of whether the Act is 'Public General', 'Private', or 'Local and Personal'. In the absence of any definition of the class of the Act it is to be assumed that it is a Private Act if passed before 1798, and a Local and Personal Act if passed between 1798 and 1860. Awards under the general Inclosure Acts mentioned above have the word 'General' before the reference to the relevant Act. In a few instances an award is made not under an Act but under an *Agreement*. The date of an *Award* is followed by an indication of any amendment, the date of enrolment where known, and the reference for the document. If the award has a simple Wiltshire Record Office (W.R.O.) number it indicates that it is the copy officially deposited with the Clerk of the Peace for Wiltshire; any reference-number preceded by 'Acc' means that the award is not the official copy but comes from another collection in the Wiltshire Record Office.

The *Commissioners* and *Surveyor*, as also the *Lord of the Manor*, *Rector*, *Vicar*, and the *lessee* of any of them, are so far as is known those at the time of the award, and those whom they have replaced or succeeded since the passing of the Act are also named. The name of a manor, rectory, or vicarage is not given when it is the same as that at the head of the abstract or subdivision.

Against the word *Area* is given the acreage of the area actually inclosed, excluding as far as possible all old inclosures subject to the award and all the exchanges of the kind that were effected by almost every award. The first figure is that given in the Act or the award; sometimes Act and award differ and a figure from each is given. The acreage printed in square brackets is of the actual area allotted, calculated by adding together the acreages of the several allotments. Following the area, each abstract gives the names of the main fields, downs, and so forth that were inclosed; minor field-names are omitted. The figure given against *Allotments* indicates the number of people or groups of people to whom allotments were made. The wording of the awards, where a single estate may be represented by several allotments, is not reflected in the abstracts, where all the parcels of land allotted to one man are counted as one allotment. Each 'public allotment', however, is separately counted. The allotments made to tenants holding by lease or copy are counted as part of the allotment to the landlord. The gross allotment to the landlord is followed in brackets by the allotments to the tenants, but it has sometimes been remarkably difficult, or even impossible, to ascertain the precise status of a tenant's holding. All those who received allotments are named; the extent of each of the larger allotments is given to the nearest acre, but private allotments of less than 15 a. are not quantified. So far as possible the figures relate to the original allotments, and take no account of the subsequent exchanges that were often recorded in the awards. The abstracts indicate the provision in an award for the responsibility of *Fencing*, whether by a general statement, by specification incorporated in the record of each allotment, or by an indication on the map.

The abstracts indicate in a general way the provision made by the awards for the commutation or extinction of *Tithes* and enumerate the *Roads* and paths of each type specified. The herbage growing along the roads was often awarded by the commissioners to the neighbouring landowners, as is indicated in the abstracts by the words 'Herbage allotted'. In those instances where the commissioners awarded the whole herbage of roads passing between allotments and old inclosures exclusively to the owners of the allotments, the fact is indicated by the words 'Herbage to neighbouring allottees only'. Against the word *Finance* is a note of how the expenses of the Act and award were met, whether by a rate or by the sale of allotments made for the purpose; sometimes special provision was made for the share of the expenses of a particular party, often the rector or vicar whose personal benefit from the inclosure might be short-lived and was neither transferable nor heritable.

An indication of the form and content of any inclosure *Map* is preceded by the name of the mapmaker and the date of the map, where they are known, and the nature of any *Schedule* is outlined. At the end of each abstract is a cross-reference to any other award affecting the same parish, and *Notes* of any interesting or significant features of the award that have not already been sufficiently described.

In the abstracts the spelling of names of towns, parishes, and villages has been rationalized in accordance with modern usage, but many of the lesser place-names and the personal names have been left in the form that they take in the awards and agreements.

ABSTRACTS OF WILTSHIRE INCLOSURE AWARDS

1 ALDBOURNE [8,490 a.]

Aldbourne and Upper Upham manors

Act 45 G.III c.92 (not printed). *Award* 10 Aug. 1809 (enrolled Court of Common Pleas, Trinity 50 G.III), W.R.O. Acc 154/5. *Commissioners* Stephen King of Overton; George Barnes of Andover, Hants; John Williams of Baydon. *Surveyor* William Church of Wantage, Berks.

Lord of Manor of Aldbourne, John Hancock; of Upper Upham, Diana Caswall.

Rector (owners of great tithes) dean and chapter of Winchester; *lessee* Stephen Neate. *Vicar* John Elderton of Gayton, Northants.

Area 3,933 a. [3,896 a.] Rooksbury Field, Grass Hill, North, South, East and West Fields, Windmill Field, the Chase and Southwood (1,000 a. together), Upham Hill Down, East and West Downs, Ewens Hill, Aldbourne Warren (800 a.).

Allotments 63. Public: chalk, sand, and gravel pits 6 a.; furze 50 a., not more than one quarter to be cut each year. William Brown 153 a.; Thomas Gould 112 a.; trustees of Thomas Hancock 337 a.; Ann Mortimer 85 a.; Stephen Neate 97 a.; George Church 197 a; Thomas Church 121 a; Robert Church 50 a.; trustees of Joseph Coleman 75 a.; John Cooke and William Wright 161 a.; Mary Pizzie 59 a.; vicar of Aldbourne 421 a. (including tithes); Mark Brown 124 a.; John Hancock 311 a. (including copy, George Church 73 a.; Robert Church 79 a.; Charles Gould); Diana Caswall 79 a.; devisees of Edne Witts 76 a.; trustees of Thomas Perfect 376 a.; James Wells 517 a.; Rev. George Foxton 38 a.; Charles Gould 44 a.; Thomas Hodder 21 a.; Sarah Chamberlaine 42 a.; John Neate 33 a.; Caleb Pizzie 30 a.; Levi Pizzie 43 a.; Sir Francis Burdett 21 a.; Mary Bunce 36 a.; William Brown 16 a.; Thomas Baskerville 23 a.; Thomas Stroud 20 a.; John Stone 24 a.; Edward Strong 16 a.; Richard Walford 34 a.; Joseph Coxhead; William Cruce; John Finch; John Fishlock; heirs of William Gwynne; Thomas Hill; James James; Stephen James; Francis Lovelock; Thomas Liddiard; Richard Blake; James Blackman; trustees of Thomas Coleman; Levi and Daniel Cook; Stephen Newth; Richard Pearce; Jacob Baker; trustees of Baydon church lands; dean and chapter of Winchester; Jane Wentworth; John Woodley; William Powell; Grace Read; John Shepherd; John Smith; Robert Salt; Sarah Sly; William Warman. *Fencing* general and with allotments.

Tithes Allotment to vicar for vicarial tithes only. The owners of the great tithes pay £40 yearly to the vicar for the rectory. £3 per annum payable to the vicar by Thomas Baskerville, for tithe of coneys, as proprietor of Aldbourne Warren. Large part (2,173 a.) not exonerated from vicarial tithes.

Roads 15 public roads, 1 public bridle way, 4 public footpaths, 12 private roads. Duties for repair and fencing set out.

Maps 1809. (1) Whole parish, common arable yellow, downs, chase and warren green, land not exonerated from vicarial tithe green. Old inclosures nos. 1–159 and 337–441. (2) Enlarged map of village with schedule of allotments.

Notes 13 a. allotted in severalty to holders of common rights over the Warren. Thomas Baskerville owner of Aldbourne Warren claimed soil rights and free warren. Watercourses not to be diverted.

2 ALDERBURY [2,265 a. excl. Pitton and Farley]
Alderbury, Ivychurch, and Whaddon

Act 43 G.III c. 96 (not printed). *Award* 2 Dec. 1809 (enrolled 24 July 1816), W.R.O. 96. *Commissioners* Francis Webb of Salisbury; Richard Richardson of London; John Hodding of Salisbury.

Lord of Manor of Alderbury and Ivychurch, of Parsonage or Rectory Manor, of Whaddon, Jacob Pleydell-Bouverie, earl of Radnor.

Rector (lay) earl of Radnor. *Vicar* George Smith.

Area 788 a. [986 a.] Shute Hill, Little Common, Whaddon Common, Treasurer's Common, Alderbury Common, Alderbury Mead.

Allotments 14. Public: 2 gravel pits 2 a.; furze 2 a. Earl of Radnor 657 a. (including tithes 257 a.; leases, Robert Head; Thomas Lake; Joshua Moody; William Osman; Anna Powell; John Pierce; copy, Henry Stevens; Elizabeth Williams); George Fort 173 a.; feoffees of Matrons' College 74 a.; vicar of Alderbury 15 a.; Robert Head 21 a.; bishop of Salisbury; William Head; Joshua Moody; Henry Fox-Strangways, earl of Ilchester; trustees of Eyre's charity for St. Thomas's, Salisbury; Samuel Whitchurch; John M. Eyre. *Fencing* with allotments and shown on map.

Tithes Rectorial tithes commuted by grant of land (257 a.).

Roads 6 public roads, 16 private roads, 1 private footpath. Herbage allotted.

Finance Sale allotments £3,161 18*s.* 10*d.*, and general rate and special rate for exchanges.

Map William Tubb and Son of Salisbury 1809. Whole parish and village shown. Allottees, acreages and fencing, the Salisbury and Southampton canal, and George Fort's estate shown. Commonable meadow and pasture outlined in green, commonable arable in yellow, old inclosures in grey. Five detached pieces of the parish. The three manors outlined.

Schedules (1) Rate for repairing private roads in full. (2) Rate for contributing to repair of private roads. (3) Rate for share of expenses.

See also No. 3.

Notes Lord's Ditch determined to be 6 feet wide and to be repaired by the earl of Radnor. Rights of George Fort to set up a hatch and take water at certain periods protected. Earl of Radnor to maintain fences round Alderbury churchyard in return for an extra allotment. Rights of Salisbury and Southampton canal protected.

3 ALDERBURY

Pitton and Farley chapelries [2,221 a.]

Act 50 G.III c. 75 (not printed). *Award* 3 Dec. 1819 (enrolled 4 Feb. 1820), W.R.O. V 108. *Commissioners* Richard Webb of Salisbury; William Jennings of Evershot, Dorset. *Surveyor* John Martin of Evershot.

Lord of Manor of Pitton and Farley, dean and chapter of Salisbury; *lessee* Henry Fox-Strangways, earl of Ilchester.

Rector and Prebendary, treasurer of Salisbury cathedral.

Area 1,500 a. (Act), 1,139 a. (Award) [Pitton 858 a., Farley 277 a.] Middle Field, Park Field, East Field, Copyhold Down, Leasehold Down, West Field.

Allotments Pitton 4. Dean and chapter of Salisbury 340 a. (leased to earl of Ilchester and sublet in smaller parcels); earl of Ilchester 472 a. (including leases, James Maton 77 a.; Thomas Maton 28 a.; representatives of John Read 88 a.; Stephen Seaward 36 a.; William Smart 17 a.; Moses Webb 62 a.; Samuel Webb 127 a.; Henry Golding; Joseph Parsons; Jane Tanner; Edward Windsor; Joseph Whitlock; Elizabeth Whitlock; John White); treasurer of Salisbury cathedral 31 a. (including warden and fellows of Winchester College 31 a.); Ann Whatley 15 a.

Farley 4. Dean and chapter of Salisbury 98 a. (leased to earl of Ilchester and sublet in smaller parcels); earl of Ilchester 120 a.; (including leases Henry Cooke 56 a.; Joseph Parsons 32 a.; Aaron Foster; Thomas Parsons; John Parsons; James Parsons; Abraham Prewett; Henry Seaward); earl of Radnor 26 a.; vicar of Pitton and Farley 32 a. *Fencing* general.

Roads Pitton, 4 public roads, 5 public footpaths, 7 private roads; Farley, 2 public roads, 4 public footpaths, 5 private roads.

Finance Rate; see Schedule 2.

Map North part of parish excluding old inclosures. Allottees, acreages, and hedges shown.

Schedules (1) Rate levied on neighbouring allottees for repair of private roads. (2) Rate levied for expenses of inclosure.

See also No. 2.

Note Not more than one shilling to be paid to view the award.

4 ALLINGTON [957 a.]

Act 35 G.III c. 16 (Allington and Winterbourne Earls). *Award* 21 Dec. 1795 (enrolled 7 Dec. 1840), W.R.O. 157. *Commissioners* Richard Richardson of Bath; John Tredgold of Chilbolton, Hants; James King of Benham, Berks. *Surveyor* William Tubb of Fisherton Anger.

Rector Thomas Fowle.

Area 921 a. including old inclosures and roads [907 a.] East and West Fields, East and West Down, Lot Meadow, Cow Down, The Ham.

Allotments 7. Public: watering place 1 a. Henry Penruddocke Wyndham 533 a.; William Child 171 a.; Robert Bunney 136 a.; trustees of Walker's charity in Amesbury 22 a.; rector of Allington 34 a.; Richard Bishop.

Roads 8 public roads, 1 public footpath, 2 private roads.

Map William Tubb 1795. Whole parish and village and allottees and acreages shown.

5 ALVEDISTON [2,534 a.]

Act 25 G.III c. 56 (Fovant, Swallowcliffe, Broad Chalke, Ebbesborne Wake, Bower Chalke, Alvediston, Bishopstone, Fifield Bavant). *Award* 3 Jan. 1792 (enrolled 17 Nov. 1794), W.R.O. V 38. *Commissioners* Richard Bloxham of West Dean; Richard Richardson of Devizes; Francis Webb of Salisbury (replacing William Corfield of Salisbury, d. 1787). *Surveyor* Benjamin Haynes (replacing William Corfield).

Lord of the Manor Henry Herbert, earl of Pembroke.

Area [597 a.] Hill Field, Long Mead, Ashland Field, North Down, Coombe North Field.

Allotments 2. Earl of Pembroke 215 a. (including copy and lease, Sarah Whitehouse 189 a.; copy, Thomas King 26 a.); Thomas King 382 a. *Fencing* general.

Roads 7 public roads, 1 public bridle way, 3 private roads. Herbage allotted.

Finance Expenses to be paid by allottees including if necessary the reversionaries.

Map East part of parish only, including the village.

Schedules (1) Lifeholders under the earl of Pembroke, whose reversionaries have paid the expenses, and who have to pay rent. (2) Charges assessed on various lifeholders under the earl of Pembroke.

Note Beast leases for cows and horses (no sheep) allotted.

6 ASHTON KEYNES [1,461 a.]

Leigh Manor

Act 7 G.III c. 39. *Award* 12 Dec. 1767, W.R.O. Acc 359/21. *Commissioners* Thomas Brown of Salperton, Glos.; Lewis Bradley of Henley in Arden, Warws.; Thomas Carter of Foxley; Benjamin Down of Bristol.

Lord of Manor George Montagu, duke of Montagu, John Montagu, marquess of Monthermer, Thomas Brudenell, Lord Bruce, Sir John Colton Bt.

Vicar Samuel Barnes.

Area 938 a. [629 a.] Bourn Lake (172 a.), Cove Wood (265 a.), Swan Lane End (18 a.), Little Moor (10 a.), Ashen Mead (155 a.), Common Field (54 a.).

Allotments 17. Public: second poor [i.e. the poor not relieved out of the rates] 20 a. Joseph and Henry Maskelyne 51 a.; lords of the manor 347 a. (including leases, Elizabeth Carter 17 a.; Christopher Gardiner 18 a.; copy, John Humphrys 28 a.; lease and copy William Haggard 24 a.; Thomas Mills; James Archard; Jane Tipper; John Gingell; John Eliot; George Coxe; Thomas Mills; Mary Turner; Thomas Boulton; Elizabeth Hawkes); William Coles 26 a.; John Hippisley Coxe 55 a.; John Packer 29 a.; James Weeks 32 a.; vicar of Ashton Keynes 24 a.; Henry Stephens; Maurice Bennett and John Brown; William Stephens; William Ware; Christopher

Gardiner; William Haggard; Robert Bath and others; John Cowley; John Carter. *Fencing* with allotments.

Roads 4 public roads, 10 private roads, 1 public bridleway, 4 public footpaths.

Finance £721.

Schedule (1) Commissioners' expenses in detail. (2) Proportions payable by allottees towards the cost.

See also No. 7.

Notes Bridge to be built close to the allotment to the second poor and £96 to be paid towards the cost. Details for widening watercourses set out. One other bridge to be built.

7 ASHTON KEYNES [2,799 a. excl. Leigh]

Act 17 G.III c. 139. *Award* 8 May 1778, W.R.O. 374/5. *Commissioners* Thomas Browne of Cowley, Glos.; George Gilbert Jones of Ford, Glos.; Timothy Lewis of Cirencester, Glos.; John Mitchell of South Weston, Oxon. ; Richard Richardson the younger.

Lord of the Manor of Ashton Keynes, Henry Whorwood (succeeding Hawkins Chapman, dead); of Minety, George Pitt, Lord Rivers.

Rector (lay) Henry Whorwood. *Vicar* Samuel Barnes. *Rector* of Shorncote, John Davies.

Area 1,981 a. excl. roads [1,976 a.] South Moor, Water Hay, Jenkins Corner, Ashton Mead, Cowbridge, North, West and East Fields, Home Common, Startletts, Broadhurst, The Hurst.

Allotments 125. Public: 6 allotments for the repair of roads 2 a.; 25 a. for the poor. Lord Rivers 147 a.; Henry Whorwood 768 a. (including 107 a. for tithes; copy, Jane Hinton 22 a.; Edmund Carter, Hugh Cotmore, Giles Hancock); vicar of Ashton Keynes 259 a.; Edward Eliot 79 a. (including copy, Hannah Taylor, Hannah Miles, George Coxe, Billy Carter, John Eliot); Thomas Master 90 a.; Robert Nicholas 98 a.; Robert and John Nicholas 81 a.; rector of Shorncote 20 a.; Elizabeth Farrington 24 a.; Mary Emerson 45 a.; Edmund Hinton 16 a.; John Cowley 21 a.; Mary Selby 17 a.; Thomas Glead 18 a.; Oliver Carter 16 a.; John Telling 28 a.; John Randall 40 a.; Henry Maskelyne 35 a.; John Packer 16 a.; John Nicholas; John Carter; Richard Fry; Thomas Wait; William Wilkins; Thomas Wilkins; Andrew Kendall; John Haynes; Maurice Bennett; Robert Selby; Martha Brain; Mary Turner; Mary Gray; William Clifford; Richard Selby; Thomas Taylor; Margaret Fry; John Humphris; Isaac Gleed; James Vincent; Robert Selby the younger; John Jones; John Carter; James Collinborne; Richard Painter; Robert Cotmore; Robert Telling; Mary Baker; Richard Kinneir; Simon Adams; William and John Stephens; perpetual curate of Ampney St. Peter; William Stephens; William Weeks; Thomas Bush; John Aish; Hannah Taylor; Richard and William Chapperlin; Isaac Telling; John Packer; Hannah Millard; Elizabeth Whitfield; Robert Whitfield; Jacob Goding; Jacob Window; Robert Berryman; Thomas Matthews; Harry Boulton; Mary Blackford; Betty Chapperlin; Thomas Telling; William Darter; Betty Telling; Ann Boulton; John

Millard; William Telling; Thomas Howse; William Dawes; Abraham Boulton; Harry Cove; churchwardens of Ashton Keynes; Mary Carter; John Kilmaster; Jane Clifford; Hungerford Whitfield; John Chapperlin; Richard Jefferies; Giles Chapperlin; Richard Messenger; Thomas Poole; Thomas Kempsford; Jane Symonds; Sylvanus Greville; William Robbins; Sarah Symonds; John Kempsford; William Cuss; Charles Cuss; John Potter; Edward Boulton; Joshua Millard; John Millard; William Carter; George Cuss; Jeremiah Telling; Thomas Carter; Edward Carter; Henry Telling; Richard Pool; John Cowley; Jonathan Telling; John Carter; Olive Telling; Harry Clifford; Mary Taylor; Edward Newman; Giles Telling; Timothy Cove; Thomas Cove; Thomas Matthews; Henry Cove; George Hathaway; William Pool; Isaac Boulton. *Fencing* general and with allotments.

Tithes Rectorial tithes commuted by allotment. South Moor (147 a.) allotted to Lord Rivers, lord of the manor of Minety for 'the impropriator, vicar, tithe owners, and commoners of Minety'.

Roads 16 public roads, 1 public bridle way, 15 public footpaths, 20 private roads. Herbage allotted.

See also No. 6.

Notes Boundaries of manors of Ashton Keynes and Somerford Keynes determined by the commissioners. Maurice Maskelyne Bennett to provide protection from his newly erected mill (erected within twenty years by Maurice Bennett deceased) for travellers on the new public road. Stone bridge with two arches to be erected on the Ashton Keynes to Cricklade road at Water Hay. Footbridge to be erected at Broad Brook. Two drains to be made and covered near the windmill, two more on the Ashton Keynes to Cerney Wick road and one on the Minety to Cricklade road. Regulations for watercourses set out. Exchanges confirmed (including a small area in Shorncote).

8 STEEPLE ASHTON

Steeple Ashton [2,864 a.], Great Hinton [676 a.], West Ashton [2,025 a.] and Semington [1,181 a.] tithings

Act 53 G.III c. 96. *Award* 13 May 1818 (enrolled 12 Jan. 1822), W.R.O. V 107. *Commissioners* George Barnes of Andover, Hants; Thomas Davis of Horningsham; Thomas Flower of Melksham. *Surveyors* Jacob Player Sturge of Bristol and John Hayward of Rowde.

Lord of Manor of Steeple Ashton, Richard Godolphin Long, John Long, and Daniel Jones Long; of Rood Ashton, Richard Godolphin Long; of Semington, Edward Seymour, duke of Somerset; of Littleton, Ann Chamberlain; of Whorwellsdown, Joshua Smith.

Vicar Samuel Hey.

Area 6,771 a. [2,173 a.] Ray Down, Dodds Mead, High Field, Albury, Middle Field, Moorfield, Lower Lain, Littleton Wood Common, Steeple Ashton Common, Little Marsh Common, West Ashton Common, Hinton Common, Southbrook, Flowers Wood, Little Wood, Little Moor Field.

Allotments 107. Lords of the manor of Steeple Ashton 1,191 a. (including lease and copy, John Adams 27 a.; George Ball 40 a.; devisees of James Coles 24 a.; Charles Tiley 22 a.; William Berrett; Charles Blake; Andrew Burbidge; John Cunditt; John Mattocks; George Taylor; leases, John Biddulph 21 a.; William Hayward 32 a.; Charles Lee 23 a.; Richard G. Long 24 a.; representatives of Walter Newman 15 a.; representatives of Rev. Thomas Owen 33 a.; Sarah Richards 27 a.; J. P. Tidcombe 59 a.; Thomas Watts 27 a.; Sarah Barrow and William Baverstock; James Beaven; William Beaven; Eleanor Berrett; William and Thomas Bruges; Samuel Eyres; Robert Griffin; Leonard Lawes; Francis Long; William Phillips; William and James Potter; Daniel Sims; Elizabeth Shepherd; Simon Taylor; Charles Timbrell; William Togwell; Richard Watts; Stephen Watts; Robert Weaver; copy, Ann Long 28 a.; John Taylor 38 a.; James Bartlett; Jane Beaven; Samuel Beaven; William Blake; Mary Blake; Ann Chamberlain; William Crook; William Dunsden; Joseph Flower; Rachel and Ann Gale; Lydia Heritage; John Kemp; John Long; Mary Mattocks; James Redman; William Stillman; John Watts; Jane Woodman); Richard Godolphin Long 208 a. (including leases, Mary Beaven; William Bell; Abraham Ludlow; Robert Weaver; Sarah Weaver; copy and lease, Arnold Joyce); duke of Somerset 61 a. (including leases, Jane Beaven; Thomas Bruges; William Bruges; Mary Cox; Thomas Flower; William Harford; John Jones; Edmund Jefferies; William Matravers; representatives of Matthew Taylor); Joshua Smith 154 a. (including copy, John Baldwin; William Brown; Jonathan Humphrey; Mary Humphrey; Catherine Hurle; Ann Price; leases, William Beaven; Thomas Brown; William Drewitt; William Price; James Sims; Thomas White; lease and copy, James Bristow); Abraham Ludlow 98 a.; George Ball 27 a.; Michael Hicks Beach 18 a.; Ann Chamberlain 22 a.; All Souls College, Oxford, 16 a.; Mary Long 34 a.; Abraham and Susannah Ludlow 98 a.; Earl Manvers 15 a.; Richard Norris 23 a.; devisees of Rev. Thomas Owen 26 a.; William Stillman 31 a.; John Adams; Thomas Angel; Cuthbert Armstrong; William Ashley; James Bartlett; Jane Beaven; Eleanor Beaven; William Beaven; Samuel Beaven; John Bell; William Berrett; Rev. Wyatt Cottle; Robert Crook; Ann Dugdale; William Dunsden; James Dunsden; churchwardens of Edington; rector of Whaddon; devisees of Francis Edwards; Sarah Ferris; Stephen Flower; Joseph Flower; Elizabeth Gaisford; William Gaisford; Rachel and Ann Gale; John Griffin; Isaac Griffin; William and Sarah Hallett; Sarah Hallett; Daniel Hayward; Laurence Howell; Robert Jefferies; James Kingman; Edmund Jefferies; Robert Long; Charles Long; Francis Long; Rev. James Long; Gorges Lowther; Magdalene College, Cambridge; William Marks; Robert Marks; William Matravers; devisees of John Matthews; John Matthews; Thomas Mayel; Charles Melsom; Thomas Mitchell; John Oatley; John Perrior; John Perrott; William Phillips; William Porter; William Price; George Pryor; John Redman; Robert Rogers; John Salter; James Selfe; Hon. and Rev. Edward Seymour; rector of East Coulston; James Sims; Stephen Sims; Elizabeth Shepherd; Henry Slade; John Smith; George Smith; Steeple Ashton second poor [i.e. the poor not relieved out of the rates]; George Taylor; Thomas Tayler; Simon Taylor; William Tayler; devisees of Matthew Taylor; Charles Tiley; John Tiley; devisees of John Togwell; Trowbridge almshouses; Rev. Thomas Turner; Gifford Warriner; James Watts; John Watts; Richard Watts; Roger Watts; Robert Weaver; West Ashton poor; devisees of John Whitaker; William Whitaker; Whitaker and Seagram; John Wild; John Winslow; Samuel Winslow; Robert Wright. *Fencing* general.

Roads 10 public roads, 69 private roads, 5 private footpaths, 18 public footpaths. Duties for repairing public and private roads set out. Herbage allotted.

Finance The share of Abraham Ludlow settled by deduction from his allotment.

Maps (1) West and Rood Ashton. (2) Steeple Ashton and part of West Ashton. (3) Hinton, Semington and Littleton. Commonable lands red, old inclosures green. Allotments numbered only.

Schedules 7 schedules of rates, being a proportion of £10, to be paid by proprietors towards the repair of roads.

Notes Very complicated manorial system. Some lands in Steeple Ashton held by copy of court roll of Edington, lands also held as of the manor of Whaddon.

Claims by Joshua Smith and five others for rights in the common fields of Steeple Ashton because of their lands in Edington, East and West Coulston, Baynton, Tinhead, and Trowbridge. Objections raised by Richard Long and two others. Commissioners decided against Joshua Smith and others whereupon Joshua Smith brought an action in King's Bench which was heard at Salisbury on 3 July 1814. Joshua Smith received 1*s*. damages and was awarded half of what he would have got if his claim had not been objected to. Each paid their own costs. The award was delayed by this and other objections.

9 AVEBURY [4.690 a.]

Act 32 G.III c.2. *Award* 21 April 1795 (enrolled 6 May 1816), W.R.O. 95. *Commissioners* Daniel Tanner of Urchfont; John Gale of Stert; Benjamin Haynes of Salisbury (in place of Richard Bloxham, dead).

Vicar James Mayo.

Area [2,307 a.] Whitelands, Tilley's Meadow, Fore Down, Down called Green Street, Wallditch, Silbury Meadow, West Hooks, West Cow Down, Houndsplott Field, Houndsplott Down, Folly Hill Field, South Meadow, Weadon Field Green, Weadon Down, South Down, Hackpen Cow Down, Ratlands Field, Thornhill Field, Beckhampton Field and Down.

Allotments 14. Adam Williamson 714 a.; Richard Thring 133 a.; Robert Nalder 182 a.; William Norris 112 a.; Charles Simpkins 204 a.; Thomas Webb Dyke 147 a.; George Spencer-Churchill, duke of Marlborough 171 a.; James Sutton 201 a.; Peter Holford 419 a.; vicar of Avebury; Sarah Nalder; William Crook; John Griffin; John Dore.

Roads 9 public roads, 3 public footpaths, 4 private roads. One road stopped up. Herbage allotted.

Maps B. Haynes of Salisbury, 1794. Part of parish only, but including the village. Allottees and acreages, Silbury Hill and Wallditch shown.

Notes Watercourse between Monkton and turnpike at Silbury Hill to be cleansed by owners of adjoining land. Water rights in Silbury Meadow divided between Peter Holford (first three days after 1 Nov.), duke of Marlborough (next three days), James Sutton (next 4 days); hatches to be repaired as follows: Peter Holford 9*s.* 6*d.* in £, duke of Marlborough 4*s.* 6*d.* in £, James Sutton 6*s.* in £. Two tithe-payments transferred from one plot to another so that they should continue to be paid to and by the same persons. Exchanges confirmed including one made 50 years previously between the late vicar and John Norris. The vicar's right of cutting two ell-ridges of wheat on certain lands of Adam Williamson transferred to another field in the same ownership. [O.E.D. suggests that an ell-ridge may have been the equivalent of 60 lugs or perches.] New watercourse from Bar Close through Waites Meadow to South Meadow. Use of this water regulated from 1 Nov. between Adam Williamson and Robert Nalder. Adam Williamson to pay two-thirds of the repairs and Robert Nalder one-third.

10 BARFORD ST. MARTIN (including parts of Grovely, Baverstock, and South Newton)

Act 49 G.III c.100. *Award* 6 Aug. 1815 (enrolled 20 Dec. 1815), W.R.O. V 94. *Commissioners* John Seagrim of Wilton; John Rogers of South Burcombe; John Charlton of Stourton. *Surveyor* James Poole.

BARFORD ST. MARTIN [2,306 a.]

Lord of Manor George Herbert, earl of Pembroke, also lord of the ancient forest of Grovely. Alexander Powell claimed the lordship of the manor of Barford St. Martin within the manor of Barford St. Martin.

Rector Edward Pole.

Area [1,986 a.] Stoney Mead, Woolver's Mead, Great Marsh, Horseshoe Marsh, East Mead, Little Field, East and West Cadford Field, North, East and West Fields, Broadham.

Allotments 13. Public: 1 stone pit 1 a.; rector of Barford St. Martin 89 a. (including 20 a. tithes); earl of Pembroke 1,251 a. (including leases, William Nicholson 172 a.; William Bennett 114 a.; Charles Bishop 26 a.; Alexander Powell 106 a.; Christopher Crouch 17 a.; Rev. Dr. Pole 62 a.; Sarah Newman and Joan Andrews 191 a.; copy and lease, William Green 164 a.; Stephen Crouch; John Nicholson; James Sidford; Nicholas Crouch; Joan Andrews; John Hazzard); Alexander Powell 468 a.; Christopher Crouch 88 a.; John Hungerford Penruddocke 38 a.; William Green 20 a.; prior, brethren, and sisters of hospital of St. John 19 a. (leased to Christopher Crouch); George Birch; Edward Griffin; Stephen Crouch; Eli Musselwhite; William Fulford. *Fencing* very detailed and set out with the allotments.

Tithes commuted by allotment. Exchange of tithes on St. Denis' farm known as St. Denis' tithes to coincide with new allotments of St. Denis' farm lands. These tithes were due to prebendary of Chute and Chisenbury and his lessee, the warden and fellows of All Souls College, Oxford, and sub-lessee Rev. Edeard Pole.

Roads 6 public roads, 14 private roads, 1 public footpath. Herbage allotted.

Maps 1812. (1) Barford St. Martin. (2) Stowford in South Newton. Acreages and allottees shown. Whole parish of Barford and the village.

Schedules (1) Proportion of expenses for repair of private road No. 1 payable by adjoining owners. (2) Amounts by which the tenants are to reimburse earl of Pembroke for paying their expenses.

Notes Exchanges allotted directly in the award. Allotments to replace rights in Grovely. Extinguished rights of common affect Baverstock also, especially in Rowden Coppice, Sandgates Coppice, Thornhills Coppice, Chilfinch Coppice, Appeldore Coppice, Hinsel Coppice, Shortengrove Coppice, all in or near Baverstock. Royalty and right of fishery from above the common bridge lately erected allotted to Alexander Powell. Responsibilities for repairing hatches and bridges and regulations and dates for watering meadows set out.

South Newton [3,502 a.]

Lord of Manor earl of Pembroke.

Area [500 a.] The Furlongs, West and East Field, Bake Field, Stowford Common, Middle Field.

Allotments 4. Alexander Powell 112 a.; earl of Pembroke 327 a. (including leases, Alice Trubridge 133 a.; William Dredge 22 a.; Solomon Dredge 24 a.); trustees of Wishford almshouse 59 a.; Richard Coombs. *Fencing* with allotments.

Map See Barford St. Martin.

11 GREAT BEDWYN

Crofton Fields

Agreement 27 Sept. 1764 between Thomas Brudenell, Lord Bruce of Tottenham, and 14 others. Award 9 Nov. 1764, W.R.O. Sav. *Referee* Thomas Blandy of Hurstbourne Tarrant, Hants.

Lord of Manor of Crofton, Lord Bruce.

Area [181 a.] Upper Field, Middle Field, Mill Field, Sand Field.

Allotments 8. Lord Bruce 171 a. (including leases, William Jackson 60 a.; John Bloxham 24 a.; copy, John Bushell 47 a.; Thomas Bushell; Benjamin Sidey; Robert Long); Thomas Tanner; William Cox; Bridget Bushell; Timothy Newman; George Wyndham, earl of Egremont; William Gale; John Chapman. *Fencing* with allotments.

Roads 5 public roads.

Finance £17 5*s*. 7*d*.; shares set out in award.

See also Nos. 12 and 13.

12 GREAT BEDWYN (including parts of Little Bedwyn and Preshute)

Act 30 G. III c. 45 (Great Bedwyn, Little Bedwyn, and Preshute). *Award* 13 April 1792 (enrolled 19 Jan. 1811), W.R.O. 68. *Commissioners* Benjamin

Pryce of Salisbury; Richard Bloxham of West Dean; Benjamin Haynes of Salisbury (replacing John Grant of Manningford, dead).

GREAT BEDWYN [9,933 a.]

Grafton and Wilton tithings

Prebendary of Great Bedwyn (lay) Thomas Brudenell-Bruce, earl of Ailesbury.

Area [2,552 a.] East and West Grafton Home Fields, East and West Grafton Further Fields, The Down, Cock Moor Common, Broad Mead, Upper and Lower Sandy Fields, Pinox Field, Dodsdown Field, Hollow Lands Field, Overlands Field, Underdown, Moor Meadow, Yonder Hill Field, Beetle Meadow, Watersend Meadow, Little Prior, Croft Field, Swath Mead, Dean Meadow, Brooklands Field.

Allotments 11. Public: 1 furze allotment 6 a., or £4 to be laid out annually if more convenient. Earl of Ailesbury 2,223 a. (including lease, William Tanner 137 a.; lease and copy, John Piper 23 a.; William Paine 52 a.; Edward Tanner 89 a.; Sarah Shepherd; John Bushell; Edward White; Zabulon Carter; John Fishlock); Simon Fenshaw 192 a. (including John Tanner; Joseph Tanner); John Hutchins 48 a.; William Paine 25 a.; dean and chapter of Salisbury 28 a. (including lease, Stephen Brown 28 a.); John Platt; William Tanner; Levi Goodman; Thomas Tanner; John White. *Fencing* shown on map.

Tithes Tithe rent-charges shown in schedule.

Roads 16 public roads, 2 public bridle ways, 7 public footpaths, 8 private roads. Roads on Grafton Green to continue. Herbage allotted.

Maps (1) Tithing of Grafton. (2) Tithing of Wilton. (3) Part of Little Bedwyn. (4) Manton tithing in Preshute. New allotments outlined in red, old inclosures exchanged in yellow, remainder in green. Allottees and acreages shown, also whether lease or copy.

Schedule Tithes payable and estates on which they are payable.

See also Nos. 11 and 13.

Notes Vicar and churchwardens gave their burgages, houses, etc. in Great Bedwyn to earl of Ailesbury in exchange for other lands.

LITTLE BEDWYN [4,343 a.]

Vicar William Harrison D.D.

Area [525 a.] North, East and South Fields.

Allotments 7. Earl of Ailesbury 70 a. (including Stephen Wentworth; Rachel Smith; Benjamin Chouls; Stephen Birch; Dorothy Tribe); guardians of William Kent 270 a.; Martha and Mary Blandy 109 a.; Stephen Wentworth 48 a.; John Pierce 21 a.; Dorothy Popham ; John Smith. *Fencing* shown on map.

Roads 2 public roads, 3 public bridle ways and private roads, 7 public footpaths, 3 private roads. Herbage to neighbouring allottees only.

Map See Great Bedwyn.

See also No. 14.

Notes Commissioners organized exchange of tithes between prebendary of Bedwyn and the vicar of Little Bedwyn, which included the provision by the prebendary of a house for the vicar. Small part of Froxfield included.

PRESHUTE [5,358 a.]

Manton tithing

Area [390 a.] Barrow Field, Upper Field, Mill Field, West, South and North Field, Laxbury.

Allotments 14. Earl of Ailesbury 171 a. (including Richard Eyles); trustees of John Braithwaite 103 a.; James Sutton 26 a.; mayor and burgesses of Marlborough for support of a free grammar school 38 a.; William Fuidge 25 a.; Thomas Brown 25 a.; James Messam; John Neate; George Brown; Thomas Lediard; Frances Ball; Jacob Furnell; churchwardens of Preshute; dean and chapter of Salisbury. *Fencing* general and on map.

Roads 3 public roads, 3 private footpaths, 3 private roads. Herbage to neighbouring allottees only.

Map See Great Bedwyn.

Notes Watercourses in Manton Marsh awarded to earl of Ailesbury and trustees of John Braithwaite for watering their meadows.

13 GREAT BEDWYN

Marten tithing

Act 52 G.III c.66. *Award* 2 Sept. 1815 (enrolled 20 Aug. 1816), W.R.O. 99. *Commissioners* George Barnes of Andover, Hants; Richard Webb of Salisbury (in place of Francis Webb, dead). *Umpire* Richard Richardson. *Surveyor* Thomas Phillips of Andover.

Lord of Manor Henry Fanshawe.

Rector (lay impropriator of prebend and of Parsonage manor) Charles Brudenell-Bruce, earl of Ailesbury.

Area [734 a.] North and South Fields, Yonder Hill Field, Little Field, Marten Down.

Allotments 4. Henry Fanshawe 384 a. (including 90 a. for great tithes and other tithes on a further 29 a.); earl of Ailesbury 272 a. (including 257 a. for prebendal tithes); Rev. William Rush Hallet Churchill and Martha his wife 43 a.; David Pinckney 35 a. *Fencing* general.

Tithes commuted by allotment of land. Two pieces of land 7 a. and 5 a. excluded.

Roads 2 public roads, 1 public footpath, 2 private roads.

Map Marten tithing. Allottees and acreages shown; also a schedule of inclosures not exchanged (201 a.). One detached portion.

See also Nos. 11 and 12.

14 LITTLE BEDWYN

Chisbury

Agreement 1 Feb. 1721 between Charles Bruce, Lord Bruce, and others. *Award* 23 May 1722, W.R.O. Sav. *Commissioners* Thomas Ambrose of Chilton Foliat; Edward Hanson of Avington, Berks.; Roger Carter of Kintbury, Berks.

Lord of Manor of Chisbury, Charles Bruce, Lord Bruce of Whorlton.

Area [252 a.] Chisbury Common, Hill Field, Shortridge Field, Church Field, Nookwood.

Allotments 7. Public: 1 chalk pit. Lord Bruce 207 a. (including John Tarrant the elder 15 a.; Stephen Birch 15 a.; Thomas Legg 63 a.; Francis Thistlethwayte 46 a.; Timothy Kimber; Richard Early; Edward Lawrence; John Smith); John Tarrant 26 a.; Thomas Street; Stephen Winkworth; John Blandy; Richard Brownjohn. *Fencing* general and with allotments.

See also No. 12.

15 BERWICK ST. JAMES [2,497 a.]

Act 29 G.III c.42. (Berwick St. James and Fisherton Anger). *Award* 5 May 1790 (enrolled 4 Dec. 1798), W.R.O. 50. *Commissioners* Richard Richardson of Devizes; Richard Bloxham of Winterslow; Thomas Fricker of Longbridge Deverill. *Surveyors* Francis Webb and William Tubb of Salisbury.

Lord of Manor none stated but allotment to James Harris, Lord Malmesbury, for rights of the soil.

Rector none stated but allotment to H. P. Wyndham for glebe.

Area 1,641 a. including roads 31 a. [1,492 a.] North and South Crofts, North, Middle and South Field, Church Marsh, Farm Meadows, Sussex Half, Bushey Ball, Home Croft, Upmarsh, The Down.

Allotments 5. Lord Malmesbury 1,102 a. (including leases, Richard Coombs 85 a.; Richard Dawkins 25 a.; Mary Parker 34 a.; George Baker 70 a.; Samuel Rolfe 38 a.; lease and copy, William Langley 72 a.; Thomas Miles 62 a.; copy, Ann Blewden 35 a.; John Gilbert 32 a.; Jane Powell 18 a.; Thomas Miles; James Carter); John Howe, Lord Chedworth 294 a.; Henry Penruddocke Wyndham 93 a.; John Saph; Henry Biggs.

Roads 6 public roads, 1 public footpath, 1 private road and public footpath, 8 private roads. Herbage allotted. Duties of repairing stiles and gates determined.

Finance Expenses paid by Lord Malmesbury who is to recoup himself by an annual rate charged on his tenants.

Notes Upmarsh watered by two sets of hatches both belonging to Lord Chedworth, one in Berwick St. James and one in Winterbourne Stoke; hatches to be repaired by Lord Chedworth and his successors and the previous scheme of watering to be continued; in return for this concession Lord Chedworth receives an improved allotment. On the downs 169 a. to be fed in common with sheep by 8 allottees, and numbers of sheep for each allottee determined; common shepherd to be appointed. In Upmarsh and Church Marsh 8a. being 6 allotments to be fed in common with cows from 12 May to 12 Dec. Of Lord Malmesbury's allotment 140 a. are to replace rights of the soil.

16 BERWICK ST. JOHN [3,725 a.]

Act 26 G.III c.48. *Award* 10 Dec. 1794 (enrolled 4 Dec. 1798), W.R.O. 51. *Commissioners* Richard Richardson of Bath; Benjamin Pryce of Salisbury;

(John Davis of Bloxham, Oxon, dead). *Surveyors* Francis Webb of Salisbury and William Tubb of Fisherton Anger.

Lord of Manor George Pitt, Lord Rivers (succeeding Anthony Ashley Cooper, earl of Shaftesbury, by purchase).

Rector Thomas Boys (succeeding Edward Rolle, dead).

Area 1,699 a. including roads 22 a. [1,678 a.] Rushmore Lawn, New Leaze Common, Tinkley Down, Costard's Common, Frying Pan Down, Staplefoot Plots, Great and Little West Field, Pigeon House Field, East Field, Horse Hill Field, Staplefoot Walk.

Allotments 11. Lord Rivers 759 a.; John Lush 33 a.; George Herbert, earl of Pembroke 228 a. (including leases, Hannah Scott; John Lush 84 a.); Hon. James Arundell 80 a.; Henry Foot 426 a.; rector of Berwick St. John 64 a.; Joseph Foot 38 a.; Thomas Grove 48 a. (including leases, Thomas Wright; Hannah Scott); William Mont Scott. *Fencing* general. Bank of earth and rails to be erected by named allottees to keep cattle from neighbouring parishes out of the woods.

Tithes not commuted; Parsonage of Rushmore Coppice and Parsonage of Staplefoot Coppice belonging to the rector of Berwick St. John were said to have been formerly taken by the rector in place of tithes of the wood.

Roads 7 public roads, 7 private roads, 1 public footpath. Herbage allotted.

Finance Expenses paid by the earl of Shaftesbury and an annual rate payable by his lease and copy holders is set out in the award.

Notes Unusual rights mentioned such as Composition Venison.

17 BERWICK ST. LEONARD [1,144 a.]

Act 58 G.III c.47 (Private, not printed). *Award* 3 Dec. 1840 (enrolled 7 Dec. 1840), W.R.O. 158. *Commissioners* Thomas Davis the younger (replacing Charles Pearson Charlton, d. 1836, replacing John Charlton of Stourton, d. 1826); John Hayward of Devizes (late of Rowde). *Umpire* Thomas Davis of Horningsham.

Lord of Manor of Berwick St. Leonard, John Benett; of Fonthill Bishop, William Beckford.

Rector Charles Henry Grove (succeeding Isaac Hodgson).

Area 1,133 a. including old inclosures [836 a.] Windmill Field, Fonthill Field, Coach Road Field, Berwick Wood, East, West and Middle Fields, Berwick Marsh.

Allotments 3. Rector of Berwick St. Leonard 109 a. (including old inclosures, and all for tithes); John Benett 724 a.; Henry King. *Fencing* Rector's allotments to be fenced by John Benett.

Tithes allotment to rector in place of tithes great and small.

Roads 5 public roads.

Map Charles Pearson Charlton. Village shown and old inclosures in pink.

Notes Very badly set out award. Exchanges with lands in Fonthill Bishop (William Beckford with John Benett) confirmed by the commissioners and signed before the main award.

18 BIDDESTONE

Biddestone St. Nicholas [1,812 a.], Biddestone St. Peter [130 a.], Slaughterford [561 a.].

Act 51 G.III c.130. *Award* 18 July 1812 (enrolled 14 July 1813), W.R.O. 88. *Commissioner* Richard Richardson of London. *Surveyor* Samuel Wharton of London (replacing Thomas Crass of London, dead).

Lord of Manor of Biddestone St. Nicholas, Paul Cobb Methuen; of Slaughterford, Hon. Charles Wyndham.

Rector of Biddestone St. Peter, Charles Daubeny, archdeacon of Sarum.

Area 266 a. excl. roads. Ancient inclosures 1,592 a. [721 a.] Shrub, Hartham Common, Weavern Mead, Harequil Coppice, Little Field, Upper and Lower Binsey, Great and Little Dry Fields, North Moor, Home Field, Hill Garston, Little Marsh.

Allotments 17. Public: 2 stone quarries. Hon. C. W. Wyndham 146 a. (including leases, D. Blake 28 a.; copy, William Little 35 a.; Mrs. Mountjoy 23 a.; John Skeate, Henry Garner, Mary Martin, trustees of John Skeate); Paul Cobb Methuen 253 a.; William Little 104 a.; Mrs. Katherine Long 137 a. (including William Gale; Francis Little); William Edwards 41 a.; archdeacon Daubeny; Isaac Little; George Neate; Mrs. Young; Daniel Edwards; John Beard; Mrs. Mountjoy; William Mountjoy; Samuel Mountjoy; Henry Shrapnell; George Gillett. *Fencing* stone walls or quickset hedges to be made 4 feet high and kept in order by allottees.

Roads 3 public roads, 1 private road and public footpath, 1 public footpath, 3 private roads.

Map Whole parish with village, allottees, and acreages shown and fences marked.

Schedule (attached to map) shows allotment number, allottee, field name, and whether allotted or not.

Notes Common Hill (6 a.) and Cloud Common (7 a.) both in Slaughterford, and the Butts (1 a.) in Biddestone St. Nicholas not inclosed but had been inclosed by the time of the tithe award (1840).

19 BISHOPSTONE (North Wilts.) [3,519 a.]

Act 49 G.III c.106 (not printed). *Award* 23 Dec. 1813 (enrolled 18 Oct. 1814), W.R.O. 91. *Commissioners* William Jennings of Evershot, Dorset; George Barnes of Andover, Hants. *Umpire* John Davis of Bloxham, Oxon. *Surveyors* John Martin of Evershot and Thomas Phillips of Andover.

Lord of Manor bishop of Salisbury; *lessee* Henry Vassall, Lord Holland.

Prebendary and Lord of Manor of Prebend, Edward Rogers; *lessee* executors of William Church. *Vicar* George Wakeman.

Area includes old inclosures 857 a. of which 236 a. were later exchanged. [2,700 a.] Lower Field, West and East Meadow, Town Down, West Field, Lord's Mead, West Coombs, Chipmead.

Allotments 6. Public: 7 gravel pits 6 a.; 1 a. to poor in place of furze. Bishop of Salisbury 1,742 a. (including lease, Lord Holland 333 a.; copy, Ann Anger 179 a.; John Anger 116 a.; William Brown 129 a.; John Batt 32 a.; John Browning 30 a.; Walter Cue 80 a.: Charles Collins 21 a.; Thomas

Chowles 19 a.; Martha Edmonds 36 a.; Stephen Goddard 24 a.; William Norris 15 a.; Thomas Newbury 20 a.; John Povey 27 a.; Rebecca Somerset 31 a.; Thomas Taylor 22 a.; representatives of John Tarrant 36 a.; James Wilson 223 a.; William Woodward 37 a.; John Pope 137 a.; Joseph Bowsher, Edward Curtis, Jane Cheer, William Chowles, Christopher Edmonds, Richard Edmonds, Henry Fairthorne, Mary Jacobs, Elizabeth Laurence, Elizabeth Morse, John Nash, Elizabeth New, Thomas Purton, Thomas Povey, Joseph Povey, William Smith, John Sayer, Elizabeth Sly, John Spicer, Ann Taylor, Sibylla Taylor, Mary Williams, Jane Wells, Henry Woodward); prebendary of Bishopstone 814 a. (including 608 a. for tithes; copy, Robert Church 99 a.; executors of Benjamin Kent 16 a.; Elijah Laurence 15 a.; James Wilson 18 a.; executors of William Church; Henry Fairthorne; Thomas Jacobs); vicar of Bishopstone 136 a. (including 124 a. for tithes); Abraham Edmonds. *Fencing* set out in award.

Tithes allotments to prebendary and vicar for greater and lesser tithes. Those with insufficient lands to pay a composition and/or give up some of their old inclosures.

Roads 10 public roads, 2 public footpaths, 13 private roads. Herbage allotted.

Map Whole parish and village, allottees and acreages, great tithes shown, exchanges coloured, common, meadows, and fields shown.

Schedule Rate for repair of private roads.

20 BISHOPSTONE (South Wilts.) [4,649 a.]

Bishopstone, Faulstone, Flambeston, Netton, Throope, Croucheston tithings.

Act 25 G.III c.56 (Fovant, Swallowcliffe, Broad Chalke, Ebbesborne Wake, Bower Chalke, Alvediston, Bishopstone, Fifield Bavant). *Award* 3 Jan. 1792 (enrolled 17 Nov. 1794), W.R.O. V 38. *Commissioners* Richard Bloxham of West Dean; Richard Richardson of Devizes; Francis Webb (replacing William Corfield of Salisbury, d. 1787). *Surveyor* Benjamin Haynes (replacing William Corfield).

Lord of Manor Henry Herbert, earl of Pembroke.

Rector William Neville.

Area [3,632 a.] West Mead, Mill Mead, Little Mead, North, South, West, East and Middle Fields, Faulston Down, Netton Down, Netton Fields, Croucheston Sheep Down, Cow Down, Little Field, Home Field.

Allotments 8. Public: 3 allotments for furze 15 a.; common chalk pit on Ragland Hill. Earl of Pembroke 3,328 a. (including leases, Amos Prowse 216 a.; executors of William Rowden 178 a.; copy, Edward Griffin 17 a.; Robert Lanham 19 a.; Robert Roberts 16 a.; John Rooke 63 a.; William Rooke 41 a.; John Baker 138 a.; Thomas Bevis 182 a.; Thomas Talbot 47 a.; William Scaplehorn 52 a.; William Clark 163 a.; Thomas Harding 92 a.; Thomas Hewitt 125 a.; Jane Deacon; Edward Hewitt; Peter Rooke; Mary Norris; Thomas Hartford; Joseph Woodlands); Edward Hewitt 233 a.; Sarah Lodge 25 a.; rector of Bishopstone 29 a; William Clark; executors of William Rowden.

Roads 24 public roads, 5 private roads. Herbage allotted. Common watering place mentioned with the roads.

Finance Sale allotment of 1 a. 10 p. to William Young for £14 6*s.* 7*d.* to pay the rector's share. Rest to be paid for by allottees including if necessary the reversionaries.

Maps (1) North part of parish including Flambeston, Netton, Bishopstone. (2) South part including Croucheston, Throope, Faulstone. Whole parish including the village. Allottees and acreages shown.

Schedules (1) Lifeholders under the earl of Pembroke, whose reversionaries have paid the expenses and who are to pay interest.
(2) Charges assessed by the commissioners on various lifeholders under the earl of Pembroke.

See also No. 195.

Notes Netton two marshes to be fed in common. Ragland Hill to be fed in common by Throope (2 a.).

21 BISHOPSTROW [1,045 a.]
(with parts of Warminster, Sutton Veny, and North Bavant dealt with in Pitmead).

Act 48 G.III c.44 (not printed). *Award* 26 Jan. 1811 (enrolled 17 Sept. 1821), W.R.O. 115. *Commissioner* John Gale of Stert.

Lord of Manor Sarah Temple.

Rector William Williams.

Area [877 a.] Cow Down, Farm Down, Bishopstrow Field, Priors Pill, Tun Mead, Ray Mead, Pitmead.

Allotments 13. William Temple 657 a. (including William Hinton); James Bayly 90 a.; William Munday 42 a.; Francis Dugdale Astley 17 a. (including William Turner, Jeremiah Morgan); Thomas Thynne, marquess of Bath 30 a.; Eton College; rector of Bishopstrow; prebendary of Warminster; William Hinton; Samuel Long; Rev. William Slade; dean and chapter of Salisbury (Warminster parsonage); John Benett. *Fencing* on map and general.

Roads 2 public roads, 1 public footpath, 3 private roads.

Maps John Hayward of Devizes. (1) Parish with allottees and acreages and five detached pieces. A fine map with hachured hills. Schedule with allottees and exchanges. (2) Pitmead with schedule of allotments under three parishes, Bishopstrow, Warminster, Norton Bavant.

Schedules (1) For repairing Bishopstrow Drove. (2) For repairing Pitmead Drove and watercourse.

See also Nos. 146, 178, 189.

Notes Old inclosures including Farm Down allotted. Payment by James Bayly of a sack of wheat at Christmas for the watering of Prior's Pile and Broad Mead not allowed for in the award and is to continue together with the customary watering. Rights of turbary and fishing reserved to lady of Bishopstrow manor and lord of Norton Bavant manor.

22 BOSCOMBE [1,688 a.]

West Boscombe

Act General, 8 & 9 Vic. c.118. *Award* 17 April 1866 (enrolled 13 July 1866), W.R.O. 185. *Valuer* Francis Attwood.

Rector Thomas Taylor.

Area [595 a.].

Allotments 3. George Matcham 555 a.; Sir Edmund Antrobus 18 a.; rector of Boscombe 22 a. *Fencing* general and with allotments and on map.

Roads 1 private road.

Map 1864. Shows West Boscombe and village. Pre-inclosure holdings shown.

Notes The Boscombe Tithe Award (1843) contains a map of the common fields. The Inclosure Award refers to numbers on the Tithe Award map.

23 BOYTON [3,944 a.]

Corton Tithing

Act 9 G.IV c.9 (Private). *Award* 19 May 1829 (enrolled 9 Sept. 1829), W.R.O. 111. *Commissioners* Thomas Davis of Warminster; Michael John Festing of Maiden Bradley; Arthur Legge of Tisbury. *Surveyor* Thomas Tillbrook of Maiden Bradley.

Lord of Manor of Corton, Aylmer Bourke Lambert.

Area 2,300 a. including roads [2,101 a.] West Wood, Corton Common Wood.

Allotments 15. Public: 1 chalk pit; 1 well. Robert Grosvenor, Earl Grosvenor (by purchase from the allottee John Farquhar) 343 a.; Aylmer Bourke Lambert 1,020 a. (including lease, William and Cornelius Churchill 19 a.; copy and lease, Ambrose Patient 346 a.; copy, William Patient 254 a.; Edward Withers 46 a.; Sarah Withers 48 a.); John Davis 115 a.; Ambrose Patient 67 a.; Richard Withers 168 a.; Sarah Withers 236 a.; William Churchill 37 a.; Cornelius Churchill 24 a.; William and Cornelius Churchill 31 a.; John Thring 26 a.; Edward Withers 33 a.; Joseph Everett; surveyors of highways. *Fencing* general and shown on map.

Roads 1 public road, 1 public bridle way, 1 public footpath, 8 private roads. Duties for repairing private roads set out; 2 footpaths stopped up.

Map Thomas Tillbrook of Horningsham. Allottees and acreages shown and coloured according to allottees. Tithing and village of Corton shown.

Schedule Rate for repair of private roads.

Notes Corton Woods (255 a.) allotted to Aylmer Bourke Lambert, and 51 a. deducted from his allotment to extinguish rights of feeding there. The 51 a. were sold to John Davis of Bapton to help meet the expenses of inclosure. Corton Common Wood (59 a.) and 5 a. of the Down adjoining were also sold to help meet expenses. Earl Grosvenor paid £820 to extinguish all rights of feeding in West Woods (343 a.). Wet Meadow and Corton Meadow to be watered as before.

24 BRADFORD ON AVON [11,478 a. including all the tithings]

Trowle Common (including parts of Trowbridge and Wingfield)

Act General, 8 & 9 Vic. c.118. *Award* 28 Oct. 1853 (enrolled 19 Dec. 1853), W.R.O. L 174. *Valuer* Jacob Henry Cotterell of Bath.

Lord of Manor of Great Trowle, John Cam Hobhouse, Lord Broughton.

Area 177 a.

Allotments 6. Charles Pierrepont, Earl Manvers 111 a.; Lord Broughton 30 a.; William Stancomb 17 a.; Charles Long and others; George and Augusta Spackman; William Applegate. *Fencing* general.

Roads 9 private roads, 3 public footpaths; 5 public roads and 3 public footpaths stopped up.

Map 1852. Allottees and acreages shown. Inclosed areas only.

See also Nos. 25 and 26.

25 BRADFORD ON AVON

Holt

Act General, 8 & 9 Vic. c.118. *Award* 2 May 1867 (enrolled 8 July 1867), W.R.O. 189. *Valuer* Francis Attwood.

Lord of Manor T. B. W. Forster.

Area [9 a.] including sale allotments 6 a. Great Common, Little Common, Ham Green.

Allotments 2. Public: churchwardens 2 r. 27 p. for recreation. T. B. W. Forster. *Fencing* with allotments and on map.

Roads 6 private roads, 2 public footpaths; 2 footpaths stopped up.

Finance 10 sale allotments, 6 a., £683 12*s.* 6*d.*

Map Allotments numbered. Recreation allotments coloured green.

See also Nos. 24 and 26.

26 BRADFORD ON AVON

Bradford Leigh Common, Forwards Common

Map only, W.R.O. Acc 748/5. T. Cruse of Bath 21 Nov. 1821. Allottees and acreages shown.

Allotments Forwards Common [10 a.] 12. J. A. Bullock; W. May; Ann Attwood; T. Rogers; Sir Benjamin Hobhouse; T. Clutterbuck; J. B. Watkin; T. Tugwell; R. Taylor; James Chapman; J. Davis; lord of the soil. Bradford Leigh Common [36 a.] 25. D. Clutterbuck; George Bush; John Bush; H. Shrapnell; J. B. Watkin; Mary Finch; A. Rainer; R. Little; J. Pearce; S. Wyld; E. Phillips; R. Tolly; John Jones; Earl Manvers; Michael Rudman; Thomas Fry; John Deverall; J. A. Bullock; lord of the soil; Sir Benjamin Hobhouse; Walter Spencer; T. C. Hellier; Jeremiah Batten; William Bush; Ann Attwood.

See also Nos. 24 and 25.

27 NORTH BRADLEY AND SOUTHWICK [1,768 a., 2,473 a. respectively]

Part of Rode Common

Act 44 G.III c.23 (not printed). *Award* 17 April 1807 (enrolled 11 May 1809), W.R.O. 75. *Commissioners* Richard Richardson of London; Thomas Davis of Horningsham; John Wilkins of Rowde.

Lord of Manor of North Bradley, Sir James Tylney Long Bt.; of Southwick, Daniel Clutterbuck; lord of Hundred of Whorwellsdown, Joshua Smith.

Rector (lay) warden and scholars of St. Mary's College, Winchester, who also claimed lordship of a manor in North Bradley. *Vicar* Charles Daubeny.

Area [930 a.] Acrefield Wood, Lambert's Marsh, Pole's Hole, Little Common, Drinham Common, Bradley Common, Picked Wood, Yarnbrook Common, Rode Common, Woodmarsh Common, Round Wood, Southwick Green, Greenhill Marsh, Mutton Marsh.

Allotments 73. Public: 2 watering places (Rode Common, Brockerswood Common). Elizabeth Crossdill 86 a.; executors of Walter Long 113 a.; executors of Caleb Bailey 83 a.; Rev. John Trenchard and Walter Long, a minor, 156 a.; executors of Sir James Tylney Long Bt. 43 a. (including 2 a. in trust that the fair may be held as before); warden and scholars of Winchester 17 a. (including glebe; copy, Rev. John Baker; William Rundell and Mary Gibbs; Jeffery Moody); William Francis 18 a.; Jeremiah Francis 20 a.; John Hooper 41 a.; Katharine Powlett, duchess of Bolton 18 a.; James Chapman 32 a.; Amy Coward 18 a.; John Greenhill 19 a.; John Whittaker 25 a.; D. Clutterbuck 26 a.; Joseph Coombs; Mary Clements; Richard Casswell; William and Edward Ferris; John Frowd; Joseph Ford; Job Francis; Richard Say; Joshua Smith; Edward Crabb; William Drewitt; Nathaniel Dalton; Isaac Elton; Mary Edwards; Nathaniel Edwards; vicar of North Bradley; William Bullock; John Bailey; William Ball; representatives of Thomas Phillips; executors of Benjamin Greenhill; churchwardens of North Bradley; John Greenhill; Joseph Greenhill; Philip Gibbs; James Guley; trustees of John Williams; Susannah Haynes; Simon Hiscocks; William Hobbs; James Jordan; Arnold Joyce; John Keates; Joshua Keates; Peter Keevil; Edward Moore; Mary Macey; Thomas Miller; Edward Moody; executors of John Pepler; Job Pickard; William Pike; Thomas Pepler; Thomas Phipps; Benjamin Rebbeck; Ann Rebbeck; Joseph Read; Rev. William Slade; Joseph Smith; Fanny Still; Elizabeth Spragg; trustees of Trowbridge almshouse; Job Usher; Rev. Robert Weaver; Robert White; Elizabeth Whittaker; Samuel Wereat. *Fencing* by allottees except for the vicar and the warden and scholars of Winchester.

Roads 6 public roads, 48 private roads, 9 public footpaths. Additional road set out on Yarnbrook Common to connect with the road authorized by the Westbury Commissioners.

Finance 36 sale allotments.

Map Jeremiah Cruse of Bath 1806. Village shown and inclosed areas.

See also No. 161.

Notes Award delayed by Joshua Smith, lord of the manors of Edington Rectory and Edington Rumsey and of Tinhead Rectory and Tinhead Rumsey, who threatened to appeal to Assizes against the decision of the commissioners to disallow his claims as lord of the above manors. Lot Meadow dealt with separately. The following woods discharged from common rights: Picked Wood 45 a.; Round Wood 43 a.; Highwood 49 a.;

Hazelwood 25 a.; Cutteridge or Ladies Wood 7 a. Sale of 50 encroachments made during the last 20 years.

28 BREMHILL [6,165 a., or 5,420 a. without Avon]

Stockham Marsh (including part of Christian Malford)

Act 15 G.III c.72. *Award* 5 Aug. 1776, amended by award of 28 May 1777 altering the public roads (enrolled 11 June 1777), W.R.O. 9 & 10. *Commissioners* Joseph Butler of York; William Gale of All Cannings; Edward Crooke of Heddington. *Surveyors* Joseph and William Dickenson of Beverley, Yorks.

Lord of Manor William Petty, earl of Shelburne.

Vicar Dr. Matthew Frampton.

Area 435 a. [389 a.] Stockham Marsh.

Allotments 10. Public: stone or gravel pit 3 a. Dr. Matthew Frampton 318 a.; earl of Shelburne 27 a.; Sir Edward Bayntun Rolt 19 a.; Sir James Tylney Long; John Pinniger; John Grant; Elizabeth Hungerford; Mary Riley; Charles Gale. *Fencing* with allotments.

Tithes both great and small exonerated, including some old inclosures (3,831 a.) by allotment of land and a rent-charge, but those on the lands of Sir Edward Bayntun Rolt and the heirs of John Bayntun were excluded by the Act.

Roads 4 public roads, 3 public bridle ways, 3 private roads, 6 public footpaths, 2 private footpaths. Herbage allotted to vicar of Bremhill except Spirthill which was allotted to Sir Edward Bayntun Rolt.

Finance £1,517 14*s*. 7*d*. including making roads and fences. Raised by rate.

Maps (1) Stockham Marsh with the inclosures about Foxham, Cadenham, Spirthill, and Charlcutt. (2) Parts of Bremhill and Christian Malford between Foxham and the river Avon 1775. (3) Tytherton with the grounds south of Avon Lane 1775. (4) Area between Charlcutt and Lebridge 1775. (5) Part of Bremhill which lies west of Lebridge Lane and Bremhill Grove and extends northwards to Wick Gate, Hydes Lane, and the estate of Sir Edward Bayntun Rolt. 1775. Maps show the glebe and lands tithable to Sir Edward Bayntun Rolt.

Schedule Money to be contributed by proprietors for expenses of inclosure.

See also No. 54.

Notes The award allots 389 a. of common land and also exonerates tithes on 3,831 a. either by allotment of land or conversion into a tithe rent-charge, which accounts for the large allotment to the vicar; 6 ditches to be made.

29 BRINKWORTH [5,680 a.]

Act 46 G.III c.28 (not printed). *Award* 19 Aug. 1808 (enrolled 7 Sept. 1827), W.R.O. 131. *Commissioners* John William Biedermann of Tetbury, Glos.; William Jennings of Evershot, Dorset; Richard Richardson of London. *Surveyor* Thomas Crass of London.

Lord of Manor John Howard, earl of Suffolk.

Rector of Brinkworth, Matthew Marsh; of Little Somerford, Henry Wightwick.

Area 500 a. (Act) [56 a.] Barnes Green, Great Common, Giles Green, Clitchbury Green, Sunday Hill, Milborne Common, Little Somerford Common.

Allotments 4. Public: 2 watering places. Rector of Brinkworth 77 a.; earl of Suffolk 423 a. (including Anne Catley, Walter Matthews, Ann Stratton, George Sutton, Mary Redways, Humphrey Hayward, Grace Nicholls, William Hayward, Elizabeth Cutts, Remmett Smith, Sarah Young, Jasper Stratton, William Stratton, Jacob Henley, Thomas Hayward, churchwardens of Brinkworth, Thomas Smith, Mary Dewell, John Fry, Walter Clark, Elizabeth Hitchcock, Richard Moody, Thomas Brook, Richard Pridy, Joshua Matthews, T. Wyatt, Isaac Hunt and G. R. Banks, William Guys, Abraham Horsell, Abraham Smith, Isaac Little, trustees of Hester Collingbourne); Lucy Heath 61 a.

Roads 5 public roads, 8 private roads and public bridle ways, 36 private roads, 6 public footpaths.

Finance 3 sale allotments 165 a. shown in red on map.

Map Henry Augustus Biedermann of Tetbury. Schedule of sale allotments, allotments numbered. Village shown but not whole parish. Several detached pieces.

Schedules (1) Increased rents due from leasehold and copyhold tenants to lord of manor to pay for fencing. (2) Rate for repair of private roads.

See also No. 171.

30 BRITFORD (including part of Downton) [3,201 a.]
East Harnham Manor

Act 56 G.III c.56 (Private, not printed). *Award* 17 March 1847 (enrolled 14 April 1847), W.R.O. 166. *Commissioners* Frederick J. Kelsey of West Lavington (replacing in 1839 Richard Webb of Salisbury, d. 1837); Francis Attwood of Salisbury (replacing in 1845 George Barnes of Andover, d. 1832).

Lord of Manor of East Harnham, Jacob Pleydell-Bouverie, earl of Radnor; of Downton, the bishop of Winchester.

Area [218 a.] East Harnham Hill, West Hill, The Roundabouts, East Field, Low Field.

Allotments 4. Public: 1 chalk pit. Viscount Folkestone 186 a. (including lease John Baker 103 a.); master and brethren of the hospital of St. Nicholas 29 a. (including lease trustees of William Boucher 29 a.); feoffees of Eyre's charity.

Roads 1 public road, 1 public bridle way, 2 public footpaths.

Map F. J. Kelsey of Salisbury. Acreages and allottees shown, village in outline only.

Note Part of the area is in Wick in Downton.

31 BROMHAM [3,519 a.]

Act 51 G.III c.190. *Award* 23 Feb. 1814, subsidiary award 1814 confirming the exchanges (enrolled 26 July 1816), W.R.O. 97. *Commissioner* John Gale of Stert. *Surveyor* John Hayward of Rowde.

Lord of Manor Sir Andrew Bayntun Rolt Bt.

Rector Henry Bayntun.

Area 260 a. [221 a.] Row Moor, Furze Down, Marsh Green, Stroud Common, Westbrook Green, Tucker's Green, Arthur's Green, Hoe Green, St. Edith's Marsh.

Allotments 18. Sir Andrew Bayntun Rolt Bt. 121 a. (including leases, William Knee; James Dunsdon; Isaac Clark; Gent and Tylee; Ann Flower; Walter Long; Edward Bayntun and Constantia his wife; Sarah Gaby; Edward Maris; Edward Wilcox; copy, Walter Breach; Susannah Gaby; Robert Crook; John Atwood; Thomas Atwood; John Gaby junior; Elizabeth Hicks; lease and copy, William Hatter); Sarah Gaby 24 a.; Wadham Locke 18 a.; Gifford Warriner; Edward Seymour, duke of Somerset; John Gaby; James Skeate; Richard Fennell; John Banks; Miss Street; David Wadworth; Mrs. Wild; Elizabeth Hicks; Rev. John Pearse; Eliza Norris; James Norris; rector of Bromham; Thomas Gaby; sale allotments 11 a. *Fencing* general and with allotments and shown on map.

Roads 7 public roads, 1 public bridle way, 16 private roads, 1 public footpath, 4 private footpaths, 1 private bridle way. Herbage allotted.

Finance Sale allotments £721 17*s.* and by rate.

Map Red for commonable land allotted, green for old inclosures. Mostly common and waste, numbered references only.

Schedule Portion of expenses due to exchanges (£276 16*s.* 4*d.*).

32 BURBAGE, COLLINGBOURNE KINGSTON, AND POULTON [3,276 a.]

Act 55 G.III c.99 (Private, not printed). *Award* 2 Feb. 1824 (enrolled 29 Jan. 1827), W.R.O. 128. *Commissioners* John Iveson of London; George Barnes of Andover, Hants; *Umpire* John Davis of Bloxham, Oxon. *Surveyor* John Iveson.

BURBAGE [3,276 a.]

Lord of Manor of Burbage Savage, Burbage Dorrells, and Burbage Esturmy, Charles Brudenell-Bruce, marquess of Ailesbury.

Prebendary of Hurstbourne and Burbage, Dr. Hurlock. *Vicar* Philip Fisher.

Area [115 a.] Steep Common, Margreen Common, Harepath Common, Short Heath Common, Burbage Down.

Allotments 7. Marquess of Ailesbury 97 a.; prebendary of Hurstbourne and Burbage; Henry Wilson; Mrs. Gaisford; John Banning; Rev. P. Fisher; William Tanner. *Fencing* general.

Roads 5 public roads, 7 private roads.

Finance 5 sale allotments 8 a. £915.

Map Allottees and acreages, exchanges marked, inclosures in green and new roads in brown. Parish in outline only and village sketched in.

Notes Lands deducted from allotments to marquess of Ailesbury and allotted to proprietors of common rights in Savernake Forest which were extinguished.

Any allotment in respect of lease or copyhold for lives or life of less value than 40*s.* per annum to be allotted to the landlord, who is to pay copyholder or leaseholder an annual sum as compensation, to be decided by the commissioners; 64 such allotments were made and the compensating sums totalled £27 0*s.* 6*d.* Similarly for holdings worth under £20, 15 allotments were made and the compensating sums totalled £168 14*s.*

COLLINGBOURNE KINGSTON [7,400 a.]

Lord of Manor of Collingbourne Kingston and Collingbourne Sunton, Charles Brudenell-Bruce, marquess of Ailesbury.

Area [1,017 a.] Furzehill Down, Hare Sleight Down, Middle Hill Down, Thornhill Down, Middle Field, North, South and East Field, Aughton Tenantry Down.

Allotments 4. Marquess of Ailesbury 911 a. (including leases, Rev. Joseph Legg 39 a.; John Ward and John Iveson in trust 91 a.); dean and chapter of Winchester 82 a. (including leases, Thomas Asheton Smith 78 a.; Robert Mackrell); Elizabeth Dean 23 a.; William Sheppard. *Fencing* general.

Roads 8 public roads.

Finance £112 10*s.* paid by marquess of Ailesbury as his share.

Map Allottees and acreages and exchanges shown. Allotments shaded in green. Boundary between Collingbourne Kingston and Aughton shown.

See also Nos. 61 and 62.

Notes Various lands exempted from inclosure: Savernake Forest, lands of Thomas Gilbert and Thomas Edwards in Collingbourne Aughton and of Edward Tanner in Oldborough Field. Boundaries between Collingbourne Kingston and Burbage straightened.

MILDENHALL [4,177 a.]

Poulton tithing

Lord of Manor of Mildenhall, Charles Brudenell-Bruce, marquess of Ailesbury.

Rector George Buxton (succeeding Charles Francis, dead).

Area [612 a.] Poulton Down, Poulton Field, Little Field.

Allotments 2. Marquess of Ailesbury 569 a. (including an estate of 267 a. bought from Viscount Bolingbroke); Rev. George Buxton 43 a. *Fencing* general.

Roads 3 public roads, 1 private road.

Map Poulton only. Allottees and acreages shown. Inclosures outlined in green.

See also No. 138.

33 CALNE [8,058 a.]

Calne, Calstone Wellington, and Blackland

Act 53 G.III c.176. *Award* 31 Dec. 1818 (enrolled 3 July 1820), W.R.O. V 110. *Commissioners* John Gale of Stert: Richard Parsons of Bath.

Umpire Benjamin Haynes of Shalbourne. *Surveyor* John Hayward of Rowde.

Lord of Manor of Blackland, John Merewether; of Prebend of Calne, and lay rectors, Hon. James Abercromby and Sir Thomas Baring as trustees for the marquess of Lansdowne; of Calne and Calstone, Henry Petty-Fitzmaurice, marquess of Lansdowne.

Prebendary of Calne, Thomas Henry Hume; *Rector* of Blackland, James Mayo; *Vicar* of Calne, Thomas Greenwood.

Area 1,980 a. [1,679 a.] North Field, The Marsh, Wenhill, Castle Field, Stockley Upper and Lower Fields; Blackland North Field, Southill, Blackland Common, Quemerford Common, Honey Garston, Abberd Mead.

Allotments 53. Trustees of marquess of Lansdowne 104 a.; devisees of John Bishop 121 a.; Hon. John Crewe 100 a.; John Merewether 104 a.; Mary Merewether 56 a.; Samuel Neate 31 a.; representatives of Arabella Walker Heneage 20 a.; marquess of Lansdowne 951 a.; devisees of Benjamin Bowman 17 a.; rector of Calstone 16 a.; Rev. William Marsh; William Northey; Katherine Oriel; devisees of Joseph Perkins; trustees of Baptist meeting house; Quakers' assembly; Mary Rawlings; James Rumming; William Savory; William Spackman; Rebecca Stevenson; devisees of Joseph Tanner; John Wayte; Robert Wetherell; James Kyrle Money; Isaac Clarke; William Clarke; Edward Eatwell; Mary Essington; Ralph Gaby; Martha Gauntlett; steward and burgesses of Calne; Joseph Gundry; Samuel Hale; devisees of T. M. Hancock; Robert Henly; John Hill; Henry King; John Ladd; dowager marchioness of Lansdowne; Mary and Martha Ashley; Daniel Bailey; William Bailey; William Bayly; George Beames; rector of Blackland; Benjamin Bodman; Thomas Button; Francis Child; churchwardens of Calne; Calne Free School; vicar of Calne; David Clarke. *Fencing* partly general and partly set out in the award. Stone wall 4ft. 6in. or quickset hedges and ditches 4ft. wide.

Tithes on the Marsh, the Alders, and Quemerford Common extinguished by allotment to the vicar of Calne.

Roads 30 private roads, 7 private footpaths, 8 public footpaths, 3 private roads and public bridle ways, 1 public bridle way.

Finance Sale allotments.

Maps (1) Calne and surrounding lands with five detached pieces. Calne lightly sketched in, allotments and old inclosures exchanged, numbered and shown on attached schedule. (2) Quemerford Common, Stockley, and Blackford, schedule as above. (3) Calstone. (4) Abberd Mead: all old inclosures with many detached pieces.

See also No. 43.

Notes The Act contains a reservation that the Alders (62 a.) is to be allotted to the marquess of Lansdowne. Great and Little Abberd, Boredown, Quemerford North and South fields excluded from the Act because they form part of other fields outside the parishes in this Act. Some lands in Compton Bassett allotted in exchange.

34 ALL CANNINGS [4,549 a.]

All Cannings and Allington tithing

Act 37 G.III c.50. *Award* 23 March 1799 (enrolled 8 Oct. 1799), W.R.O. 56. *Commissioners* Francis Webb of Salisbury; John Gale of Stert; William Jennings. *Surveyor* William Tubb of Fisherton Anger.

Lord of Manor of All Cannings and Fullaway, Nicholas Nicholas; of Allington, Henry Fox-Strangways, earl of Ilchester.

Rector John Fullerton.

Area 3,302 a. (All Cannings 2,243 a., Allington 1,059 a.) [All Cannings 2,145 a., Allington 1,038 a.]. *All Cannings* Long Mucket Hill, Cannings Marsh, Clifford's Hill, Gall Sand, East Hams, Red Meads, Woodway Field, Tenantry Down, Stanton Ford, Applepye Grounds, Windmill Ball, Snipe Mead, Little Westbrook Field, Farrell, Short Wetlands, Lain's Field, Whitefoot Mead, Great and Little Costacres, Upper Cusborough, Cusborough Meads, Bean Ham, Ford's Mead, Collett's Mead, Limborough Grounds, Hither and Farther Coomb, Great and Little Oxmore, Little Cow Leaze. *Allington* East and West Field, Mansole, Hither Combe.

Allotments All Cannings 16. Nicholas Nicholas 1,459 a. (including lease, William Green; copy, Thomas Andrews 38 a.; John Chamberlayne 102 a.; Hannah Durnford 51 a.; William Fowle 153 a.; Rev. George Gibbs 45 a.; Martha Hamlen 23 a.; Harry Hitchcock 103 a.; trustees of George Jaques 38 a.; Mary Maslen 25 a.; William Miell 28 a.; James Noyes 60 a.; Joseph Pearce 142 a.; executors of Sarah Pearce 29 a.; John Popejoy 119 a.; Stephen Pricter 31 a.; William Rivers 68 a.; James Stratton 18 a.; Stephen Durnford; Jacob Giddings; Susannah Giddings; William Green; Thomas Hibbard; Jane Lane; John Maslen; Thomas Maton; John Neale; William Nash; John Palmer; John Shipman; Thomas Tucker; William Waylen; William Green); Gifford Warriner 48 a.; Harry Hitchcock 397 a.; Ann Lavington 139 a.; John Hope 43 a.; rector of All Cannings 37 a.; John Matthews; William Maslen; William Rivers; William Miell; William Green; James Stratton; James Sutton; trustees of Stanton charity; Jane Springford; Robert Tucker.

Allington 5. Earl of Ilchester 772 a.; (including leases, Daniel Parry 156 a.; William Hill 45 a.; Joseph Pearce 39 a.; Daniel Maslen 26 a.; John Sims 33 a.; John Godwin 38 a.; copy, Jesse Beak 44 a.; John Pile 35 a.; Paul Perrott 18 a.; lease and copy, Thomas Parry 130 a.; Joseph Parry 179 a.; Robert Neate; John Chamberlayne; John King; Thomas Skeates; William Maslen); John Giddings 195 a.; Paul Perrott 18 a.; Isaac Hamlen 32 a.; Thomas Parry. *Fencing* general with bank 2ft. high.

Roads All Cannings, 5 public roads, 1 public bridle way, 8 public footpaths, 16 private roads. Allington, 2 public roads, 9 private roads, 1 private bridle way. Herbage allotted.

Finance Lands deducted from allotments to Nicholas Nicholas and the rector and granted to John Grant and Harry Hitchcock who are to pay the expenses for All Cannings and Allington, and rate.

Maps (1) Parish north of Calne-Pewsey road. (2) South part including village. Allotments numbered and acreages shown. Wansdyke, Rybury Camp and Kennet and Avon canal shown. Boundary between All Cannings and Allington marked. Whole parish including village.

Schedule Sums to be paid by proprietors for expenses of inclosure and roads.

Notes Allotment to Thomas Parry, lessee of parsonage of Allington, of 1 a. in respect of his right of keeping a bull on the late Cow Down. Certain lands to be depastured in common; sets out regulations and numbers of sheep. William Maslen and William Rivers to repair a bridge in their allotments. New boundary between All Cannings and Allington determined by commissioners.

35 BISHOP'S CANNINGS

Coate tithing

Act 18 G.III c.62. *Award* 4 Aug. 1780 (enrolled 2 Feb. 1781), W.R.O. 13. *Commissioners* Daniel Tanner of Urchfont; Richard Bloxham of Winterslow; William Gale of All Cannings. *Surveyor* John Clements of Avebury.

Lord of Manor Thomas Erle Drax.

Rector Dean and chapter of Salisbury; *lessee* Rev. Thomas Abdy Abdy. *Vicar* Arthur Dodwell.

Area [851 a.].

Allotments 10. Thomas Erle Drax 546 a. (including leases, John Brown 45 a.; Simon Cook 32 a.; Rachel and Anne Jacques 42 a.; Margery Lawrence 53 a.; John Neate 20 a.; George Sloper 49 a.; Richard Shergold 45 a.; Rev. Charles Gibbs; Francis Merewether; William Neate; Daniel Neate); committee of Thomas Knight, a lunatic, 209 a. (including leases, Richard Hiscock; John Neate; George Ruddle); trustees of Jonathan Weston 66 a.; Thomas Brown; trustees of Coate charity; Mary Hood; Ambrose Hood; John Smith; Michael Tichborne; dean and chapter of Salisbury. *Fencing* fencing of rector's allotment to be paid for by rest of allottees.

Tithes Vicar to take his great tithes, lately due from the common fields, from 8 a. on the east side and from part of the allotment to trustees of Jonathan Weston.

Roads 3 public roads, 3 private roads, 2 public footpaths.

Finance £599 8*s*. 9*d*. General rate, except for dean and chapter of Salisbury. The schedule of amounts due from allottees not attached.

See also Nos. 36, 37.

36 BISHOP'S CANNINGS, CHITTOE, AND MARDEN

Roundway, Bedborough, and Chittoe tithings and Marden

Act 34 G.III c.52. *Award* 11 Sept. 1812 (enrolled 11 Sept. 1813), W.R.O. 89. *Commissioners* Richard Richardson of London; Thomas Wyatt of Wargrave, Berks. (late of Rowdeford); John Gale of Stert. *Surveyors* Francis Webb of Salisbury and William Tubb of Fisherton Anger.

BISHOP'S CANNINGS [8,872 a. excl. Southbroom]

Lord of Manor of Bishop's Cannings, bishop of Salisbury; *lessee* Thomas Grimston Estcourt (replacing James Sutton, dead); of Cannings Canonicorum, Thomas Grimston Estcourt (succeeding dean and chapter of Salisbury); *lessee* Thomas Abdy Abdy.

Rector (lay) Thomas Grimston Estcourt (succeeding dean and chapter of Salisbury). *Vicar* Arthur Dodwell.

Area [3,348 a.] Blackenhill, Sand Field, Lower Field, Hill Field, Crocombe Down, Home Field, West and East Fields, Roundway East, South and North Fields, Coate Grove, Roundway Down, Shearing Down.

Allotments 8. Bishop of Salisbury 2,809 a. (including lease, Thomas Grimston Estcourt 704 a.; copy, William Salmon 1,188 a.; James Gent 455 a.; Susannah Ruddle 118 a.; Mark Sloper 137 a.; Daniel Parry 16 a.; William Crook; Walter Ashley; Joan Ashley; William Brown; Michael Pound; Robert Nash; Joseph Pierce; William Maslen; Thomas Matthews); holders of lands in Bourton and Easton 118 a.; Eleanor Sutton 298 a.; guardians of George Ruddle 88 a.; Sir Andrew Bayntun Rolt Bt.; devisees of George Norris; Sir John Smith Bt.; feoffees of parish lands.

Tithes Allotments to bishop of Salisbury and Thomas Grimston Estcourt in place of tithes.

Roads 11 public roads, 25 private roads, 1 public bridle way, 6 public footpaths. Herbage allotted.

Finance Bishop of Salisbury's share paid by deduction of 114 a. from his allotment which was sold to Thomas Grimston Estcourt who is to pay expenses. Deduction from lay rectory (T. G. Estcourt) of 18 a. and sale to T. G. Estcourt who is to pay expenses.

Maps (1) Tithings of Roundway and Bedborough. (2) Bishop's Cannings village. (3) Bishop's Cannings, Horton, Easton, Bourton. Allottees and acreages shown.

See also Nos. 35 and 37.

Notes 118 a. to be fed in common by holders of lands in Easton and Bourton. Allotments for rights of the soil and for demesne to Thomas Grimston Estcourt as lessee of the manor. Large number of exchanges confirmed including some from freehold estates.

CHITTOE [1,100 a.]

Lord of Manor Bishop of Salisbury; *lessee* Sir Andrew Bayntun Rolt Bt.

Area [105 a.] Chittoe Heath, Silver Street Common, Burton's Green.

Allotments 2. Sir Andrew Bayntun Rolt 97 a. (including lease, John Rains 21 a.; and 17 a. sale allotments); Rev. John Pearse.

Roads 3 public roads, 3 private roads. Herbage allotted, private roads to be kept up by beneficial allottees.

Finance Two allotments to Sir Andrew Bayntun Rolt who is to pay the expenses.

Map Part of the tithing in outline only, village shown.

Notes Parts of Bromham included in Chittoe. Boundary between Chittoe and Bromham redrawn by commissioners.

MARDEN [1,286 a.]

Lord of Manor Eleanor Sutton (succeeding James Sutton, dead).

Rector Dean and chapter of Bristol; *lessee* Jenny Hayward. *Vicar* Francis Simpson of Tarrant Gunville (succeeding Edward Bowles).

Area [1,154 a.] Eystone, Lake's Common, Lot Meadow, Hill Mead, Icelick, Bell Crofts, Clay Field, Ruslet Common, Green Hill, Gooseham, Sandfield, North Meadow.

Allotments 5. Elanor Sutton 1,102 a. (including leases, executors of Benjamin Hayward 33 a.; Daniel Chandler; copy, Joseph Gilbert 51 a.); dean and chapter of Bristol 37 a. (including lease, Jenny Hayward 37 a.); Mrs. Heneage; Betty Hayward; Jenny Hayward.

Tithes Exchange of tithes between the rectory and vicarage, leaving 165 a. tithable wholly to the vicar and the rest wholly to the rector.

Roads 4 public roads, 2 public footpaths, 2 private roads, other previous and unspecified roads to continue. Herbage allotted. Repairs to private roads to be made by beneficiary allottees.

Finance Sale allotment to Jenny Hayward of 2 a. to pay expenses of rectory allotment.

Map Allottees and acreages shown, whole parish including village.

37 BISHOP'S CANNINGS

Bourton, Easton, Horton, Nursteed, and Wick tithings

Act 55 G.III c.17 (Private). *Award* 6 March 1819 (enrolled 26 April 1829), W.R.O. 109. *Commissioners* Richard Richardson of London; Richard Webb of Salisbury; Young Sturge of London. *Surveyors* William Tubb of Fisherton Anger and John Hayward of Rowde.

Lord of Manor Bishop of Salisbury; *lessee* Thomas Grimston Estcourt.

Rector (lay) T. G. Estcourt.

Area [2,639 a.] Kitching Barrow, Shute Common, Horton Sand Field, Horton Cleaves, Easton Sheep Down, Horton Field, Stone Acre Mead, Easton Cow Down, Devizes Green, Lower Wick Green, Ashmans Green, Bourton Field, Bourton Down, Breach Field, Easton Field, Horton Ox Down, Dunsett Down.

Allotments 11. Bishop of Salisbury 1,682 a. (including lease, T. G. Estcourt 1,682 a. and sublet as follows by copy, William Salmon 1,461 a.; James Gent 20 a.; William Brown 60 a.; Michael Cook 48 a.; William Maslen 16 a.; John Nash 18 a.; Joseph Pierce 16 a.; Mark Sloper 34 a.; Martha Ruddle; Walter Ashley; William Crook; Charles Croome); T. G. Estcourt 386 a.; Dame Elizabeth Smythe 189 a.; George Worall 214 a.; Thomas Brown 74 a.; Thomas Giddings 74 a.; William Brown; feoffees of Bishop's Cannings church lands; Kennet and Avon canal; William Salmon; John Tylee.

Tithes both great and small on the demesne allotted to T. G. Estcourt, as his freehold, in exchange for 19 small closes and 131 a. Great and small tithes on his copyholds allotted to T. G. Estcourt in exchange for 66 closes and 207 a.

Roads 2 public roads, 4 private roads and public bridle ways, 1 public bridle way, 9 private roads, 1 public footpath, 1 private road and public footpath.

Finance deduction of 6 allotments (58 a.) from the allotments to the bishop of Salisbury are allotted to T. G. Estcourt who is to pay the bishop's share of the expenses.

Maps (1) Horton. (2) Bourton and Easton. (3) Southbroom, Nursteed and Wick. Commonable land red, old inclosures exchanged green. Schedules of allotments and exchanges with each map.

Schedules Repair of roads, (a) Bourton and Easton rate, (b) Horton road rate.

See also Nos. 35 and 36.

Notes The precise standing of T. G. Estcourt is difficult to determine. He seems to have leased Bishop's Cannings manor from the bishop yet is referred to as lord of the manor and receives an allotment for rights of the soil. At the same time he was lord of the manor of Cannings Canonicorum and held the rectory with its tithes in his own right, the dean and chapter of Salisbury having sold their rights to Sir Anthony Abdy who had conveyed them to T. Sutton, ancestor of Mrs. Estcourt. See *V.C.H. Wilts.* vii. 189.

38 BOWER CHALKE [2,985 a.]

Act 25 G.III c.56 (Fovant, Swallowcliffe, Broad Chalke, Ebbesborne Wake, Bower Chalke, Alvediston, Bishopstone, and Fifield Bavant). *Award* 3 Jan. 1792 (enrolled 17 Nov. 1794), W.R.O. V 38. *Commissioners* Richard Bloxham of West Dean; Richard Richardson of Devizes; Francis Webb (replacing William Corfield of Salisbury, d. 1787). *Surveyor* Benjamin Haynes (replacing William Corfield).

Lord of Manor Henry Herbert, earl of Pembroke.

Vicar William Coles.

Area [2,576 a.] South, East, Middle and West Fields, Sheep Down, Knoyle Green.

Allotments 12. Public: furze 10 a. Earl of Pembroke 2,266 a. (including leases, Edward Heasell 249 a.; executors of Isaac Savage 57 a.; copy, Hannah Adlam 44 a.; Elizabeth Gould 46 a.; Henry Herrington 91 a.; Sarah Lodge 225 a.; John Target 36 a.; copy and lease, John Newman 100 a.; Mary Foyle; Joseph Goodenough; Edward Gould); John Rebbeck 61 a.; Henry Rebbeck 74 a.; Richard Bingham 133 a.; provost and scholars of King's College, Cambridge, 22 a.; churchwardens of Broad Chalke; John Good; Morgan Herrington; Henry Norris; Charles Penruddocke; Jeremiah Cray.

Roads 9 public roads, 3 public bridleways, 6 public footpaths, 13 private roads. Herbage allotted. Roads in Bower Chalke woods to remain at accustomed width.

Finance 4 sale allotments to pay expenses of provost and scholars of King's College, Cambridge (£18 4*s.* 2*d.*), and one for those of Joseph Goodenough (£1 6*s.*). Expenses to be paid for by allottees, including if necessary the reversionaries.

Maps (1) North part of parish. (2) South part. Whole parish shown, including village. Allottees and acreages marked.

Schedules (1) Lifeholders under the earl of Pembroke whose reversionaries have paid the expenses and who are to pay interest. (2) Charges assessed by the commissioners on various lifeholders under the earl of Pembroke.

See also No. 39.

Notes Horse and cow leazes allotted, also 97 a. winter feed allotted to freeholders. Regulations for occupying Bower Chalke Cow Down and common woods. Furze allotted in proportion to beast leazes. Cowherd to be paid in proportion to number of cows.

39 BOWER CHALKE

Act General, 8 & 9 Vic. c. 118. *Award* 1 Oct. 1860 (enrolled 20 Nov. 1860), W.R.O. 181. *Valuer* Francis Attwood.

Lord of Manor Robert Henry, earl of Pembroke.

Area [1,099 a.] Cow Down, Furze Dole, Chase Woods.

Allotments 6. Public: 10 a. for labouring poor. Earl of Pembroke 1,046 a. (including leases, William Parham 100 a.; William Chizlett; William Coombs); Richard Bingham 27 a.; Elizabeth Bracher; Alexander Powell; John Rebbeck. *Fencing* in award and with allotments and on map.

Roads 2 public roads. 1 public road stopped up and 1 public footpath diverted.

Map Inclosed areas only shown and allotments numbered.

See also No. 38

40 BROAD CHALKE [6,966 a.]

North and South tithings, East Gerardston, and Stoke Verdon tithings.

Act 25 G.III c.56 (Fovant, Swallowcliffe, Broad Chalke, Ebbesborne Wake, Bower Chalke, Alvediston, Bishopstone, Fifield Bavant). *Award* 3 Jan. 1792 (enrolled 17 Nov. 1794), W.R.O. V 38. *Commissioners* Richard Bloxham of West Dean; Richard Richardson of Devizes; Francis Webb (replacing William Corfield of Salisbury, died 1787). *Surveyor* Benjamin Haynes (replacing William Corfield).

Lord of Manor Henry Herbert, earl of Pembroke.

Vicar William Coles

Area [3,453 a.] South tithing East, Middle and West Fields, North tithing West, Middle and East Fields, Stoke Farm Down, Cow Down, Tenantry Down, Chicken Grove Copse, East Hookland Field, Tenantry Sheep Down, West and East Hill Field, West and East Low Field, Mountsorrel Field, Anthony's Gore, Moody's Gore, Parsonage Gore, Gerrardston Mead, Green Man Mead.

Allotments 18. Public: 5 common watering places; 3 allotments of furze for the poor 24 a. Earl of Pembroke 2,072 a. (including leases, Mary Dove 41 a.; Nicholas Folliat 40 a.; Joseph Goodenough 111 a.; William Penny 27 a.; Samuel Parrett 43 a.; Stephen Witt 59 a.; Humphrey Pellew 297 a.; copy, John Butler 33 a.; Benjamin Emm 43 a.; Isaac Gulliver 28 a.; Mary Hazell 36 a.; Elias Ingram 28 a.; James Lawes 60 a.; John Newman 52 a.; Henry Penn 18 a.; John West 19 a.; Richard Alley 19 a.; Thomas Batt 20 a.; Sarah Lodge 27 a.; Mary Steevens 17 a.; John Younge 29 a.; copy and lease, Henry Crine 151 a.; Josiah Gould 1,101 a.; William Bond; Stephen Crine; John Good; David Lawes; William Moody; Joseph Perry; Moses Read; Charles Smith; Hannah Randall; Thomas Hayden; Elias Read; Henry Savage); George Randall 96 a.; Thomas Thynne, Viscount Weymouth [*recte* marquess of Bath] 451 a.; Jeremiah Cray 200 a.; provost and scholars of King's College, Cambridge, 275 a. (including leases, Henry Bankes 123 a.; Viscount Weymouth 47 a.; Sarah Lodge 103 a.; John West); master of St. Nicholas's Hospital, Salisbury, 232 a. (including lease, George Randall 232 a.); James Lawes 31 a.; Jane Marsh 17 a.; vicar of Broad Chalke 24 a.; Henry Bankes; John Butler; Josiah Gould; John Lawes; William Slater; William Hussey; churchwardens of Broad Chalke. *Fencing* 12 in. landshards to be left.

Roads 34 public roads, 4 public bridle ways, 3 public footpaths, 16 private roads. Herbage allotted.

Finance to be paid by allottees or if necessary by the reversionaries. 6 sale allotments to pay expenses of King's College, Cambridge (4), St. Nicholas's Hospital, Salisbury (1), and the vicar of Broad Chalke (1).

Maps (1) North part of Broad Chalke. (2) South part of Broad Chalke. (3) New furze allotments in South Tithing. (4) New furze allotments in North Tithing and Stoke Verdon. Village shown but not entire parish. Allottees and acreages marked.

Schedules (1) Lifeholders under the earl of Pembroke who are to pay rent or interest because the reversionary has paid the expenses. (2) Charges assessed by the commissioners on various lifeholders under the earl of Pembroke.

See also No. 41.

Notes New common fields set up, rights of common of pasture and numbers of beast leases for sheep and cows allotted. *North Tithing:* 186 a. to be fed in common, 419 sheep leases; regulations for opening the Fallow field, Wheat Stubble field, Barley Stubble field, and Clover field and for stemming the sheepfold. *South Tithing:* 436 a. of allotments to be fed in common, 1,857 sheep leases; regulations as above. *Stoke Tithing:* 194 a. of allotments to be fed in common, 643 sheep leases; regulations as above. Regulations for common woods. Furze on Tenantry Sheep Downs allotted in proportion to holdings.

41 BROAD CHALKE AND CHILMARK

Act 54 G.III c.155. *Award* 11 Dec. 1861 (enrolled 22 Sept. 1866), W.R.O. V 188. *Commissioners* James Poole of Sherborne (replacing Charles Pearson Charlton, d. 1834, replacing John Rogers, d. 1820); William Robson of Wilton (replacing William Thring, d. 1852, replacing John Seagrim, d. 1832). *Umpire* John Hayward of Devizes (replacing Christopher Ingram, dead). *Surveyor* Charles Pearson Charlton.

BROAD CHALKE

North and South tithings

Lord of Manor of Broad Chalke, Robert Herbert, earl of Pembroke (succeeding George Herbert, earl of Pembroke, d. 1827); of Chalke Prebend, provost and scholars of King's College, Cambridge.

Vicar Rowland Williams.

Area 3,577 a. [2,285 a.] Card's Marsh, Church Marsh, Vernditch Woods, Anthony's Gore, Gawen's Gore.

Allotments 10. Public: 1 watering place; furze on 139 a. Earl of Pembroke 1,553 a. (including leases, William Fryer 32 a.; Cornelius Gould 37 a.; copy, Thomas King 43 a.; William Woodcock; George Young); King's College, Cambridge, 163 a. (including 75 a. for tithes); George Young 311 a.; trustees of marriage of William Woodcock 74 a.; vicar of Broad Chalke 15 a.; Thomas King 30 a.; John Floyer; Cornelius Gould. *Fencing* general and on map.

Tithes partly commuted. Rights of King's College for 6 ridges of wheat and 1 acre of wood from lands of the earl of Pembroke in Chalke manor farm and Knowle farm, for tithes, replaced by an allotment.

Roads 14 public roads, 2 public footpaths.

Maps Poole and Newman of Sherborne 1861. Broad Chalke mostly south of the river, lands in Bishopstone and Bower Chalke included in the award. Allotments numbered only.

See also No. 40.

Notes 66 old inclosures included in the award but excluded from this abstract. Some lands in Fonthill Bishop and Bishopstone exchanged under this award. 'King Harry's Hut' of the previous award is called 'Harry King's Hut'.

CHILMARK [3,210 a.]

Lord of Manor Robert Herbert, earl of Pembroke (succeeding George Herbert, earl of Pembroke).

Vicar Charles Tower.

Area Chilmark [851 a.]; Rudge [641 a.] Lady Down, Chilmark Down, Rudge Down.

Allotments Chilmark 2. Earl of Pembroke 849 a.; Frederick King. Rudge 2. Earl of Pembroke 641 a.; Frederick King. *Fencing* general and on map.

Roads Chilmark: 7 public roads, 1 public footpath, 4 private roads. Rudge: 8 public roads.

Maps Poole and Newman of Sherborne 1861. Allotments numbered only; whole parish with village.

Schedule Rate for repairing road as a proportion of £1.

Notes 102 old inclosures given up to be included in the award (not included in this abstract).

42 CHARLTON ST. PETER [1,734 a.]

Act 20 G.III c.14. *Award* 8 Oct. 1780 (enrolled 9 Jan. 1781), W.R.O. 16. *Commissioners* Thomas Browne of Sevenhampton, Glos.; John Grant of Manningford Bruce; Richard Richardson of Devizes. *Surveyor* Francis

Webb of Stow on the Wold, Glos., and his assistant Joseph Harris.

Lord of Manor Rev. William Davenport and Martha his wife.

Rector Dean and chapter of Christ Church, Oxford.

Area 1,356 a. [1,601 a.] North, West and South Fields, The Cleeve, Farm Summer Down, Thornham Down, Cow Down, South Winter Down, Ruslet Common, Lammas Meadow.

Allotments 6. Rev. William Davenport 1,035 a. (including leases, Thomas Fowle 284 a.; Henry Fowle 101 a.; Francis Giffard (of Upavon) 103 a.; William Pinkney 78 a.; Mary Palmer 42 a.; John Chamberlain 42 a.); Thomas Erle Drax 145 a.; Francis Giffard 135 a.; Thomas Walter 15 a.; Henry Fowle; Mary Still.

Roads 12 public roads, 1 public footpath, 6 private roads.

Note Boundary with Market Lavington determined.

43 CHERHILL [1,904 a.]

Cherhill and parts of Calne, Calstone Wellington, and Compton Bassett

Act 1 G.IV c.44 (Private). *Award* 25 Oct. 1822 (enrolled 13 March 1827), W.R.O. 129. *Commissioners* John Hayward of West Lavington; George Barnes of Andover, Hants. *Umpire* Thomas Davis of Horningsham. *Surveyor* George Hayward of Devizes.

Lord of Manor of Cherhill, devisees of late William Hunt Grubbe (T. G. Estcourt, Wadham Locke, W. W. Salmon); of Prebend of Calne and *Rector* Rev. Thomas Hume, treasurer of Salisbury Cathedral; *lessees* trustees of marquess of Lansdowne (Hon. James Abercrombie and Sir Thomas Baring Bt.).

Vicar of Cherhill, John Henry Hume (succeeding Thomas Greenwood, dead); of Calstone Wellington, Charles Townsend; of Calne, John H. Hume.

Area [1,193 a] not including Calne 365 a., Compton Bassett 7 a., Calstone 7 a., Cherhill Low, Cherhill Pen, Great and Little Abberd, Ball Mead, Quemerford North and South Field, Bore Down, The Breaches, Cherhill Field, Marsh Lane Common.

Allotments Cherhill 17. Public: 2 chalk pits 2 a. Devisees of William Hunt Grubbe 740 a. (including leases, William Flower 26 a.; Ann Neate 40 a.; copy, William Caswell 43 a.; Edward Flower 31 a.; James Neate 34 a.; William Pottow 27 a.; Roger Pottow 25 a.; Uriah Pottow 29 a.; John Spackman 20 a.; Peter Spackman 15 a.; devisees of Mrs. Heneage 17 a.; lease and copy, George Church 47 a.; Edward Hunt 96 a.; Thomas Neate 25 a.; Ann Pottow 73 a.; trustees of Uriah Pottow 66 a.; John Rawlings 38 a.; Richard Alderman; Mary Bromham; Ann Bradfield; John Dyke; Clare Flower; Mary Hillier; Oriel Viveash); devisees of Mrs. Arabella Heneage 273 a.; Thomas Neate 66 a.; vicar of Calne 44 a.; marquess of Lansdowne 22 a.; surveyors of highways for Cherhill; surveyors of highways for Calne; John Gabriel; John Spackman; Richard Tanner; John Gale; Edward Hunt; William Northey; Richard Lewis; Jabez Bailey; prebendal manor of Calne. Calstone Wellington 1. Devisees of Mrs. Heneage. Compton Bassett 3. Devisees of Mrs. Heneage; trustees of William Prowess; John Spackman. Calne 14. Public: 1 chalk pit 1 a. Marquess of

Lansdowne 117 a. (including representatives of Samuel Hale; Katherine Oriel, Thomas Sketch); Thomas Poynder 53 a.; devisees of Mrs. Heneage 53 a.; Prebendal Manor 56 a. (including lease, trustees of marquess of Lansdowne 56 a.); Lt. Gen. the Hon. John Crewe 33 a.; Rev. George Wyld 15 a.; rector of Blackland; William Northey; William Pottow; Thomas Neate; Sarah Rawlings; John Smith; rector of Calstone. *Fencing* general and with allotments on map.

Roads 5 public roads, 2 private roads and public bridle ways, 18 private roads, 2 public bridle ways, 4 public footpaths.

Finance 6 sale allotments £1,087, and rate on exchanges.

Maps (1) Inclosed area. (2) Three detached pieces, exchanges only. Schedules of allotments and exchanges. Allotments numbered only. Commonable lands allotted coloured red, old inclosures exchanged green. Village shown.

Schedules (1) Rates for Pen Low and Marsh Lane road, for Cherhill Fields road, and for Abberd Meadow road. (2) Regulations for stocking Low and Marsh Lane commons under devisees of William Hunt Grubbe, showing the allotment, proprietor, tenure, beast leases, sheep leases; 1 horse equivalent to 2 beasts; horses 14 May to 23 Nov. and sheep 23 Nov. to 14 Feb.

See also No. 63.

Notes Surveyors of public roads appointed. Exchanges confirmed, including some in Bremhill.

44 GREAT AND LITTLE CHEVERELL

Act 37 G.III c.147. *Award* 30 Sept. 1802 (enrolled 10 July 1805), W.R.O. 63. *Commissioners* Richard Davis of Lewknor, Oxon.; Richard Richardson; Francis Webb. *Surveyor* William Tubb of Fisherton Anger.

GREAT CHEVERELL [1,846 a.]

Lord of Manor keeper and poor men and women of the almshouse of Walter and Robert Hungerford of Heytesbury.

Rector Richard Laurence.

Area 1,463 a. including roads 40 a. [1,485 a.] The Marsh, Great Meadow, Middle, West and East Sand Field, Middle, West and East Clay Field, Moams Land, East Hill Field, Great Sand Ground, Hilliers Bottom, Drove Acre, Garston Field, North Meadow, Causeway Ham, Spratts Meadow.

Allotments 17 Public: furze 5 a. Heytesbury almshouse 717 a. (including copy, William à Court 23 a.; Job Gibbs 84 a.; James Slade 38 a.; Joshua Smith 37 a.; Robert Pile 15 a.; William Bartlett 36 a.; Samuel Adlam 24 a.; Richard Staples 17 a.; William Chandler 23 a.; James Bartlett 16 a.; William Young 16 a.; lease and copy, Gifford Warriner 288 a.; William Butcher; William Dowse; Bridget and Elizabeth Legg; Catherine Shergold; Jenny Potter; Mary Potter; William Purnell; William Giles; John Butcher; Mary Boulter; John and William Cotes alias Newberry; Thomas Purnell; Samuel Purnell; Frances Post; William Giles; Isaac Axford); trustees of John Wadman 170 a.; Jacob Pleydell-Bouverie, earl of Radnor 140 a.

(including lease, William Purnell 8 a.); rector of Great Cheverell 330 a. (including 316 a. for tithes); Gifford Warriner 18 a.; Joshua Smith 17 a.; Job Gibbs 26 a.; John Pile 35 a.; William Dowse 19 a.; James Potter; Mary Dowse; trustees of John Wadman; executors of John Giles; William Bartlett; trustees of Free School; Abraham Newman.

Tithes allotments of land in place of tithes.

Roads 1 turnpike road, 4 public roads, 4 public footpaths, 14 private roads.

Finance £1,517 7*s*. 4*d*. by rate, including Little Cheverell, the shares determined in the award.

Maps Great and Little Cheverell (1) south of Lavington-Westbury road; (2) north of Lavington-Westbury road. Whole of both parishes shown with allottees and acreages and both villages.

Schedule Old inclosures in Great Cheverell not exonerated from tithes by allotment of land and left subject to money payment; 15 a. in all, £3 10*s*. 9*d*.

LITTLE CHEVERELL [1,025 a.]

Lord of Manor Earl of Radnor.

Rector William Richards.

Area [778 a.] West Clay Field, Forehill Common, East and West Sand Fields, Lord's Mead, Long Leaze Common, Hill Field.

Allotments 2. Earl of Radnor 555 a. (including copy, John Axford; William Purnell); rector of Little Cheverell 223 a.

Tithes allotments of land in place of tithes.

Roads 2 public roads, 2 public footpaths.

Finance see Great Cheverell.

Maps see Great Cheverell.

Schedule Old inclosures in Little Cheverell not exonerated from tithe by allotments of land and left subject to money payments; 43 a. in all, £9 7*s*. 4*d*.

45 CHICKLADE [1,085 a.]

Act 21 G.III c.14. *Award* 10 Nov. 1781 (enrolled 1781), W.R.O. 22. *Commissioners* Richard Richardson of Devizes; Thomas Fricker of Longbridge Deverill; Richard Bloxham of Winterslow.

Rector Benjamin Blatch.

Area 989 a. [971 a.] Middle Field, East Field, Little Field, Bockerley Field, Cow Down, Sheep Down, Farm Down.

Allotments 13. John Russ, clerk, 193 a. (including leases, William Blake; William Beckett); Nathan Wright 145 a.; Thomas Waters 122 a.; Richard Randall 172 a.; Thomas Hull, John Williams, and Elizabeth Burnett 129 a.; Elias Lucas 59 a.; Martha Burnett 20 a.; William Bracher 16 a.; John Vincent 42 a.; Harry Edgell 29 a.; rector of Chicklade 34 a.; Richard Withers; Solomon Bright.

Roads 4 public roads, 2 private roads, 1 public footpath. Herbage allotted.

Finance £334 10*s*. by rate assessed on major allottees.

Map [none, but reference to a plan already made for the commissioners by Joseph Singer.]

46 CHILTON FOLIAT [2,202 a. in Wilts., 1,292 a. in Berks.]

Act 49 G.III c.45 (not printed). *Award* 27 Aug. 1813 (enrolled in Chancery 19 July 1814), W.R.O. Acc 735/43. *Commissioners* George Barnes of Andover; John Davis of Bloxham, Oxon. *Surveyor* Thomas Phillips of Andover.

Lord of Manor of Chilton Foliat with Soley, Edward Leyborne Popham; of Leverton, John Pearse.

Rector Edward Popham D.D.

Area 400 a. [401 a.] Hoe Lane Common, Little Down, North Field, South Field, Upper and Lower Marsh, Crooked Soley, Soley Lot Mead.

Allotments 23. Public: 2 gravel and chalk pits 2 a.; 1 public watering place. Edward Leyborne Popham 173 a. (including leases, William Pearse 37 a.; George Holloway); Fulwar Craven 133 a.; rector of Chilton Foliat 19 a.; John Martin 29 a.; John Pearse; heirs of Henry Burton; Robert Bence; Mary and Esther Drew; William Deadman; Hannah Ellenton; George Goldring; Fettiplace Hopkins; trustees of James Hill; James Martin; Benjamin Mallam; Susannah Neate; Thomas Pontin; Elizabeth Simmons; John Smith; James Wiltshire; Jeremiah Yorke. *Fencing* general.

Tithes commuted by allotments and tithe rents £916 15*s*. 7*d*.; 2 a. allotted to rector in place of tithes of under 5*s*. per annum; £56 11*s*. 10*d*. paid for exoneration.

Roads 4 public roads, 1 public footpath, 6 private roads.

Maps to show allottees and acreages; whole parish shown, including village, the area not subject to inclosure being numbered for tithe.

Schedules (1) Yearly tithe rents and quantity of wheat at 8*s*. 6*d*. per bushell. (2) Annual value of tithes of less than 5*s*., and sums paid for exoneration.

Notes Manner of assessing tithes fully described. Two common drains 8ft. wide set out. Several old inclosures are indistinguishable and have been included in the abstract.

47 CHIPPENHAM

Tytherton Lucas tithing [580 a.] and Langley Burrell

Act General (unspecified). *Award* 19 March 1856, W.R.O. Acc 542. *Commissioners* national.

Vicar of Chippenham, Lewis Purbrick.

Area [52 a.] Westham Mead, Bull Mead, Humborne Common.

Allotments 5. Mary Langton 17 a.; William Porter 30 a.; Broome Pinniger; vicar of Chippenham; John Large. *Fencing* with allotments.

Map William Bryan Wood of Chippenham 1854. Inclosed area only; allotments numbered.

See also Nos. 48 and 121.

48 CHIPPENHAM AND LANGLEY BURRELL

Act General, 8 & 9 Vic. c.118. *Award* 1 March 1869 (enrolled 16 May 1870), W.R.O. 192. *Valuer* William Bryan Wood of Chippenham.

Area [Chippenham 38 a., Langley Burrell 13 a.] Allington Mead.

Allotments 4. Chippenham: trustees of late earl of Mornington 38 a.;

Langley Burrell: Hugh Beames; trustees of earl of Mornington; Ann Wood. *Fencing* with allotments and general.

Map William Bryan Wood of Chippenham 1866. Allotments numbered and boundary between Chippenham and Langley Burrell shown.

See also Nos. 47 and 121.

49 CHIRTON [1,926 a. including Conock]

Chirton excluding Conock

Act 39 & 40 G.III c.80 (Private and Personal, not printed). *Award* 9 Sept. 1808 (enrolled 23 Aug. 1809), W.R.O. 77. *Commissioners* Richard Richardson of London; Christopher Ingram of Amesbury; John Gale of Stert. *Surveyor* William Tubb of Fisherton Anger.

Lord of Manor trustees of Heytesbury Almshouse.

Rector (lay) keeper and poor men and women of Heytesbury almshouse. *Vicar* Samuel Clarke.

Area 1,091 a. [1,049 a.] Sandfield, East and West Clay Field, North Barrows, Chirton Down, Pitt Meadow, Mill Meadow, Lulland Meadow, South Field, Green Hill, Hill Field, Gooseham, Middle Field, Broad Bridge Field.

Allotments 12. Public: 1 stone pit 1 a. Heytesbury almshouse 468 a. (including leases, George Griffin Peirce 138 a.; John Burge 94 a.; Robert Hayward 17 a.; copy, Gifford Warriner (son) 55 a.; Michael Burgess 55 a.; copy and lease, William Bruges 61 a.; executors of Gifford Warriner; John Wells; John Reeves; Margaret Davis; William Clift; Mary Reeves; John Durnford; Thomas Palmer; Daniel Chandler; Thomas Sheppard); trustees of Froxfield almshouse 265 a.; trustees of Bradford charity (Rev. Frederick Blomberg, vicar of Bradford, and Rev. Edward Lambert, rector of Freshford, as devisees under the will of John Curll) 138 a.; William Bruges 60 a.; executors of John Pearce 88 a.; vicar of Chirton; John Burgess; Mary Barnes; Daniel Chandler; Benjamin Hayward; William Tinker.

Roads 6 public roads, 5 public footpaths, 6 private roads. Herbage allotted whole width, except where there are allottees on both sides when half width only.

Map Chirton without Conock, village shown and allottees and acreages.

See also No. 50.

Notes Down depastured in common by Chirton and Conock divided between the two by the commissioners and staked. Great tithes due to the vicar of Chirton transferred from one set of allotments to another; Heytesbury almshouse entitled to rest of great tithes.

50 CHIRTON

Conock

Act 54 G.III c.212. *Award* 8 Aug. 1816 (enrolled in King's Bench 9 Sept. 1816), W.R.O. Acc 402/3. *Commissioners* George Barnes of Andover, Hants; John Hayward of Rowde.

Lord of Manor the two chaplains and thirteen poor men of Ewelme, Oxon.

rea 660 a. [647 a.] Wedhampton Field, Chirton Field, Bottom Field,

Great Down, Little Down, Farm Down, Honey Down, The Ridge, Hitch Field.

Allotments 3. Public: 1 chalk pit 1 a. Ewelme almshouse 633 a. (including lease, trustees of William Bruges 24 a.; copy, Sarah Coster; Mary Biggs; Richard Tyler; John Pierce; Josiah Huntley; lease and copy, Gifford Warriner 573 a.); Gifford Warriner. *Fencing* with allotments and general.

Roads 1 public road, 2 private roads. Duties for repairs set out.

Map William Walmesley of Andover, Hants; leaseholds green, copyholds blue, freeholders yellow. Acreages and allottees shown. Whole tithing including hamlet.

Schedule shows proprietor, allotment, arable or otherwise, acreage, tenure, date of last grant, yearly value, quite rents and heriots.

See also No. 49.

Notes Ditches, drains, and watercourses to be repaired by neighbouring owners; 131 a. of old inclosures included in the award but excluded from this abstract.

51 CHISELDON [4,917 a. excl. Draycot Foliat 706 a.]

Badbury

Act (to confirm an agreement) 21 G.II c.7. *Award* 15 Oct. 1748 (enrolled 28 Oct. 1749), W.R.O. 5 (Q.S. enrolled document 82). *Commissioners* Robert Carter of Purton Stoke; Thomas Brown of Overton; Anthony Southby of South Marston; Michael Haines of Hannington; John Withers of Bishopstone; Jonathan Wirdnam of Shrivenham, Berks. *Surveyors* John Povey of Broad Hinton and Stephen Neat of Lower Upham, Aldbourne.

Lord of Manor of Badbury, John Stone.

Area 685 a. [685 a.] East and West Fields.

Allotments 13. John Stone 524 a.; Theodora and William Morse (her son) 59 a.; Walter Hardyman 36 a.; Anthony Allen 22 a.; John Allen; Thomas Smart; Anna Maria Walker and William (her son); Thomas Woolford; Mary and Charles Horton; John Crisby; Elizabeth and Richard Little; Edward Ballard; Elizabeth Miles. *Fencing* allottees responsible for their own fencing.

Roads 5 public roads.

See also No. 52.

Notes Proprietors of lands to be inclosed to be given one month in which to cut, grub up, and carry away pollards, bushes, trees, and hedges on lands which belonged to them before inclosure.

52 CHISELDON

East and West Chiseldon and Hodson tithings

Act 19 G.III c.95. *Award* 14 Jan. 1780 (enrolled 29 June 1780), W.R.O. 12. *Commissioners* Richard Richardson the younger of Devizes; John Grant of Manningford Bruce; John Mitchell of South Weston, Oxon. *Surveyor* John Clements of Avebury.

Rector (lay) Thomas Browne Calley. *Vicar* William Rich Stock.

Area 1,280 a. [1,176 a.] West End Field, Hodson Common, North Field, Pinkcomb Hill, Hodson East and West Fields, The Narrows, Waldron's Hill, Tuff Lynch, Chiseldon North and West Field.

Allotments 31. Thomas Browne Calley and the vicar of Chiseldon for tithes 396 a.; T. B. Calley 122 a.; William Morse 72 a.; William Bailey 50 a.; William Drury and Elizabeth Ballard 55 a.; John Brown 56 a.; Samuel Hawkes 62 a.; Thomas Herring 79 a.; Stephen Lambert 33 a.; Thomas Crook 24 a.; William Dyke 43 a.; Mary Kemble 15 a.; William Stratton 39 a.; Richard Webb 44 a.; Philip Pearce the elder 15 a.; John Phelps 34 a.; Sarah Pope 15 a.; trustees of poor of Highworth; Mary Day; Joseph Looker; William Goddard; Charles King; Joseph King; Jacob Pleydell-Bouverie, earl of Radnor; John Berry; Edmund Cook; Philip Pearce the younger; Mary Seymour; Margaret Allen; Edward Arman; vicar of Chiseldon. *Fencing* with the allotments and to be fenced with quickset within 12 months.

Tithes Rectorial and vicarial tithes commuted by grant of land (396 a. of which 77 a. were for old inclosures).

Roads 10 public roads, 1 public bridle way, 4 public footpaths, 10 private roads.

Schedule Old inclosures exonerated from tithe.

See also No. 51.

Notes Water-course to be repaired at expense of neighbouring allottees. Numerous later requests for exchanges.

53 CHITTERNE

[Chitterne All Saints 4,449 a., Chitterne St. Mary 1,218 a.]

Act 55 G.III c.67 (Private), repealing 50 G.III c.18 (not printed) for inclosing lands in Chitterne St. Mary. *Award* 5 May 1818 (enrolled 14 July 1818), W.R.O. 105. *Commissioners* Thomas Davis of Horningsham; John Hayward of Rowde. *Surveyor* Charles Pearson Charlton of Stourton.

Lord of Manor Paramount lord of manors of Chitterne All Saints and Chitterne St. Mary, Paul Methuen (succeeding Paul Cobb Methuen, dead); of Chitterne All Saints, Robert Michell.

Rector of Chitterne St. Mary, dean and chapter of Salisbury; *lessee* Paul Methuen. *Vicar* of Chitterne All Saints, William Macdonald; of Chitterne St. Mary, William S. Wapshare (succeeding John Batchellor, dead).

Area 5,784 (Act), 5,574 (Award) [4,934 a.] Wormsey Down, London Way Field, Heytesbury Way Field, Woehill Field, Parker's Mead, Crandown.

Allotments 6. Vicar of Chitterne St. Mary 180 a. (including 107 a. for tithes); Paul Methuen 2,889 a.; Louisa Michell 1,569 a.; Robert Michell 133 a.; Ann Compton 121 a.; vicar of Chitterne All Saints 42 a. and corn rents of £151 0*s*. 5*d*. *Fencing* shown on map and generally in award, hedges to be 4ft. inside boundary.

Tithes Vicarial tithes commuted by allotments and corn rents.

Roads 2 public roads, 16 private roads, 3 public bridle ways.

Map 1818. Both parishes with village, boundary between parishes marked by red line. Arable, yellow; meadow and pasture, green.

Schedules (1) Rate for expenses of private roads. (2) Corn rents payable to vicar of Chitterne All Saints in place of tithes.

Notes Boundary between Chitterne All Saints and Chitterne St. Mary determined by the commissioners. Vicar of Chitterne St. Mary to pay 6*s*. in £ towards repair of hatches and has right to take water in Parker's Mead. Crandown to be depastured in common, Paul Methuen 240 sheep, Ann Compton 180 sheep. Award contains perambulation of Chitterne St. Mary and Chitterne All Saints. No rectory glebe.

54 CHRISTIAN MALFORD [3,185 a. excl. Avon 180 a.]

Dole Mead in Christian Malford and Bremhill

Act General, 6 & 7 W.IV c.115. *Award* 7 April 1843 (enrolled 12 July 1843), W.R.O. 161. *Commissioner* Robert Davis Little of Chippenham.

Area 24 a. including roads. Dole Mead.

Allotments 4. Henry Petty Fitzmaurice, marquess of Lansdowne 19 a.; trustees of Popham's Charity; Hungerford Crewe, Lord Crewe; Arthur Long Wellesley. *Fencing* general.

Roads 1 private road, 1 public footpath.

Map Henry Weaver 1843.

See also Nos. 28 and 164.

55 CHUTE [3,256 a.]

Act 48 G.III c.40 (not printed). *Award* 4 Nov. 1820, W.R.O. Acc 304/1. *Commissioners* Richard Parsons of Hungerford, Berks.; Benjamin Haynes of Shalbourne. *Umpire* George Barnes of Andover. *Surveyor* George Barnes of Andover.

Lord of Manor of Chute, George Smith (by purchase from Strickland Freeman); of Collingbourne Kingston, Thomas Brudenell-Bruce, earl of Ailesbury.

Prebendary Robert Blayney of Northampton.

Area 592 a. [595 a.] Upper Deep Field, Lower Hackney Field, Shaw Down, Chute Slay, Ladies Lawn, Banks Hill, Butts Common, Chute Heath, Honey Bottom, Chute Down, Amblens Coppice Ground.

Allotments 35. Public: 2 gravel pits; 2 watering places. George Smith 249 a.; (including copy, Major Baily; James Knight; Mary Bower; representatives of George Bennett; representatives of George Palmer; Daniel Wilkins; representatives of Ann Cook; Thomas Fisher; John Mills; representatives of John Phillimore; representatives of William Smart; Ralph Broad; Thomas Mills; Francis Breadmore; representatives of Thomas Smart; representatives of John Nicholls); George Soley Foyle 171 a. (including representatives of Joseph Norris; representatives of James Batchelor; representatives of William Smith; Edward Broad; representatives of Blandena Bennett; representatives of Mary Arnold); Evelyn Meadows 85 a.; earl of Ailesbury 37 a.; Philip Pulse 34 a.; John Webb; Charles Tylee; John and Thomas Gale; William Barnes; Henry Spreadbury; Jane Wild; William Wild; Charles Cook; Catherine Knight; Thomas Knight; representatives of Thomas Cook; Joseph Miles; Thomas Butler; representatives of Thomas Hopgood; representatives of Sylvan Sturgess; Thomas Phillimore; representatives of Henry Hutchins; representatives of Jane Belcher; John Smith; Peter Webb; William Broad; representatives of Joseph Norris; Richard Hopgood; Mary Bower; representatives of Martha Crouch; James Wayte; John Mitchell; Charlotte Poore. *Fencing* with allotments.

Roads 12 public roads, 9 public footpaths, 4 private roads.

Notes Doubts about whether Banks Hill was in Chute or Collingbourne Kingston settled by the commissioners' decision that the Great Ditch was the boundary. The Commissioners also settled the boundary between Chute and the extra-parochial liberty of Chute Forest. Old inclosed allotments omitted from this abstract, but partly inclosed allotments included.

56 CODFORD ST. MARY [2,129 a.]

East Codford

Act General, 6 & 7 W.IV c.115. *Award* 30 Oct. 1844 (enrolled 7 March 1845), W.R.O. V 164. *Commissioners* Thomas Waters of Stratford sub Castle; James Combes of Tisbury; *Umpire* Francis Attwood. *Surveyor* Thomas Tilbrook of Horningsham.

Lord of Manor Harry Biggs.

Rector George Webster.

Area 2,123 a. (Act) [1,267 a.] West Field, Home Field, Yonder Field, Middle Field, Hermitage Hill, Sandhill Field.

Allotments 6. Public: 2 chalk pits. Harry Biggs 639 a. (including lease and copy, William Bennett 108 a.); William Bennett 328 a.; Rev. James Ingram 92 a.; rector of Codford St. Mary 169 a.; James Slade 39 a.

Roads 3 public roads, 1 public bridle way.

Map 1844. Whole parish and village, allottees and acreages. Inclosures outlined in green.

Schedule Allotments and exchanges.

57 CODFORD ST. PETER [1,668 a.]

Act 48 G.III c.49 (not printed). *Award* 19 Sept. 1810 (enrolled 9 Sept. 1829), W.R.O. 137 & 138. *Commissioners* Thomas Davis of Horningsham; William Jennings of Evershot; William Tubb of Fisherton Anger. *Surveyor* John Tubb of Fisherton Anger.

Lord of Manor Henry Fox-Strangways, earl of Ilchester.

Rector John Dampier.

Area 600 a. [697 a.] Hakefield, Mead Field, West Hill, Borth Mead, Hookland Field, Braydon Hill.

Allotments 17. Public: 1 stone pit. Earl of Ilchester 254 a. (including leases, devisees of James Slade 161 a.; Robert Kellow 15 a.; John Harding; Mary Cotterell; Hester Ingram; copy and lease, Henry Ingram 41 a.); devisees of James Slade 324 a.; William Parry 21 a. (including lease, Richard Haynes 21 a.); John Crouch 32 a.; Benjamin Rebbeck 19 a.; Col. Bingham; Robert Kellow; Hester Ingram; Sarah Bingham; William Hinton; John

Ruxworthy; Aylmer Lambert; William Trowbridge; churchwardens of Codford St. Peter; churchwardens of Codford St. Mary; rector of Codford St. Peter. *Fencing* on map.

Roads 2 public roads, 3 private roads, 2 public footpaths.

Map John Tubb of Fisherton Anger (William Tubb and Son). Whole parish except Ashton Giffard shown, including the village. Allottees, acreages, and tenure shown.

Schedule Private roads to be repaired by neighbouring allottees.

See also No. 58.

58 CODFORD ST. PETER

Ashton Giffard tithing

Act 54 G.III c.86. *Award* 3 Oct. 1815 (enrolled 9 Sept. 1829), W.R.O. 135 & 136. *Commissioners* John Hayward of Rowde; Ambrose Patient of Corton; John Rogers of Burcombe. *Surveyor* John Daniell of Warminster.

Lord of Manor Harry Biggs.

Rector John Dampier.

Area [693 a.] Blissets Common, Ashton Giffard Down, The Marsh.

Allotments 9. Public: 1 gravel pit. William Hubberd 307 a.; Hester Ingram 154 a.; Richard Bingham 52 a. (including lease, Sarah Bingham 52 a.); James and John Slade 108 a.; William Hinton 25 a.; John Ruxworthy 26 a.; executors of James Trowbridge 16 a.; Harry Biggs.

Roads 3 public roads, 3 private roads, 1 public bridle way.

Finance by deduction from allotments and sale, £484 7*s.* 11*d.*

Map John Daniell of Warminster 1815. Ashton Giffard tithing only, shown with village. Allotments numbered only and acreages shown.

Schedule Repair of private roads: seven proprietors and rate in £.

See also No. 57.

59 COLERNE [3,928 a.]

Act 25 G.III c.12. *Award* 30 April 1787 (enrolled *c.*1788), W.R.O. 30. *Commissioners* John Davis of Bloxham, Oxon.; Samuel Kingdon of Milverton, Som.; Richard Richardson of Devizes. *Surveyors* William Kingdon of Milverton and Edward Webb of Stow, Glos.

Lord of Manor of Colerne, warden and scholars of New College, Oxford; of Thickwood, governors of the Charterhouse; or Euridge cum Yatton, Wentworth Parsons.

Rector John Oglander. *Vicar* Nathaniel Bliss.

Area 1,446 a. including arable 1,308 a., Colerne Down 138 a. [1,293 a.] North and West Fields, Little or East Down Field, Great or West Down Field, Gassons Field, Great and Little Ashley Field, Medley's Field.

Allotments 11. Public: 10 allotments for repair of roads. Warden and scholars of New College, Oxford 423 a. (including lease, representatives of George Drewitt 48 a.; copy, Mary and Ann Drewett 127 a.; Hugh Blatchley 20 a.; William Smith 26 a.; Mary Sumsion 29 a.; John Greenway 18 a.; Thomas Aust 43 a.; Paul Methuen; William Sheats; Richard Read; Walter Edwards; Thomas Tyley; William Rawlins; Philip Smith; Robert Marler;

John Showring; Ferdinando Aust; Mary Knight; Peter Drewett; Richard Aust; Elizabeth Ford); Wentworth Parsons 527 a. (including leases, Elizabeth Browning 94 a.; John Edwards 23 a.; Michael Ford 16 a.; Richard Milsham; — Smart; Sarah Greenway); governors of the Charterhouse 187 a. (including copy, Mary and Ann Drewett; Thomas Tyley; John Browning; Daniel Davis; Daniel Sumsion); Paul Methuen 132 a.; Mary and Ann Drewett; Sir William Codrington; Joseph Pinchin; Richard Phelps; Samuel Drewett; Thomas Parry. *Fencing* with allotments.

Tithes Rectorial and vicarial tithes commuted for a tithe rent-charge only, with leave to amend after 20 years.

Roads 7 public roads, 25 private roads, 10 public footpaths. Herbage allotted.

Finance general rate, 40*s.* per acre (Wentworth Parsons £472 10*s.* 4*d.*)

Maps (1) South-west of church. (2) North-east of church. (3) Colerne, on a larger scale, and the village of Thickwood. Lands of the following coloured separately: New College, Oxford, W. Parsons, governors of the Charterhouse, Paul Methuen, other freeholders.

Schedules (1) List of proprietors with acreage of their fields, old inclosure allotments and parcels taken in exchange. (2) Owners, tenants, acreage, value of tithes, quantity of wheat equal thereto, proportion due to W. Parsons, rector, and vicar, yearly tithe rent-charge due to W. Parsons, rector, and vicar. (3) List of persons assessed for expenses of inclosure and amounts paid out.

Notes Inclosures made during the last 14 years to be included and allotted. Surveyor to be appointed to fence and repair the roads and report in 2 years. Exchanges confirmed but timber thereon not included.

60 COLLINGBOURNE DUCIS [3,431 a.]

Agreement 10 Oct. 1773 between Thomas Bruce, Lord Bruce, the bishop of Oxford, the rector of Collingbourne Ducis, and others. *Award* 31 Aug. 1775, W.R.O. Sav. *Arbitrators* John Watts of Sulgrave, Northants.; James Poore of East Woodhay, Hants.

Lord of Manor of Collingbourne Ducis or Lower Collingbourne, Thomas Bruce, Lord Bruce.

Rector William Tomlins.

Area Common fields 1,078 a., common downs 485 a. [1,313 a.] Wick Heath, Widgerly Down, Coleridge Rails, Snail Down, Little Slay, Dewberry, White Dick, Middle Field, West Field, East Field, Out Field.

Allotments 4. Public: Slough Pond to be a public watering place. Lord Bruce 985 a. (including lease, John Hutchins 44 a.; copy, Dr. William Batt 77 a.; Mary Black 59 a.; Daniel Black 40 a.; Matthew Hutchins 58 a.; Edward Andrews 33 a.; Robert Marshment 35 a.; Thomas Marshment 19 a.; David Black; John Lawrence; Thomas Lewis; Giles Shepherd); bishop of Oxford 283 a. (including leases, Matthew Hutchins; Edward Shepherd; Thomas Marshment; John Mortemer); rector of Collingbourne Ducis 45 a. *Fencing* with allotments.

Roads 7 public roads, 9 public bridle ways, 2 public footpaths. Soil coming from the new road to be used for filling up the old road.

Finance £290 10*s*. 1*d*. Schedule of proportions payable mentioned in text but not attached to award.

Notes 237 a. of the downs to be fed in common. Very detailed instructions for feeding with sheep and rotation of crops. Number of sheep leases determined. West, East, Middle and Out Fields to continue to be subject to one-course husbandry.

The Cow Down is referred to as an old inclosure in the award, and its inclosure seems to have been effected by two previous agreements (W.R.O. Sav. 13/107/1 and 2), dated 27 Aug. 1731 and 16 March 1737, in which 1,000 a. including Sheep House Down, Cow Down, Black Down, Little Slay, Snail Down, Wiggelly Down, Wick Ash Down, Wick Heath, Lickford Mead, East and West Fields were involved. Under the second of these agreements between Charles Bruce, Lord Bruce, and 30 others the farm lands leased to Richard Callow were to be inclosed and broken up. The tithes were reduced by half for four years on account of the increased value of the land when broken up.

61 COLLINGBOURNE KINGSTON [7,400 a.]

Aughton

Agreement 26 Jan. 1761 between Thomas Bruce, Lord Bruce, and 12 others. *Award* 17 Jan. 1763, W.R.O. Sav. *Arbitrators* James Poore of Crux-Easton, Hants; Thomas Compton of Cholderton; Richard Rawlins of Hilldrop Farm.

Lord of Manor Thomas Bruce, Lord Bruce.

Area [712 a.] Duck Puddle, Falstone Pond, North and South Fields, Low Field.

Allotments 5. Lord Bruce 406 a. (including leases, Thomas Cannon 52 a.; Richard Legg 35 a.; Fulke Greville 85 a.; copy, Elizabeth Norris 89 a.; Thomas Collins 43 a.; Mary Collins 29 a.; Elizabeth Chandler 16 a.; lease and copy, Ralph Tanner 57 a.); Thomas Gilbert 238 a.; John Dean 26 a.; John Edwards 32 a.; Ralph Tanner. *Fencing* with allotments.

Roads 8 public roads.

See also Nos. 32 and 62.

Notes Abbots Down (145 a.) to be fed in common and not divided. Various allotments in South Field and North Field are not intended to be inclosed owing to the barrenness of the soul. Rest of Scrub or Shrubb Down 66 a. to be fed in common.

62 COLLINGBOURNE KINGSTON

Collingbourne Vallance

Agreement 29 May 1798 between Thomas Brudenell-Bruce, earl of Ailesbury, and 6 others. *Award* 1 Nov. 1799, W.R.O. Sav. *Arbitrators* John Gale of Stert; John Butcher of Wexcombe.

Area [759 a.] Slough Field, Harley Field, Coombe Field, Stonehill Field The Ham.

Allotments 5. Slough Pond to be a public watering place. Earl of Ailesbury 344 a. (including lease, Thomas Edwards 201 a.; copy, Michael Ford 18 a.); William Ludlow 278 a.; Dummer Andrews 84 a.; Thomas Edwards 53 a.
Roads 7 public roads, 4 private roads, 1 public bridle way, 1 public footpath. Herbage allotted.
See also Nos. 32 and 61.

63 COMPTON BASSETT (including exchanges with Cherhill) [2,576 a.]
Act 1 W.IV c.2 (Private). *Award* 12 April 1837 (enrolled 27 March 1838), W.R.O. 152. *Commissioner* Thomas Davis. *Surveyor* George Barnes of Andover.
Lord of Manor of Compton Bassett and Compton Comerwell, George Heneage Walker Heneage.
Rector Richard Musgrave.
Area [63 a.] The Hill.
Allotments 6. George Heneage Walker Heneage 51 a.; rector of Compton Bassett; William and Jane Thring; trustees of Richard Dugdale; Winifred Pyke; Robert White.
Roads 3 private roads.
Map Allotments numbered. Two detached pieces in Cherhill. New inclosures in red.
See also No. 43.

64 COOMBE BISSETT [2,212 a.]
Act 42 G.III c.84 (Private and Personal, not printed). *Award* 18 Sept. 1806 (enrolled 8 July 1819), W.R.O. 106. *Commissioners* Francis Webb of Salisbury; Richard Richardson of London; John Hodding the elder of Salisbury.
Lord of Manor (1) Warden, scholars, and clerks of St. Mary College, Winchester; (2) Jacob Pleydell-Bouverie, earl of Radnor.
Prebendary of Coombe and Harnham, Rev. William Douglas; *lessee* Joseph Tanner.
Area 1,946 a. [1,955 a.] North, East and West Fields, North Down, Middle Field, Little Field, Coombe Green, East Hill.
Allotments 8. Public: 1 stone or gravel pit. Warden, scholars, and clerks of St. Mary College, Winchester 650 a. (including copy, Elizabeth Bowles 26 a.; Ann Curtis 52 a.; John Flower 193 a.; David Feltham 21 a.; Elizabeth and Mary Hibberd 103 a.; Edith Shergold 99 a.; Thomas Heale 20 a.; William Baker; William Gravel; Mary Meaden; Samuel Meaden; George Sandy); earl of Radnor 1,007 a. (including lease, John Rogers 21 a.; John Harwood; Samuel Meaden; James Macie; Mary Warren); John Flower 102 a.; prebendary of Coombe and Harnham 155 a. (including lease, Joseph Tanner 155 a.); Elizabeth and Mary Hibberd 15 a.; George Sandy 22 a.; trustees of Margaret Strahan.
Roads 10 public roads, 6 private roads and public bridle ways, 1 private road and public footpath, 2 private roads, 1 public footpath. Directions for repair of public and private roads.

Finance £2,098 9*s.* 5*d.* Schedule mentioned in award but not attached.
Maps William Tubb of Fisherton Anger 1806. (1) North part of parish north of Blandford-Downton road. (2) South part. Whole parish and village shown.
Notes Inclosures within the last twenty years to be included. First shear in Homington Mead also allotted.

65 CORSHAM [6,604 a.]
Act 56 G.III c.42 (Private). *Award* 31 March 1819 (enrolled 17 July 1823), W.R.O. 121. *Commissioner* Thomas Davis of Horningsham. *Surveyor* Charles Pearson Charlton.
Lord of Manor Paul Methuen.
Area 52 a. [36 a.] Street Green, Chappel Nap, Elly Green, Greenhill Common, Moor Green Common, Lypiatt, Lock's Cross, Pound Pill, Dainy Green, Westwells, Rudge Side, Great and Little Minety Mead, Great Pound Mead, Lot Mead.
Allotments 7. Paul Methuen 23 a. (including copy, Audley Hervey; Letitia Day; William Hulbert; feoffees of Corsham parish; Kirby's charity; Hezekiah Hayward; Mary Leir; Susanna Michell; James Kerr; Thomas Peirce; Robert Sadler; William Stump; Robert Fowler; Caleb Dickenson; trustees of Richard Higgs; Margaret Coker; Elizabeth Dickenson; Anthony Guy; Mary Collett; Emma Dickenson; Thomas Eldridge; John Edwards; Mary Guy; Ralph Gaby; Richard Godolphin Long); bailiff of manor of Corsham; Thomas Eldridge; John Edwards; John Merewether; Sir Harry Neale Bt.; Sir George Ducket. *Fencing* in award.
Roads 4 public roads, 18 private roads. Grass and herbage awarded separately in award.
Finance Sale allotments (5 a.) £149.
Maps (1) Waste, common, and detached pieces. Lypiatt Common, Street Green, Dainy Green, Moor Green, West Field Common. Schedule of allottees. (2) Lypiatt Farm, Hartham, and many detached pieces, coloured according to owners.
Schedule Rate for repairing private roads.

66 CRANBORNE CHASE
Act 9 G.IV c.14 (Private), disenfranchising Act. *Award* 29 Sept. 1829 (enrolled 19 Sept. 1831), W.R.O. V 141. *Commissioner* Philip Williams of London.
Owner of franchise called Cranborne Chase, William Pitt-Rivers, Lord Rivers.
Maps 44 (of which 35 relate to Dorset); Berwick St. John 3, Donhead St. Andrew 1, Fifield Bavant 1, Ebbesborne Wake 2, Bower Chalke 2.
Note The document is not an inclosure award but an agreement under which Lord Rivers agreed to accept £1,800 per annum as compensation for extinguishing his right to allow deer to roam over the chase. The numbers of deer were estimated at 12,000—20,000.

The proportions payable were as follows: *Berwick St. John and Donhead St. Andrew:* Rev. Richard Downes £11 11*s.* (for 42 a.); William Wyndham

£37 3*s*. 6*d*. (76 a.); earl of Pembroke, earl of Malmesbury, Lord Heytesbury, and Hon. Henry Clive £254 1*s*. 7*d*. (531 a.). *Bower Chalke:* George Young 12*s*. (4 a.); General Richard Bingham £2 2*s*. 3*d*. (143 a.). *Ebbesborne Wake:* E. M. Pleydell £9 0*s*. 2*d*. (326 a.); marquess of Bath £24 4*s*. 7*d*. (35 a. in Ebbesborne and 140 a in Fifield Bavant). *Tollard Royal:* Thomas Grove £7 6*s*. 4*d*. (348 a.).

Lands handed over instead of payment: *Berwick St. John and Donhead St. Andrew:* earl of Pembroke and others £254 1*s*. 7*d*. (438 a.); Rev. R. Downs £11 11*s*. 0*d*. (19 a.); William Wyndham £37 3*s*. 6*d*. (55 a.). *Ebbesborne Wake:* marquess of Bath £16 (35 a.).

67 CRICKLADE [6,243 a. including Widhill]

Great and Little Chelworth manor and tithing

Act 26 G.III c.58. *Award* 25 Sept. 1788 (enrolled 10 Nov. 1796), W.R.O. 40. *Commissioners* Richard Bloxham of Winterslow; Richard Davis of Lewknor, Oxon.; Richard Richardson of Devizes. *Surveyor* Edward Webb of Stow on the Wold.

Rector dean and chapter of Salisbury; *lessee* Dr. William Heberden.

Area 740 a. [705 a.] Middle Field, Far Field, 150-Acres Common, South Meadow, Maskelyne's Meadow, Hitchin Field, Redlands Field, Queen Ham.

Allotments 56. Dean and chapter of Salisbury 76 a. (including lease, Dr. William Heberden 76 a.); Jonathan White 62 a.; Sarah Bristow 98 a.; Richard Kinneir 53 a.; Edward Eliot, Lord Eliot 18 a.; William Heberden 33 a.; devisees of Thomas Bush 23 a.; John Nesbitt 17 a.; Thomas Gunn 16 a.; John Byrd 32 a.; George Adams 16 a.; William Fry 15 a.; William Maskelyne 30 a.; Ann Mabson; John Hinton; the reeve; earl of Shaftesbury; earl of Ilchester; Richard Selfe; Edward Dorell; executors of Olive Mills; Thomas Plummer; John Brown; Thomas Ansell; Morgan Byrt; Mary Archer; Charles Poulton; William Lawrence; Richard Townsend; trustees of Cricklade wayland; George Kempster and others; Edward King; Sylvia Trinder; Crook Godby; Edward Wilbraham; Elizabeth Jones; John Carter; vicar of Cirencester (for the poor of Cirencester); Robert Maskelyne; William King; Christopher King; warden and fellows of Merton College, Oxford; Mary Norman; Alexander Hughes; Robert Nicholas; Maurice Vincent; Thomas Ride; John Collinborne; Robert Stratford; William Telling; Edward Williams; William Roberts; William Forrester; Thomas Moulder; William Johnson; poor of Cricklade. *Fencing* with allotments and on map.

Tithes not dealt with under the award, but some areas are shown as being already tithe-free both in the award and on the map.

Roads 1 public road, 1 public bridle way and private road, 10 private roads, 1 public footpath, 3 private footpaths.

Maps (1) 150-Acres Common. (2) Middle Field, Far Field, Redlands, Great Hitchin, Trinder's Piece. (3) South Meadow, Maskelyne's Meadow. Maps do not cover the entire parish and the town is not shown. Allottees. acreages, and tithe-free areas shown.

Schedule Sum required from proprietors for repairs to private roads in (a) late common fields, (b) late common meadow, (c) South Meadow, Maskelyne's Meadow.

Note The maps relating to the award are in Cricklade Museum; photocopies are in W.R.O.

68 CRICKLADE

Great and Little Chelworth manor and lands within the Inner Boundaries of the late Forest of Braydon

Act 54 G.III c.160, amended by 55 G.III c.48 (Private) to rectify inaccuracies in earlier Act. *Award* 30 Aug. 1824 (enrolled 13 Nov. 1832), W.R.O. 143. *Commissioners* Daniel Trinder of Cirencester, Glos. (replacing Robert Wright Hall, dead); Frederick Phelps of Cheltenham, Glos. (replacing John Edmonds, mad). *Surveyor* Richard Hall of Cirencester.

Lord of Manor of Cricklade and Great and Little Chelworth, Joseph Pitt.

Vicar of Cricklade St. Sampson, Henry Gauntlett; of Cricklade St. Mary, David Middleton.

Area [771 a.] Cricklade Common (212 a.), Lanes etc. (60 a.), North Meadow (120 a.), Cricklade Common, Frogham, Normead, Read's Knap, Little Hitching, Rushey Meadow, Spital Meadow, Calcot Meadow, Calcot Field, Small Meadow, Causeway Furlong, Upper and Lower Chelworth Green, Sinderums Field, Pages Green, Ragmans Ground, Great and Little Wallenger, Hailstone Hill, Bawdhouse Ground.

Allotments 65. Rev. Thomas Heberden 120 a.; Joseph Pitt 44 a.; Susannah Adams 29 a.; representatives of Elizabeth Adams 36 a.; feoffees of Cricklade waylands 18 a.; devisees of Morgan Byrt 17 a.; Richard Champernowne 21 a.; William Champernowne 38 a.; executors of Henry Cullerne 33 a.; Richard King 39 a.; Robert Maskelyne 23 a.; representatives of Ann Poulton 37 a.; Richard Kinneir 35 a.; earl of St. Germans 27 a.; Thomas Collingbourn; John Compton; William Cuss the elder; William Cuss the younger; David Archer; Edward Barnes; representatives of John Boote; Jacob Carter; George Bevir; Richard Dafter; John Dowsell; Daniel Edmonds; vicar of Cricklade St. Sampson; — Gleed; Mary Golding; Francis Heath; dean and chapter of Salisbury; Mary Hinton; Thomas Hitchman; Thomas Hull; Catherine Jackson; Thomas Jenner; Alice Jenner; Christopher King; John Lucas; Charles Poulton; trustees of Powell's charity; William Quarrel; Rev. Ralton; representatives of Michael Reynolds; Thomas Roberts; Edmund Ruck; John Slatter; Edmund Smith; John Stone; William Maskelyne; John White the younger; John Williams; John Wood; rector of Cricklade St. Mary; Robert Nicholas; William Ockwell; John Pinniger; William Wells; Elizabeth White; executors of Robert White; Robert Strange; William Talmage; William Trinder; William Ware; William Worne. *Fencing* with allotments.

Roads 5 public roads, 2 public bridle ways and private roads, 12 private roads, 13 public footpaths. All roads crossing the inclosures and not mentioned in this and previous awards to be stopped up.

Finance 4 sale allotments (20 a.) £898 7*s.* 7*d.*

Maps (1) West of Cricklade. (2) Calcot to Seven Bridges. Coloured according to allottees. Allotments numbered and allottees shown.

Schedule Lands allotted and not allotted.

See also No. 67.

Notes New drain set out in Normead. In Normead or North Meadow, Thomas Heberden and others had right to mow first vesture; holders of houses in Cricklade had right to depasture from 12 Aug. to 12 Feb. 'The commissioners do set out allot and award the said common meadow called Normead otherwise North Meadow unto and among the several persons owners of the first vesture or hay crop thereof but so far only as regards such vesture or hay crop.' In this abstract old inclosures are not included except for those that were allotable or intermixed. Lanes and wastes in Great Chelworth were excepted from the award.

69 CRUDWELL [4,899 a.]

Act 56 G.III c.69 (Private, not printed). *Award* 20 March 1841 (enrolled 4 March 1842), W.R.O. 160. *Commissioner* Daniel Trinder of Cirencester.

Rector William Maskelyne.

Area [1,071 a.] Honeyham Field, Riding Field, Newport Field, Hill Field, Far Ridgeway Field, Murcoat Meadow, Chelworth Field, Crudmore Meadow.

Allotments 8. Public: 1 stone pit. Thomas de Grey, Earl de Grey 513 a. (including leases Joseph Mill 22 a.; Joseph Pitt 55 a.; Luke Cole 15 a.; Rev. Henry Boucher); Joseph Pitt 329 a. (including leases, Luke Cole 23 a.; John Hankey 20 a.); Toby Sturge 98 a.; John Hankey 28 a.; rector of Crudwell 26 a.; Joseph Mill 18 a.; Robert Peacey 18 a.; Thomas Brown; devisees of John Buckland; John Seager Buckland; devisees of Isaac Berry; Elizabeth Buckland; John White; George White; Henry Hayes; William Hayes; Thomas Ricketts. *Fencing* with allotments.

Roads 7 public roads, 8 private roads, 1 private road and public bridle way, 1 public bridle way, 5 public footpaths.

Map Coloured according to allottees, village shown.

Schedule Old inclosures given up and exchanges.

70 WEST DEAN [2,818 a.]

East Grimstead tithing [951 a.]

Act General, 6 & 7 W.IV c.115. *Award* 26 March 1849 (enrolled 2 June 1849), W.R.O. V 169. *Commissioner* Francis Attwood of Salisbury.

Lord of Manor trustees of John Head Burdett and Henry Moore, marquess of Drogheda.

Area [479 a.]

Allotments 7. Trustees of John Burdett and marquess of Drogheda 315 a.; Charles Baring Wall 86 a.; George Brown 48 a.; William Willoughby Cole, earl of Enniskillen, and others 17 a.; Robert Futcher and others; charity trustees; Richard Bingham. *Fencing* only three laid down in award.

Roads 2 public roads, 2 public bridle ways, 1 public footpath.

Map 1848. Tithing and village only, allottees and acreages shown.
Notes Boundary between East and West Grimstead shortened and set out by commissioner. The award quotes the relevant parts of the various acts for each part of the award.

71 KINGSTON DEVERILL [2,738 a.]
Act 22 G.III c.19. *Award* 21 Nov. 1785 (enrolled 1786), W.R.O. 17. *Commissioners* Richard Richardson of Devizes; Thomas Fricker of Longbridge Deverill; Richard Bloxham of West Dean. *Surveyor* Thomas Webb late of Warminster, since deceased.
Lord of Manor Thomas Thynne, Viscount Weymouth.
Rector Millington Massey.
Area 2,509 a. [2,499 a.] King's Hill, Cucknell Field, Rodmead Field, Peasecombe, Cow Down, Church Field, North and South Down, Upper and Lower Dean Bottom, West Field, Court Hill, Kilton.
Allotments 9. Rector of Kingston Deverill 350 a.; Viscount Weymouth 1,507 a. (including William Blake 23 a.; Thomas Davis 153 a.; Michael Humphry 23 a.; John Marvin 111 a.; Henry Sturgis 22 a.; George Townsend 23 a.; John Blake; Philip Garrett; William Garrett; Thomas Humphry; Robert Hurle; John Hurle; Lucy Norris; Elizabeth and Rachel Oborne; William Reynolds; William Turner; George Young); William Ballard 128 a.; Mary Bleek 115 a.; Peter Delme 234 a.; William Slade 151 a.; trustees of Crey's charity school; dean and chapter of Oxford; dean of Salisbury. *Fencing* determined in the Act and recited in the preamble to be at expense of proprietors.
Tithes exonerated by grant of land to rector (see schedules).
Roads 8 public roads, 1 public road and private carriage way, 1 public bridle way, 3 public footpaths, 4 private roads.
Finance Rate on general proprietors. Viscount Weymouth empowered to charge £433 on certain lands to defray his expenses. The rector also empowered to charge for erecting new buildings.
Map Thomas Webb of Warminster 1782. Whole parish and village shown, allotments lettered and shaded grey, old inclosures numbered.
Schedules (1) Old inclosures exonerated from tithes by deduction from the allotments, allotted to the rector in place of tithes. (2) Old inclosures from which money payments are payable to the rector.
Notes The rector had both great and small tithes except a £4 composition due to William Chafyn Grove, lessee of the dean of Salisbury; this was also exonerated by an allotment of land. Cost of grass seed to be borne by allottees.

72 LONGBRIDGE DEVERILL
Longbridge Deverill, Hussey Deverill, and Monkton Deverill
Act 30 G.III c.18. *Award* 23 June 1795 (enrolled 14 June 1797), W.R.O. 43. *Commissioners* Richard Richardson of Bath; Thomas Davis of Longleat (in place of Thomas Fricker of Longbridge Deverill, d. 1792); Francis

Webb of Salisbury (replacing Richard Bloxham of West Dean, d. 1793). *Surveyor* W. Tubb.

Lord of Manor Thomas Thynne, marquess of Bath.

LONGBRIDGE DEVERILL [3,811 a.]

Vicar John Dobson.

Area 2,140 a. including old inclosures [1,631 a.] Sandfield, West Field, Crockerton Common, Deverill Marsh, Great Marsh, Long Iver Field, East Common, Clay Field, Many Man's Mead, South Field, Cow Down, Broom Common.

Allotments 3. Marquess of Bath 1,619 a. (including leases, executors of Mary Adlam 32 a.; Edward Collinson 19 a.; William Dowson 27 a.; Thomas Gilbert 26 a.; Samuel Long 69 a.; representatives of Fanny Maskelyne 20 a.; John Moore 46 a.; executors of Benjamin Rebbeck 30 a.; assignees of Mary Rogers 148 a.; Dennis Sturgis 20 a.; Stephen Sturgis 30 a.; John Sturgis 58 a.; Rebecca Sturgis 20 a.; executors of James Wickham 39 a.; James Aldridge; William Adlam; Edmund Adlam; James Brookman; John Baker; John Butcher; Jane Bedbury; executors of Edward Butcher; Richard Carpenter; executors of Edward Dewcey; John Dicks; John Dobson; representatives of John Gilbert; Thomas Heall; William Hodgson; executors of Rebecca Long; Edward Lombard; William Merett; Thomas Morgan; William Marshall; Mary Moore; John Moody; John Pearce; John Randall; Elizabeth Snelgrove; Edward Snelgrove; Thomas Starr); churchwardens of Longbridge Deverill; vicar of Longbridge Deverill.

Tithes Marquess of Bath to take over those great tithes which are due to the vicar and pay him annually £84 7*s.* 7*d.*

Roads 10 public roads, 4 private roads and public bridle ways, 10 private roads.

Finance Sale of 277 a. to marquess of Bath.

Map Draft map with allotments inked in red; shows village but not parish west of Shearwater. W.R.O. Acc. 845.

Schedule Allotments to be fenced by owners.

MONKTON DEVERILL [1,813 a.]

Rector (lay) marquess of Bath. *Vicar* John Dobson.

Area 1,149 a. [1,127 a.] Great and Little Cow Down, East Field, The Pen, Boarsmead, Sheep Down, Saunders Mead, Boarsbottom.

Allotments 6. Marquess of Bath 905 a. (including leases, executors of John Phillips; 167 a.; assignees of John Miller 117 a.; James Gibbs 209 a.; executors of Thomas Hurle 35 a.; executors of William Taplin 225 a.; Charles West; Henry Phillips; Edward Dredge); executors of William Taplin 211 a.; John Methuen Rogers; William Turner; heirs of William Buckler; churchwardens of Monkton Deverill. *Fencing* in schedule.

Tithes not commuted but marquess of Bath to take over the great tithes due to the vicar and pay him a rent for them.

Roads 5 public roads, 3 private roads, 3 public bridle ways, 2 public footpaths, 2 private sheep droves (and one private watering place).

Map 1791. Draft map showing the position before inclosure with the inclosures superimposed in red ink. W.R.O. Acc. 845.

Schedule Allotments to be fenced by new owners.

Note Powers given to marquess of Bath to charge up to £1,200 on his lands to pay the charges of inclosure.

73 DINTON AND TEFFONT MAGNA [Dinton 2,567 a., Teffont Magna 1,734 a.]

Act 3 G.IV c.30 (Private). *Award* 11 Jan. 1837 (enrolled 11 Feb. 1837), W.R.O. V 150. *Commissioners* James Poole of Sherborne (replacing John Charlton, dead, and Charles Pearson Charlton, dead); William Woodcock of Fugglestone St. Peter (replacing John Seagrim, dead). *Umpire* John Hayward of West Lavington. *Surveyor* Charles Pearson Charlton.

Lord of Manor Robert Herbert, earl of Pembroke.

Vicar Henry Linton D.D.

Area [Dinton 2,170 a., Teffont Magna 1,501 a.] Sheriff's Mead, Teffont Common, Common Grounds, Upper East Field, Lower Field, Gaston, Higher Field, The Woores, Bowers Mead.

Allotments Dinton 5. Public: 1 watering place (2 a.). Earl of Pembroke 1,510 a. (including leases, Walter Bailey 1,004 a.; William King 105 a.; James and William King 233 a.; Thomas Jesse 27 a.; Mary Wright 51 a.; Thomas Barnes 24 a.; William Douty 66 a.); William Wyndham 601 a.; vicar of Dinton 41 a.; William Barnes 18 a.

Teffont 6. Walter Fitz 287 a.; William Wyndham 184 a.; earl of Pembroke 1,015 a. (including copy, William Macey 17 a.; lease and copy, representatives of John Lush 245 a.; James Humby); representatives of John Lush; John Hayter; churchwardens of Teffont Magna.

Roads 5 public roads, 11 private footpaths, 1 public footpath.

Finance Expenses paid by earl of Pembroke.

Maps (1) Teffont and Dinton with boundary between them marked. (2) Exchanged lands in Fovant. Whole parish and villages.

Schedules (1) Allotments. (2) Exchanges.

Notes Inclosures made within the last 20 years to be included. Some lands in Fovant included in the exchanges. 297 a. of Groveley Wood included.

74 DONHEAD ST. MARY [5,227 a.]

Act General, 8 & 9 Vic. c.118. *Award* 1 Aug. 1867 (enrolled 5 Sept. 1867), W.R.O. 190. *Valuer* John Waters of Salisbury.

Area [535 a.] East, Middle and West Fields, Charlton Common Field.

Allotments 2. Robert Graves 520 a.; Thomas Grove. *Fencing* with allotments on map.

Roads 2 private roads, repair duties set out.

Map John Waters of Salisbury 1866. Allotments numbered only, old inclosures shown. Charlton Common fields and Broad Down only.

Note This is the last inclosure of common fields in Wiltshire.

75 DOWNTON [12,495 a. excl. Nunton and Bodenham]

Charlton tithing

Act 41 G.III c.74 (Private and Personal, not printed). *Award* 11 Nov. 1807, supplementary award 2 Dec. 1809 with exchanges (enrolled 10 April 1812), W.R.O. 83 & V 85. *Commissioners* Francis Webb of Salisbury; John Bailey of Redlynch; Moses Boorn of Romsey, Hants. *Surveyor* William Tubb of Fisherton Anger.

Lord of Manor of Downton, bishop of Winchester, *lessee* Sir Philip Hales Bt.

Area 1,600 a. [1,503 a.] Parrots Mead, North Mead, North Ground, New Court Mead, Broad Meadow, North, South and Middle Fields, Great Home Close, Gore Close, Bodenham Meadow, Highworth Ground.

Allotments 23. Henry Dawkins 337 a.; John Lord Willoughby de Broke as trustee for estate of late Anthony Duncombe, Lord Feversham 131 a.; trustees of Peter Rooke 616 a.; John Newman 50 a.; Frances Humby 45 a.; Jacob Pleydell-Bouverie, earl of Radnor 244 a.; James and Margaret Noyce 58 a.; bishop of Winchester; Elizabeth Newman; Joseph Chubb; Frances Tanner; Samuel Ockarell or Ockamor; John Flower; John Lewis; Mary Wheeler; George Bound; Mary Bailey; Henrietta Bailey; John Bailey; John Serrin; Mary Young; Mary Atwater; Jane Bailey; Joshua Tanner and William Cooper.

Roads 2 public bridle ways, 4 public roads, 2 private roads. Herbage allotted.

Finance £2,140 8*s*. 3*d*., see schedule.

Map William Tubb of Salisbury 1806. Whole tithing including village shown. Allottees. Old inclosures outlined in colour. Lord Feversham yellow, Henry Dawkins sap green, trustees of Peter Rooke lake red, Frances Humby pea green, John Newman orange, James and Margaret Noyce vermilion, Thomas Attwater brown, earl of Radnor blue.

Schedule Proportion of expenses of £2,140 8*s*. 3*d*. (£2,840 8*s*. 3*d*. according to the award) to be paid by the eight principal proprietors.

See also Nos. 76 and 77.

Notes Inclosures made in the last twenty years included. Clearbury Ring planted by the late Lord Feversham. Holdings are described as copy, lease or freehold, bondland, boordland, and knightamhold, but the amount of each is difficult to assess; fines were reserved on certain properties. Very great number of old inclosures and messuages allotted. All rights and duties attached to original holdings transferred to new allotments. A difficult award to interpret especially as it is inaccurate in some respects, e.g., it gives two different dates for the Act. No mention made of water-meadows although there were evidently some there.

76 DOWNTON

East Downton tithing and Hamptworth manor

Act 53 G.III c.148. *Award* 18 Oct. 1822 (enrolled 28 July 1823), W.R.O. V 122. *Commissioners* John Davis of Bloxham, Oxon.; George Barnes of Andover, Hants. *Surveyor* William Tubb of Fisherton Anger.

Lord of Manor of Downton, bishop of Winchester; of Hamptworth, Robert Eden Duncombe Shafto.

Vicar Thomas Lear.

Area [Downton 1,213 a., Hamptworth 954 a.] Paccomb Common, Morgan's Hill, Downton Common, Morgan's Bottom, Woodfalls, Bohemia, Warminster Green, Franchise Common, Loosehanger, Barford Park, Hamptworth Green.

Allotments Downton 94. Public: 4 chalk pits; 4 watering places. Bishop of Winchester 674 a. (including copy, under lessee, Jacob Pleydell-Bouverie, earl of Radnor, Susannah Eyre 76 a.; William Nelson, Earl Nelson 69 a.; Robert Shafto 135 a.; Rev. Charles Shuckburgh 67 a.; Jacob Pleydell-Bouverie 268 a.; William Bowles; representatives of John Baily; John Brothers; James Bryant; Samuel Bungay; Thomas Bolton; John Chalk; George Dixon; Henrietta Gibbs; William Hooper; Joseph Jellyman; John Kerville; James Kemish; representatives of Francis Kelleway; representatives of John Kerville; Betty Lush; Rev. Thomas Lear; William Mitchell; Mrs. Moody; John Mussell; Thomas Newman; David Park; John Pearson; John Purkess; Andrew Pope; John Reeves; Hannah Radcliffe; George Snelgrove; representatives of John Street; Ambrose Shelly; Ann Wentworth; representatives of John Wheeler; Samuel Whitchurch); Corpus Christi College 76 a. (including lease, Mary May 76 a.); warden and scholars of Winchester College 68 a. (including copy, Susannah Eyre 19 a.; Phoebe Barter; representatives of James Bailey; Elizabeth Chalk; representatives of Henry Harris; Mary Howe; Ann Innis; representatives of Francis Kelleway; Thomas Lear; William Nicholas; John Reeves; Ezekiel Spare; earl of Radnor; Robert Shafto); Mary May 99 a.; Robert Shafto 70 a.; representatives of John Baily 16 a.; William Arney; John Arney; Samuel Arney; representatives of William Absolem; John Blake; representatives of James Baily; L. Bound; James Bryant; representatives of William Bundy; Tabitha Bungay; Samuel Bunday; Thomas Bolton; Samuel Chalk; William Cockerell; Charles Cove; representatives of Ralph Cooper; Mary Cooper; John Collins; William Dear; John Damon; Susannah Eyre; Thomas Bolton; James Forder; Joseph Ford; Joseph Fulford; Joseph Fulford the younger; John Fulford; George Goulding; Elizabeth Gray; representatives of Henry Harris; Mary Howe; Ann Holding; John Ings; Joseph Jellyman; representatives of Francis Kelleway; John Lass; representatives of John Lush; Betty Lush; Thomas Long; Elizabeth Light; Joseph Littlecott; representatives of Thomas Mitchell; George Moody; Mrs. Moody; William Musselwhite; Mary Meech; representatives of Charles Newman; John Newman; representatives of John Newman; Thomas Newman; William Nicholas; William Nicholas the younger; James Nicholas; Josiah Nicholas; Sarah Newman; Earl Nelson; David Park; John Paler; John Pearson; James Perrin; Andrew Pope; Charles Poore; representatives of Hannah Poulton; William Poulton; Samuel Pilgrim; earl of Radnor; John Reeves; representatives of John Russell, representatives of Matthew Read; George Snelgrove; Ezekiel Spare; representatives of John Street; George Street; James Shelly;

Ambrose Shelly; Rev. Charles Shuckburgh; Peter Templeman; George Tucker; Frederick Webb; Thomas Webb; John Weeks; Robert Whitmarsh; Samuel Whitchurch; Samuel Wort; Daniel Wilkins; vicar of Downton; trustees of poor of Downton.

Hamptworth: 7. Public: 1 chalk pit; 1 watering place. Robert Shafto 556 a. (including leases, representatives of Sarah Ashley 17 a.; Ann Rice 28 a.; David Park 50 a.; John Andrews; representatives of James Andrews; James Eldridge senior; James Eldridge junior; John Batten; William Hodson); Frederick Webb 395 a.; John Rice; representatives of John King; Mark King.

Roads East Downton: 11 public roads, 4 public footpaths, 31 private roads. Hamptworth: 4 public roads, 1 public bridle way, 9 private roads.

Finance Sale allotments (837 a.) £7,006.

Maps William Tubb of Fisherton Anger. (1) Tithing of East Downton. (2) Manor of Hamptworth. Acreages and allotments; 4 detached pieces.

See also Nos. 75 and 77.

Notes Allotments for turbary. 11 sale allotments of timber, £4,661 9*s*. 3*d*. Fees laid down for admission to copyholds: admission 1*s*., use 1*s*., copy 7*s*. 6*d*., for extracting each particular 6*s*. 8*d*., each boundary 6*d*., hayward 6*d*.

77 DOWNTON

Wick Tithing

Act 56 G.III c.56 (Private, not printed). *Award* 17 March 1847 (enrolled 14 April 1847), W.R.O. V 167. *Commissioners* Francis Attwood of Salisbury (replacing George Barnes, d. 1832); Frederick J. Kelsey of West Lavington (replacing Richard Webb, d. 1837).

Lord of Manor of Downton, bishop of Winchester; *lessee* Sir Philip Hales Bt.

Area [959 a.] Hind Town Furlong, North, Middle and South Fields, Stanbury Field, Scotland Field.

Allotments 8. Public: 1 gravel pit; 1 pond. Bishop of Winchester 374 a. (including copy, devisees of Jacob Pleydell-Bouverie, earl of Radnor 114 a.; trustees George Matcham 173 a.; John Gibbs Baily 25 a.; Sarah Heather 28 a.; Frances Taunton 19 a.; trustees of William Pleydell-Bouverie, earl of Radnor; John Harvey; Frederick Caiger; John Westcomb; John Mussel); Jacob Pleydell-Bouverie, Viscount Folkestone 388 a.; John Gibbs Baily 148 a.; trustees of marriage of George and Harriett Matcham 47 a.; Silas Taunton; Samuel Whitchurch.

Roads 3 public roads, 1 public bridle way, 6 private roads.

Maps (1) F. J. Kelsey of Salisbury 1846. Tithing of Wick only. Acreages and allottees. (2—5) Exchanges only.

See also Nos. 30, 75, and 76.

Note Fee for copy of court roll for new allotments to be £1 1*s*. payable to the steward.

78 DURNFORD [3,820 a. including Normanton]

North End tithing and Hungerford Durnford manor

Act 33 G.III c.43. *Award* 30 Jan. 1794 (enrolled 22 Sept. 1794), supplementary award 18 Dec. 1795 containing exchanges between Lord Malmesbury and Jane Duke, W.R.O. 36 & 52. *Commissioners* Richard Richardson of Bath; John Hodding of Salisbury; Henry Stephens of Salisbury (replacing Richard Bloxham of Winterslow, dead). *Surveyor* William Tubb of Fisherton Anger.

Lord of Manor of Hungerford Durnford, James Harris, Lord Malmesbury.

Prebendary and Rector George Watts; *lessee* trustees of Lord Malmesbury. *Vicar* John Raven.

Area 957 a. [891 a.] North Mead, Catsbrain, Tenantry Sheep Down, Woodway Field, Farm Down, Ogberry, Farm Field, Long Breach Furlong, Middle Field, North Field, Cow Common Field, Dean's Mead.

Allotments 6. Prebendary of Durnford 281 a.; Lord Malmesbury 503 a. (including copy, William Flower; William Gilbert; William Cable; James Amor; churchwardens of Durnford); Jane Duke 71 a. (including leases, Lord Malmesbury, 22 a.; John Bussell; George Hayter); vicar of Durnford 35 a.; Philip Pinkney; prebendary of Wilsford.

Tithes commuted by allotments of land to prebendary and vicar.

Roads 5 public roads, 4 public footpaths, 2 private roads, 3 private footpaths. Herbage allotted.

Map 1793. Allotments coloured red, old inclosures exchanged blue. North End only, including the village.

See also No. 79.

Notes Exchanges are allotted directly to the final owner, which is unusual. Inclosures within last sixty years included.

79 DURNFORD

South End, and Salterton and Newtown manors

Act 1 & 2 G.IV c.3 (Private). 5 May 1824 (enrolled 10 Nov. 1834), W.R.O. 147 & 148. *Commissioners* Thomas Davis of Warminster; Elias Saph of Salisbury. *Umpire* Richard Nightingale of Lyndhurst, Hants. *Surveyor* Richard Webb of Salisbury.

Lord of Manor of Durnford South End or Durnford Parva, James Harris, earl of Malmesbury; of Netton, John Swayne.

Area [Durnford 488a., Netton 294 a.] Durnford Cliff, Upper and Lower Ham Field, Tenants Marsh, North, South and Middle High Fields, Little Down, Little Lowfield, The Beak, The Hookland.

Allotments Durnford 9. Earl of Malmesbury 166 a.; Richard Webb 106 a.; Stephen Smith 85 a.; Francis Smith 32 a.; devisees of William Newman 21 a.; Thomas Harris 18 a.; Frances Smith 23 a.; guardians of William Smith 22 a.; John Hyde.

Netton 3. John Swayne 178 a.; devisees of William Newman 72 a.; devisees of George Flower 44 a.

Roads 6 public roads, 3 private roads, 1 public bridle way, 1 private sheep drove.

Finance Expenses to be paid by proprietors in possession (but not in reversion); Mr. Webb paid the earl of Malmesbury's share by purchase of 25 a. for £533 5*s*.

Maps Allottees and acreages. (1) Durnford South End. (2) Netton; whole tithing shown.

See also No. 78.

Notes Netton Elm on Netton Green mentioned. Intercommoning between Salterton and Netton regulated. Inclosures within the last twenty years included. Boundary between Salterton and Netton manors straightened.

80 DURRINGTON [2,702 a.]

Durrington, and Knighton tithing in Figheldean

Act 59 G.III c.13 (Private). *Award* 12 Dec. 1823 (enrolled 1 Jan. 1833), W.R.O. 144 & 145. *Commissioners* Edward Corfield of London; Richard Webb of Salisbury; Elias Saph of Salisbury. *Surveyor* John Hayward of Rowde.

Lord of Manor of Durrington West End, warden, scholars, and clerks of St. Mary College, Winchester; of Durrington East End and of Knighton, dean and chapter of Salisbury; *lessee* Sir John Methuen Poore.

Rector dean and chapter of Winchester; of Figheldean, Thomas Henry Hume, treasurer of Salisbury Cathedral; *lessee* Edward Dyke Poore.

Area [Durrington 2,506 a., Knighton 612 a.] Knighton Mead, Knighton Hams (no field names given for Durrington).

Allotments Durrington 11. Public: chalk pits, 10 feet each side of Bulford to Shrewton road from Bulford Bridge to Durrington Down. Winchester College 1,555 a. (including copy, William Fowle 184 a.; Sarah Edmonds 139 a.; Elizabeth Moore 102 a.; Jane Pinckney 189 a.; John Scamell 268 a.; Jane York 65 a.; William Young 55 a.; Sarah Blatch; John Brown; William Dowling; John Kellow; Job Mead; Charlotte Poore; James Rose; Mary Rose; Charles Sheppard; William Sheppard; David Smith; Jane White); dean and chapter of Salisbury 228 a. (including copy, executors of George Moore 228 a.); Sir Edward Poore 91 a.; Charlotte Poore 74 a.; devisees of George Moore 266 a.; John Methuen Rogers and William Wroughton Salmon 286 a. (including copy, Charlotte Poore 282 a.; — Collier; John Hayden; Benjamin Rumbold; David Smith); John Scamell; David Smith; Archibald, Lord Douglas; Sarah Edmonds.

Knighton 4. John Methuen Rogers and William Wroughton Salmon 239 a. (including Charlotte Poore 239 a.); Charlotte Poore 200 a.; devisees of George Moore 158 a.; treasurer of Salisbury Cathedral.

Roads 10 public roads, 7 private roads.

Finance By allotments deducted from warden and scholars of Winchester and dean and chapter of Salisbury; some tenants refused. Sale allotment (22 a.) £550 19*s.* 10*d.* to pay expenses of Winchester College and William Fowle.

Map John Hayward. Whole parish and village; allottees and acreages; green for Durrington parish, red for tithing of Knighton.

Schedules (1) Rate for repair of private roads in Durrington. (2) Rate for repair of private roads in Knighton.

See also No. 89.

Notes Regulations for division of duties between Charlotte Poore, Jane Pinckney, and John Scamell for erecting and repairing hatches and for rent to be paid to Milston Mill for water; stems to commence 29 Oct. and 4 May: Jane Pinckney and John Scamell to have first stem for five days and Charlotte Poore for nine days; Charlotte Poore to repair the water carriage going through the lands of the other two. Allotments for the two manors set out separately.

81 EBBESBORNE WAKE [2,884 a.]

Act 25 G.III c.56 (Fovant, Swallowcliffe, Broad Chalke, Ebbesborne Wake, Bower Chalke, Alvediston, Bishopstone, Fifield Bavant). *Award* 3 Jan. 1792 (enrolled 17 Nov. 1794), W.R.O. V 38. *Commissioners* Richard Bloxham of West Dean; Richard Richardson of Devizes; Francis Webb of Salisbury (replacing William Corfield of Salisbury, d. 1787). *Surveyor* Benjamin Haynes (replacing William Corfield).

Lord of Manor Henry Herbert, earl of Pembroke.

Rector Charles Tarrant, succentor of Salisbury. *Curate and officiating clergyman* William Evans.

Area [2,187 a.] Great North Field, Cow Down, North and South Tenantry Down, Mead Hill Cliff, Long Meadow, Pond Hill, West, East and South Field, Yew Tree Hill, Bitcombe Field, Tenantry Mead, Long Mead, Great Forlorn Coppice, Great and Little Coker Coppice.

Allotments 9. Public: 9 a. furze in Cow Down. Earl of Pembroke 1,631 a. (including leases, Sarah Carey 231 a.; Henry Philpot 57 a.; copy, Thomas Scammell 18 a.; lease and copy, Benjamin Pryce 257 a.; John Coombes; William Jenkins; George Younge; John Younge; Thomas Fox); Edward Morton Pleydell 211 a. (including lease, William Coles 211 a.); John Rebbeck 99 a.; George Jackson 102 a. (including leases, Henry Rebbeck 55 a.; Rebecca Rebbeck; Richard Lawes; William Purchase; Joseph Younge); provost and scholars of King's College, Cambridge, 16 a.; succentor of Salisbury 44 a.; Hon. Everard Arundell; Stephen Emm.

Roads 13 public roads, 3 public bridle ways, 6 public footpaths, 5 private roads. The roads through Ebbesborne woods confirmed in their ancient course.

Finance not stated, except that 2 r. 27 p. allotted to the rector was sold to John Rebbeck for £25 3*s*. 11*d*. on his promising to pay the expenses of the rector and 1 r. 16 p. allotted to provost and scholars of King's College, Cambridge, was sold to John Rebbeck for £13 9*s*. 8*d*. on his promising to pay their expenses. The rest to be paid by allottees or if necessary by the reversionaries.

Maps (1) North part of parish. (2) South part including the village. Whole parish shown except the north-east corner (Ebbesborne Farm). Allottees and acreages shown.

Schedules (1) Lifeholders under the earl of Pembroke whose expenses have been paid by the reversionaries and who have to pay rent (interest). (2) Charges assessed by the commissioners on various lifeholders under the earl of Pembroke.

Note Regulations for watering Long Mead and for erecting hatches.

82 EDINGTON [5,765 a.]

Cowleaze

Act General, 8 & 9 Vic. c.118. *Award* 5 June 1865 (enrolled 10 July 1865), W.R.O. 183. *Commissioners* William Ferris of Draycot Fitz Payne (replacing Samuel Ferris of Bulkington, dead).

Lord of Manor of Tinhead, Simon Watson Taylor.

Area [89 a.] Tinhead Cowage.

Allotments 2. Simon Watson Taylor 87 a.; trustees of marriage of William and Ann Hicks. *Fencing* general and on map.

Roads 1 public bridle way, 1 private road. Regulations for upkeep.

Map 1863. Old inclosures outlined in red, allotments in green. Cowleaze only.

83 ENFORD [7,253 a. excl. West Chisenbury]

Compton Manor

Act 10 G.III c.27. *Award* 30 June 1772 (enrolled 29 Dec. 1772), W.R.O. 7. *Commissioners* William Wapshare of Salisbury; John Hibberd of Rockbourne, Hants; Edward Hewett of Martin (replacing John Poore of Longstreet, refused). *Surveyor* John Overton of Devizes.

Rector (lay) Henry Howe, Lord Chedworth. *Vicar* William Cooke.

Area 1,008 a. [1,008 a.] Lammas Mead.

Allotments 5. William Hussey 877 a.; vicar of Enford 59 a.; Mary Attwood 44 a.; Jane Rolf and others 27 a.; Robert Bawden. *Fencing* with each allotment, very detailed instructions about ditches.

Tithes Rectorial tithes commuted into a rent-charge, vicarial tithes extinguished by allotment of lands.

Roads 5 public roads, 1 public footpath, 2 private roads.

See also Nos. 84, 85, 86, and 142.

Notes Bridge from the Lime Kiln to be repaired by the inhabitants. Allottees to pay previous holders for trees; detailed prices for elms, withies, and ash trees recorded.

84 ENFORD

Coombe, Fifield, Longstreet, and East Chisenbury

Act 45 G.III c.104 (not printed). *Award* 1 March 1809 (enrolled 26 Feb. 1810), W.R.O. 79. *Commissioners* Joseph Pennington of Lee Place, Godstone, Surrey; George Barnes of Andover, Hants; John Charlton of Stourton (replacing Thomas Davis of Horningsham, dead). *Surveyor* John Charlton.

Lord of Manor of Enford and Fifield, John Benett; of East Chisenbury, master of hospital or free chapel of St. Katherine near the Tower of London and the brothers and sisters of the hospital; *lessee* executors of William Chafin Grove.

Rector (lay) devisees of John Howe, Lord Chedworth. *Prebendary* of Chute and Chisenbury, Rev. Robert Charles Blayney. *Vicar* John Prince.

Area [2,870 a.] Ellstubb, Cow Down, Man Mead, Annis Mead, Fifield Sheep Down, The Stert, The Island.

Allotments 10. Vicar of Enford 221 a. (and 157 sheep leases); John Benett 770 a. (including copy, William Herne 40 a.; Richard White 24 a.; John Phillimore 23 a.; George Griffin Pierce 32 a.); devisees of John Howe, Lord Chedworth 726 a. (including lease, William Munday 124 a.); dean and chapter of Winchester 376 a. (including lease, Daniel Hearne 376 a.); Andrew Baden 309 a.; St. Katherine's Hospital 133 a. (including lease, executors of William Chafin Grove 133 a.); executors of William Chafin Grove 280 a. (including copy, Thomas Timbrell the younger 45 a.; William Baden 177 a.; Richard Stretch 31 a.; Thomas Maton; Moses Giddings; Philip Pearce); prebendary of Chute and Chisenbury 54 a. (including Thomas Timbrell 22 a.; William Baden 16 a.; Edward Bailey; Thomas Maton; Philip Pearce; John Nicholas); William Barnes; executors of Robert Baden.

Tithes Allotment to vicar for small tithes.

Roads 12 public roads, 8 private roads.

Maps (1) Enford and west part of parish. (2) Fifield and west part of parish. (3) Coombe and Longstreet and east part of parish. (4) East Chisenbury and east part of parish. Acreages and allottees shown.

See also Nos. 83, 85, 86, and 142.

85 ENFORD

Littlecot

Act 54 G.III c.75. *Award* 12 March 1817 (enrolled 14 May 1829), W.R.O. 133. *Commissioner* Thomas Davis of Horningsham.

Lord of Manor of Littlecot, John Moore.

Vicar John Prince.

Area 719 a. [674 a.] Upper, Middle and Lower Field, Pook Linch, Littlecot Sheep Down, The Marsh.

Allotments 6. John Moore 332 a.; William Akerman 222 a.; vicar of Enford 111 a.; Andrew Baden; John Coward; Thomas Herne.

Tithes Vicarial tithes (except those on the glebe) allotted to William Akerman in exchange for 14 a. Rectorial tithes exchanged for 14 a.

Roads 2 public roads, 2 private roads, 1 public footpath.

Map Thomas Tilbrook 1817. Allottees and acreages shown. Village and tithing of Littlecot only. Arable red, pasture and down green.

See also Nos. 83, 84, 86, and 142.

86 ENFORD

East Chisenbury

Act General, 8 & 9 Vic. c.118. *Award* 6 Nov. 1856 (enrolled 18 Dec. 1856), W.R.O. 177. *Valuer* Francis Attwood.

Area [944 a.]

Allotments 6 (including three money allotments). Hospital of St. Katherine 369 a. (including lease, William Chafyn Grove 369 a.); William Chafyn Grove 193 a.; Ecclesiastical Commissioners 382 a. (including lease and copy, William Chafyn Grove 382 a.). Money payment instead of allotments for those entitled to allotments worth less than £5. *Fencing* with allotments.

Roads 2 private roads.

Maps John Waters of Salisbury 1856 (1) East of River Avon. (2) Northern part. Village included. New allotments have red numbers.

See also Nos. 83, 84, 85, and 142.

87 ERLESTOKE [2,054 a.]

Act 17 G.III c.138. *Award* 16 Jan. 1782 (enrolled 5 Nov. 1782), W.R.O. 21. *Commissioners* Thomas Wyatt (replacing William Wyatt of Burton-upon-Trent, d. 1780); Richard Bloxham of Winterslow; William Simpson of Walcot, Bath. *Surveyors* John Dugmore of Tamworth, Warws., and John Powell of Chippenham.

Rector dean and chapter of Salisbury. *Vicar* John Newton, vicar of Melksham.

Area 1,643 a. excl. ancient inclosures 373 a. [1,624 a.] The Marsh, The Hill, Great Hill Common, Hill Wood, West Lands, Sharpe, Southlands, North Sands, Low Field, Lower Low Field, Upper Low Field.

Allotments 6. Dean and chapter of Salisbury 331 a. (including lease, Peter Delme 331 a.); Peter Delme 748 a. (including copy, Esther Howell 21 a.; Hannah Oram); John Wadman 489 a. (including copy, Mary Tilley); vicar of Melksham 44 a.; John Axford; William Bartlett. *Fencing* with allotments.

Tithes commuted by allotment.

Roads 3 public roads, 2 public bridle ways, 2 private roads, 4 public footpaths. Herbage allotted.

Finance £1,400. Expenses including those of ring-fencing the vicar's allotments to be paid by the three allottees named in Schedule 2. Fixed money rents to be paid by copyholders.

Schedules (1) Old inclosures given up to Peter Delme for open-field lands, and the value comprised in the allotments to John Wadman, Mary Tilley, and Esther Howell. (2) Proportion of expenses to be paid by allottees.

Notes John Wadman and his heirs and the owners and occupiers of Hill Farm shall be allowed to water their sheep at Well Head Pond at such times only as no water can be found in the well or ponds on the Brunkers Hill Farm sufficient for that purpose. Water running from Erlestoke shall be turned into the ditch by the side of the road under the hedge that leads from the corner of Skimcroft to Pudnell for the use of John Wadman, Peter Delme, the dean and chapter of Salisbury, and the tenants of Erlestoke having the right to take a sufficient quantity of water to water their cattle in their lands late the Marsh.

88 FIFIELD BAVANT [1,161 a.]

Act 25 G.III c.56 (Fovant, Swallowcliffe, Broad Chalke, Ebbesborne Wake, Bower Chalke, Alvediston, Bishopstone, Fifield Bavant). *Award* 3 Jan. 1792 (enrolled 17 Nov. 1794), W.R.O. V 38. *Commissioners* Richard Bloxham of

West Dean; Richard Richardson of Devizes; Francis Webb of Salisbury (replacing William Corfield of Salisbury, d. 1787). *Surveyor* Benjamin Haynes (replacing William Corfield).

Rector Henry Diggle.

Area [812 a.] West Field, Maple Field, Middle Field, East Field, Fifield Down, Stony Croft, Barn Croft.

Allotments 5. Thomas Thynne, Viscount Weymouth (marquess of Bath), 755 a. (including lease, Joseph Heasall 21 a.); Charles Lisle 33 a. (including lease, Lord Weymouth 23 a.); rector of Fifield 23 a.; John Rebbeck; Thomas Bond.

Roads 7 public roads, 1 public bridle way. Herbage allotted.

Finance 1 sale allotment (1 r. 10 p.) to Viscount Weymouth for £6 8*s* to pay the rector's expenses.

Map Allotments and acreages shown. Whole parish and village.

Note Fifield Bavant was transferred to Ebbesborne Wake parish in 1894.

89 FIGHELDEAN [5,439 a.]

Agreement, under General Act, 6 & 7 W.IV c.115, 22 June 1842. *Award* 27 June 1844 (enrolled 10 Oct. 1844), W.R.O. V 162. *Commissioners* Francis Attwood of Salisbury; James Combes of Fonthill.

Lord of Manor bishop of Salisbury; *lessee* Edward Dyke Poore.

Rector Liscombe Clarke.

Area 1,375 a. [1,449 a.] Sheer Barrow Field, South Field, Gallows Barrow Field, Newton Mead, Upper and Lower North Field, Cow Down, North Mead, Costard, Tenantry Down, Middle Field.

Allotments 5. Bishop of Salisbury 1,025 a. (including lease, Edward Dyke Poore 296 a.; copy, Thomas Gilbert 564 a.; William Dyke Poore 152 a.; Henry Whitmarsh); Robert Herbert, earl of Pembroke 357 a. (including lease, Edward Poore 357 a.); Edward Dyke Poore 23 a.; rector of Figheldean 39 a.; Thomas Simpkins.

Roads 8 public roads, 2 private roads, 2 public footpaths. Rules for repair of private roads incorporated in the award. Herbage allotted to neighbouring allottees only.

Finance £740 (bishop £497 15*s*.; earl of Pembroke £183 10*s*.).

Map James Combes junior. Village shown but not Ablington or Choulston. Allottees and acreages.

Schedule Rate for mending private road No. 1 expressed as proportion of £1.

See also No. 80.

Note Right of feeding the river on both sides 'as far as cattle can reach' and right of cutting sedge allotted to lessee of bishop of Salisbury.

90 FISHERTON ANGER [320 a.]

Act 29 G.III c.42 (Berwick St. James and Fisherton Anger). *Award* 5 May 1790 (enrolled 4 Dec. 1798), W.R.O. 53. *Commissioners* Richard Richardson of Devizes; Richard Bloxham of Winterslow; Thomas Fricker of Longbridge Deverill. *Surveyors* Francis Webb of Salisbury and William Tubb of Salisbury (late of Cranborne).

Rector Edward Davenport.

Area 205 a. including 6 a. roads [190 a.] Church Field, Long Lands, Broad Mead Drove, Brick Field, Middle Field, St. Ann's Stile, Little Field, North Field, Parsonage Mead, Spring Ditch Mead.

Allotments 8. James Harris, Lord Malmesbury 107 a. (including leases, George Page, Peter Hunt); William Hayter 67 a.; trustees of Sarah Neave; churchwardens of Fisherton Anger; James Feltham; Elizabeth Boney; rector of Fisherton Anger; William Meaden. *Fencing* with allotments, hedges to be protected from sheep for seven years.

Roads 4 private roads, 2 public footpaths.

91 FISHERTON DELAMERE [2,834 a.]

Agreement 14 March 1807 between (1) William Davis, the vicar of Fisherton Delamere, John Davis of Bapton, John Gilbert, and William Doughty and (2) the Commissioners. *Award* 8 May 1807 (enrolled 15 May 1807), W.R.O. 71. *Commissioners* Christopher Ingram of Amesbury; Richard Parsons of North Standen, Berks.; Thomas Perrier of Deptford.

Lord of Manor of Fisherton Delamere, William Davis; of that part of the said manor of Fisherton Delamere situate at Bapton, John Davis.

Vicar Edward Meyrick.

Area [164 a.] East Field, Paradise, Pillmead.

Allotments 2. William Davis 143 a. (including lease, William Doughty; copy and lease, John Gilbert 100 a.); vicar of Fisherton Delamere 20 a.

Tithes Allotment to vicar for his glebe and certain tithes mostly on corn and hay. The glebe and tithes were then allotted to William Davis.

Finance £109 16*s*. ½*d*. borne by William Davis, but interest of 5 per cent per annum to be paid to William Davis by his tenants for their shares.

Map Only part of parish shown, with allottees and acreages.

See also No. 92.

92 FISHERTON DELAMERE

Bapton tithing

Agreement 2 July 1810 between (1) John Davis of Bapton, Benjamin Rebbeck of Woodhay, Hants, and James Slade of Bapton and (2) the Commissioners. *Award* 5 Oct. 1810 (enrolled 3 April 1811), W.R.O. 82. *Commissioners* Christopher Ingram of Amesbury; Thomas Perrier of Wylye.

Lord of Manor of Bapton, John Davis.

Rector (lay) John Davis; *lessee* Benjamin Rebbeck.

Area [54 a.] Rangers, West Field, Hickes Marsh, Patients, Millpond Meadow.

Allotment 1. John Davis 54 a. (including copy, James Slade 28 a.; Benjamin Rebbeck 23 a.).

Tithes on Benjamin Rebbeck's holding extinguished by deduction of lands in lieu. James Slade's holding remained tithable.

Roads General instruction that 'accustomed roads' are to continue.

Finance £84: John Davis £77, Benjamin Rebbeck £3 10*s*., James Slade £3 10*s*.
See also No. 91.
Note Arrangements for watering meadows to continue.

93 FITTLETON [3,213 a.]
Act 34 G.III c.32 (Keevil, Idmiston, Fittleton, and Chisenbury de la Folly). *Award* 20 Aug. 1796, W.R.O. 45. *Commissioners* Thomas Sheppard D.D. of Basingstoke; Francis Webb of Salisbury; John Gale of Stert (replacing Thomas Verry, dead). *Surveyor* John Verry of Bristol.
Lord of Manor Michael Hicks Beach.
Rector Stephen Jenner of Berkeley, Glos.
Area [710 a.] Combe Mead, Vals Hill, Common Mead, Fittleton Down.
Allotments 2. Michael Hicks Beach 678 a.; rector of Fittleton 32 a.
Roads 4 public roads, herbage allotted.
Map John Verry. Manor of Fittleton including the village but not including Haxton or Fittleton Down Farm.
See also No. 94.

94 FITTLETON
Haxton
Act General, 6 & 7 W.IV c.115. *Award* 4 Sept. 1839 (enrolled 12 Oct. 1839), W.R.O. 154. *Commissioners* William Ruddle Brown of Chiseldon; Richard Stratton of Upavon. *Umpire* Thomas Washbourne of Cholsey, Berks. *Surveyor* William Bryan Wood.
Lord of Manor of Hacklestone and Fittleton, Sir Michael Hicks Beach, Bt.
Area 915 a. [918 a.]
Allotments 3. Sir Michael Hicks Beach 682 a. (including copy, William Lawes 5 a.); John Perkins 224 a. (including Prosnary Lands 65 a.); Felix Harris.
Roads 2 public roads, 1 private road, 1 public footpath.
Map W. B. Wood. Haxton tithing including village.
Schedule Old inclosures and allotments, allottees and acreages.
See also No. 93.
Notes Sir Michael Hicks Beach as owner of the dissolved free chapel of Fittleton was entitled to part of the tithes on 279 a. in Haxton called Prosnary or Portionary lands and these tithes were not affected by the award. Boundary between Haxton and Fittleton determined.

95 FOVANT [2,203 a.]
Act 25 G.III c.56 (Fovant, Swallowcliffe, Broad Chalke, Ebbesborne Wake, Bower Chalke, Alvediston, Bishopstone, Fifield Bavant). *Award* 3 Jan. 1792 (enrolled 17 Nov. 1794), W.R.O. V 38. *Commissioners* Richard Bloxham of West Dean; Richard Richardson of Devizes; Francis Webb of Salisbury (replacing William Corfield of Salisbury, d. 1787). *Surveyor* Benjamin Haynes (replacing William Corfield).
Lord of Manor Henry Herbert, earl of Pembroke.
Rector Thomas Eyre.

Area [1,017 a.] Broad Mead, Oddy Mead, Hill Land Field, Acre's Edge Field, Townsend, East Limbway Field, East and West Hays Field, North and South Middle Field, Ivers Field, Barter's Oak Field, the field against Compton, Fovant Down. *New Common Fields* Down Field, Shaftesbury Road Field.

Allotments 14. Public: 1 furze allotment 10 a. Earl of Pembroke 925 a. (including leases, Edward Bracher 124 a.; John Blundell 79 a.; Francis Blundell 37 a.; rector of Fovant 30 a.; copy, Mary Martin 46 a.; Osmond Martin 44 a.; Thomas Reading 28 a.; William Nightingale 24 a.; George Younge 17 a.; Richard Mills; Thomas Hartford; William Macey and Nathaniel Rowden; Thomas Harrison and Edward Bracher); Francis Blundell 17 a.; Walter Eve 16 a.; Osmond Martin; Henry Goodfellow; Edward Brickle; Richard Mills; John and Henry King; Edward Bracher; William Goodfellow; Thomas Goodfellow; Roger Barnes; overseers of poor.

Roads 7 public roads, 1 public bridle way, 1 public footpath; 10 private roads. Herbage allotted.

Finance to be paid by allottees including if necessary those holding reversions. Osmond Martin granted part of the rector's allotment on condition that he pay all the rector's expenses and his own.

Map Whole parish including the village. Allottees and acreages.

Schedules (1) Lifeholders under the earl of Pembroke who are to pay interest, as the reversionaries have paid the expenses. (2) Charges assessed by the commissioners on various lifeholders under the earl of Pembroke.

Notes The award dealt with inclosures in eight different parishes, 16,720 a. in all; see also Nos. 5, 20, 38, 40, 81, 88, 179. Except for Fifield Bavant they are all parishes in which the earls of Pembroke had a major interest and they are remarkable in several ways. In some, although the old common fields were inclosed and allotted to the several proprietors, new common fields were set up under the award, certain areas of downland were appointed to be fed in common, and new regulations drawn up for regulating the cropping of the new common fields. The arrangements for finance were that the lifeholders under the earl of Pembroke were assessed for their share in Schedule 2 of the award. Those who could not pay their share had it paid for them by the reversionary (the earl of Pembroke) and had to pay an increased rent, set out in Schedule 1.

96 FROXFIELD AND MILTON LILBORNE

Act 58 G.III c.56 (Private, not printed). *Award* 5 May 1823, W.R.O. 119. *Commissioner* John Gale of Devizes. *Surveyor* John Hayward of Rowde.

FROXFIELD [2,291 a.]

Lord of Manor trustees of Somerset Hospital.

Area [441 a.] Froxfield Field.

Allotments 5. Trustees of Somerset Hospital 306 a. (including copy, William Merewether 27 a.; Mary Drury 34 a.); Edward Leyborne Popham 91 a. (including lease, William Merewether 20 a.); dean and canons of Windsor

30 a.; Charles Brudenell-Bruce, marquess of Ailesbury; Henry Hurle. *Fencing* general and on map.

Roads 2 public roads, 1 public bridle way and private road, 2 private roads.

Map Allottees and acreages shown, 7 detached pieces some in Ramsbury and Little Bedwyn. Whole parish, except tithing of Oakhill and area to the west marked Hensett and Puthall. Late commonable lands allotted, marked red, old inclosures exchanged, green.

MILTON LILBORNE

Fyfield manor

Surveyor Charles Pearson Charlton of Brook House, Wilts.

Lord of Manor John Hungerford Penruddocke.

Area [487 a.] Martins Hill Down.

Allotments 2. Trustees of Somerset Hospital 132 a.; John Hungerford Penruddocke 355 a. *Fencing* general.

Map 1822. Fyfield manor only, allottees and acreages shown. Areas not allotted are numbered only.

See also No. 140.

97 FUGGLESTONE ST. PETER [1,818 a.]

Quidhampton tithing

Agreement 10 Oct. 1796 between (1) George Herbert, earl of Pembroke; (2) John Howe, Lord Chedworth; (3) 24 others including Rev. William Coxe, the mayor of Wilton, and the sisters of the hospital of St. Giles. *Award* 1798, in archives of the earl of Pembroke. *Commissioners* John Seagrim of Wilton; John Good of Shaftesbury; Adam Powell of Bulbridge.

Lord of Manor George Herbert, earl of Pembroke.

Rector William Coxe.

Area 548 a. including common lands 70 a., common marsh 40 a. [542 a.] Little Ham, West Mead, Spear Ham, Gore Mead, King's Mead, East Field, West Field, Middle Field, Higher Field, Wiremead.

Allotments 9. Public: 1 sheep pond to be common to those who have sheep leases. Earl of Pembroke 130 a. (including Joseph Williams 21 a.; William Batten; Richard Jeffery; William Holmes; Margaret and Catherine Hawes; William Whitmarsh; Joseph Gibbs; Richard Earlsman; William Hussey); Lord Chedworth 24 a.; dean and chapter of Salisbury 16 a.; Rev. John Hopkins; John Eastman; Rev. William Coxe as rector of Bemerton; Mrs. Hawes; hospital of St. Giles; 349 a. to continue to be fed and cropped in common. *Fencing* with allotments.

Roads 11 (whether public or private not stated), 2 footpaths.

Finance Rate on free-, lease-, and copyholders, but not on their undertenants.

See also No. 195.

Notes The net result of the provision that 349 a. of the allotments were to continue to be fed and cropped in common was that the old strips were done away with and the old common fields reallotted in larger holdings which, however, were still farmed on the open system, the number of fields being reduced from five to four. The area affected lay north of the Wilton-Salisbury road and right up to the parish boundary but excluding a narrow strip by the Wilton–Salisbury road. The area in the marshes between Quidhampton and the river was not included in this arrangement but was finally allotted in severalty. Sheep leazes were also awarded and regulations made for numbers of sheep and times of stocking. Any occupier of an allotment in the wheat field could fold one night for each acre in the field.

98 WEST GRIMSTEAD (including part of Whiteparish)

Act 42 G.III c.85 (Private and Personal, not printed) (West Grimstead and Whiteparish). *Award* 19 Feb. 1805 (enrolled 18 March 1817), W.R.O. 100. *Commissioners* Francis Webb of Salisbury; Thomas Charlton of Stourhead; Richard Richardson of London.

Lord of Manor Jacob Pleydell-Bouverie, earl of Radnor.

Rector Joseph Griffith.

Area 466 a. [483 a.] East and West Fields, Inner and Outer Down Field, East Field, Middle Field, Willowslade, Tenants Meadow, Dartford Common, Crockford Green, Pound Meadow.

Allotments 10. Public: 1 stone and gravel pit. Earl of Radnor 267 a. (including leases, Joel Rowden 61 a.); Thomas Edward Baker 93 a.; William Emmett 59 a.; George Maton 39 a.; Ann Roles 25 a.; rector of West Grimstead; Thomas Roles as parish clerk; — Bingham; Thomas Chubb. *Fencing* set out in award.

Roads 5 public roads, 2 public bridle ways and private roads, 2 private roads. Herbage allotted to neighbouring allottees only.

Finance £1,035 5*s.* 11*d.*, and in addition public roads £51 15*s.* 1*d.* and private roads £1 6*s.* 5*d.*

Map William Tubb of Salisbury 1804. Whole parish and village, allottees and acreages shown.

Schedule shows proprietor, amount payable for expenses, and amounts payable for repairing public and private roads.

See also No. 191.

Notes Inclosures within the last twenty years included. No cattle to be depastured on any allotments for seven years to protect the hedges.

99 HAM (including a small part of Buttermere) [1,652 a.]

Act 7 & 8 G.IV c.2 (Private). *Award* 24 Oct. 1828 (enrolled 25 Aug. 1829), W.R.O. 134. *Commissioners* George Barnes of Andover, Hants; James Comely of Compton, Hants. *Umpire* James Blackman J.P. *Surveyor* William Walmesley of Andover, Hants.

Lord of Manor dean and chapter of Winchester.

Rector William Gomm of Bramdean, Hants.

Area 639 a. including old inclosures 975 a. Great Field, Little Field, Pidgett Field, Several Mead, Home Meadow.

Allotments 5. Dean and chapter of Winchester 1,191 a. (including copy, Thomas Harding 25 a.; John Sheppard 57 a.; lease and copy, John Watts 1,061 a.; William Elton 52 a.; Rev. James D'Avenant; Elizabeth Winterbourne); Thomas Cowderoy 240 a.; Francis Watts 77 a.; rector of Ham 20 a.; John Watts. *Fencing* general.

Roads 4 public roads, 2 private roads, 1 public bridle way, 1 public footpath.

Map 1828. Whole parish and village, allottees and acreages shown. Copyhold red, leasehold yellow, freehold green.

100 HANKERTON [2,203 a.]

Act 48 G.III c.33 (not printed). *Award* 24 Aug. 1809 (enrolled 7 Sept. 1827), W.R.O. 132. *Commissioners* John William Biedermann of Tetbury, Glos.; Robert Wright Hall of Cirencester, Glos.

Lord of Manor of Hankerton, John Howard, earl of Suffolk; of Cloatley, Joseph Pitt.

Vicar James Wiggett.

Area [522 a.] Hankerton Purlieus, Hither and Further Home Commons, Windmill Hill Common, Cloatley Common, Straight Mead.

Allotments 12. Earl of Suffolk 293 a. (including leases, George Beale; Henry Biedermann; John Bishop; Hannah Butler; Henry Golding; John Hayward; Susannah Hall; William Hughes; Thomas Law; Edward Matthews; William Matthews; John Matthews; Henry Perring; William Perring; James Ratcliff; James Sisum; Richard Sisum; John Sparrow; William Sparrow; John Tanner; Charles Tanner; William Westmacott; William Waite; Thomas White; John White; William Woodhead; copy, Jane Woodland; copy and lease, John White); John White 52 a.; Christopher Cole 126 a.; Joseph Pitt; vicar of Hankerton; George Skuse; Mary and Ann Beale; corporation of Gloucester, as governors of the hospital of St. Bartholomew; Richard Constable; churchwardens of Hankerton; Zachariah Huggins; Jacob Huggins. *Fencing* general and in the award.

Roads 3 public roads, 8 private roads, 1 public footpath. Rules for repair of roads and erection of swing gates and stiles set out.

Map Samuel Wharton of London. Allotments coloured according to allottees.

Schedule For repair of private roads.

Note Boundaries between Hankerton and Charlton and between Hankerton and Crudwell determined by the Commissioners.

101 HANNINGTON [2,518 a.]

Agreement 16 May 1632 between Richard Swayne, John Stubbs, Sir Thomas Freke, Thomas Saverye, William Batson, and others; in possession of Ambrose Hussey-Freke Esq. of Hannington Hall. *Commissioners* Abraham Allen, Richard Trender, John Hunt.

Lord of Manor Richard Swayne, holding on behalf of his nephew Sir Thomas Freke.

Rector (lay) Richard Swayne, as above.

Vicar Richard Stubbs 1615-1628; John Stubbs 1630.

Area 1,806 a. West, East and South Fields, Broad Mead, Oxlease, Cow

Lease, Nelland, Ham Furlong, Northedge, Berryton, Adwell, Parsonage Mead, Ningram Lake, Lord's Meadow, Chessell Piece, Donnington, Mascalls, Pibworth, Woodcockes, Jewry Lane, Bidlam Meadow, Sterte Meade, Sourelands, Starling Hill, Brocke Furlong.

Allotments 3. Richard Swayne 1,688 a. (including 156 a. for tithes; copy, Agnes Berryman 35 a.; John Yorke 36 a.; Elizabeth Willier 35 a.; John Harper 73 a.; Thomas Matthewe 15 a.; Humphry Boulton 19 a.; Richard Marshe 18 a.; Thomas Beckett 67 a.; John Jenkins 28 a.; widow Sanders and John Sanders 22 a.; Robert Boulton 46 a.; Walter Boulton 26 a.; Thomas Shermore 77 a.; Walter Weston 76 a.; Robert Marshe 67 a.; William Ballowe 34 a.; William Plomer 52 a.; William Batson 135 a.; John Batson 49 a.; Thomas Plomer 29 a.; Jeoffrey Pynnell 87 a.; Humphry Yorke 18 a.; Thomas Savery senior 64 a.; Thomas Savery junior 89 a.); Thomas Savery 71 a.; vicar of Hannington 47 a. (for tithes).

Tithes commuted in part by allotments of land.

Notes 'The said common fieldes were lying in a deep watrye part of the county, were subject oftentymes to overflowing of water . . . and the grasse spoyled.' Four parcels of land employed of ancient time for the repair of the bridge leading over the Thames called Hannington Bridge and for the repair of Hannington church called Bridge Lands and Church Akers. Walter Beckett refused to allot lands in place of tithes and must pay tithe on all his lands except Harpers Laynes; so also Walter Weston and Thomas Matthews; Thomas Plomer for his mill to pay 5*s.* yearly; farm of Sir Thomas Thinne to pay tithes as before. Agreements over footpaths and tracks for harvest carrying only. Thomas Strotton named as steward of the court. Horwell tithes (formerly due to the abbess of Wherwell, Hants, whereof one John Arden was lately propriate) owned by Sir Thomas Freke. Lanes and bridges to be repaired by each owner proportionately by providing one load of stones yearly for each 5 a. he owned. Customs of manor set out.

102 WEST HARNHAM [1,179 a.]

Act 23 G.III c.36 (Odstock, Homington, West Harnham, and Netherhampton). *Award* 17 March 1787 (enrolled 17 Sept. 1787), W.R.O. 27. *Commissioners* Benjamin Pryce of Wilton; Richard Bloxham of Winterslow; Richard Richardson of Devizes. *Surveyor* William Corfield of Salisbury.

Lord of Manor of West Harnham, Henry Herbert, earl of Pembroke; of West Harnham Walrons, Jacob Pleydell-Bouverie, earl of Radnor.

Rector and Prebendary of Coombe and Harnham, Edward Emily; *lessee* committee of William Hayter.

Area 499 a. [503 a.] The Cliff, Home Field, Little Field, West Dean Field, Pissing Bush Field, The Down, Pigg's Marsh.

Allotments 8. Prebendary of Combe and Harnham 269 a. (including lease, committee of William Hayter 269 a.); earl of Pembroke 150 a. (including copy, Solomon Sweetapple); earl of Radnor 53 a.; representatives of Thomas Walter Young 25 a.; representatives of John Hibberd; master, chaplain, brothers and sisters of hospital of St. Nicholas; Rev. John Baker.

Tithes commuted by allotments of land or by rent-charge.

Roads 2 public roads, 1 public bridle way, 1 public footpath, 4 private roads. Herbage allotted.

Map (No map with the copy of the award deposited with the Clerk of the Peace, but there is a copy with a map attached in the Salisbury City archives). 1787. Whole tithing of West Harnham shown, with allottees and acreages and field names; also shows the boundary between the manors of West Harnham and West Harnham Walrons.

Schedules (1) Lands remaining tithable (19 a.). (2) Cottages and gardens (three) for which a composition in money is to be made.

See also No. 30.

Notes Description of manor of West Harnham, and its bounds determined. The earl of Pembroke agreed that any manorial rights over this manor were to be extinguished, and his rights in the rest of the parish were confirmed. Boundary between West Harnham and Britford fixed.

103 HEDDINGTON [1,697 a.]

Act 6 G.III c.8, to confirm an *agreement* of 21 Nov. 1765. *Award* 26 Jan. 1767 (enrolled 31 Jan. 1767), W.R.O. 6. *Commissioners* John Nalder of Kennett; William Wapshare of Salisbury; John Bishop of Calne (nominated by seven parties); Michael Smith of Alton; John Gaby of Bromham (nominated by the rest). *Surveyor* John Clements of Avebury.

Lord of Manor Anthony Brooke.

Rector Francis Rogers.

Area 786 a. [786 a.].

Allotments 12. Thomas Hunt Grubbe 177 a.; George Willy 82 a.; Henry Brooke 150 a.; Anthony Brooke 192 a.; trustees of Thomasin Maundrell 50 a.; Nicholas Pearse 28 a.; Jenevera Sympson 40 a.; Benjamin Stephens 35 a.; David Hill; Phebe Townsend; rector of Heddington; John Hood. *Fencing* with allotments, and to be on lands of allottees; rector excused fencing duties.

Roads 1 public road, 1 public bridle way, 3 public footpaths, 1 private road.

Finance Rate on allottees according to the annual value of their lands (except the rector).

Note Old inclosures of less than twenty years included.

104 HEYTESBURY [5,198 a. including Tytherington]

Heytesbury and Tytherington with small areas of Sutton Veny and Horningsham

Act 23 G.III c.5. *Award* 26 Nov. 1785 (enrolled 10 Nov. 1786), W.R.O. 25. *Commissioners* Richard Richardson of Devizes; Thomas Fricker of Longbridge Deverill; Richard Bloxham of West Dean. *Surveyor* Thomas Webb of Warminster.

Lord of Manor of Heytesbury and Tytherington, William Pierce Ashe à Court.

Rector and Prebendary of Heytesbury, dean of Salisbury; *lessee* W. P. Ashe à Court.

Prebendary of half the prebend of Horningsham and Tytherington, seised of half the appropriate rectory of Tytherington, James Stirling Samber D.D.;

lessee Thomas Thynne, Viscount Weymouth; of the other half, Charles Greene; *lessee* Richard Crowch.

Prebendary of Swallowcliffe, Thomas Osborne D.D.; *lessee* Arundell Frome.

Area 4,910 a. [4,951 a.] North and South Field, Heytesbury Down, Cow Down, Tytherington Down, East and West Mead, Broad Mead, Eaken Mead, Slater's Mead, West Garston, Tytherington West Field, The Croft, The Sea, East Hanging.

Allotments 15. Dean of Salisbury 977 a. (including lease, W. P. Ashe à Court 977 a.); W. P. Ashe à Court 3,021 a. (including leases, John Sloper and William Tinker 457 a.; Thomas M. Biggs 313 a.; James Raxworthy 104 a.; Roger House 95 a.; Richard Snelgrove 110 a.; William Marsh 75 a.; Joseph Everett 81 a.; William Hooper 17 a.; Thomas Exten 103 a.; Samuel Long 23 a.; copy, Obadiah Flower 18 a.; Mary Crowch 16 a.; John Rodwell 25 a.; lease and copy, John Sloper and William Tinker 457 a.; William Everett 233 a.; Simon Dyer 27 a.; Thomas Cousens; trustees of Thomas and Frances Cousens; John T. Wickham; Richard Crowch; William Giddings; William Dyer; Thomas Flower; Isaac Flower; William Fry; Hannah White; Christian Prior; Robert Snelgrove; Richard Withers; Thomas Prangley; Thomas Smith; Thomas Snelgrove; Jane Flower; John Gale Everett); dean and chapter of Salisbury 65 a. (including Giles Halliday 26 a.; Richard Sheppard 31 a.; Jane Flower); John Gale Everett 115 a.; prebendary of half the prebend of Horningsham and Tytherington 185 a. (including lease, Viscount Weymouth 185 a.); prebendary of the other half 167 a. (including lease, Richard Crowch 167 a.); Richard Crowch 147 a.; Viscount Weymouth 57 a. (including Stephen Long 46 a.; Giles Halliday); Rebecca Long 24 a.; John Walker Heneage 52 a. (including Rebecca Long 52 a.); Thomas Osborne 37 a.; Samuel Long; William Giddings; prebendary of Heytesbury as appropriator of parsonage of Knook; representatives of James Frampton; — Hayward of Knook. *Fencing* Only Broad Mead, East Mead, and Little Oxen Lease specified.

Tithes Allotments in place of tithes awarded to dean of Salisbury and his lessee and to the prebendary of Swallowcliffe. Rent-charge levied on those with insufficient lands in the common fields. Lord Weymouth pays for all his tithes, on about 400 a. of meadow and pasture in Longleat Park, a customary rent of 4*s*. per annum as appears by the Parliamentary Survey of 1649.

Roads Turnpike roads to be 40 feet wide. 6 public roads, 3 public bridle ways, 26 private roads, 1 public driftway to a well, 1 public footpath and private road, 10 public footpaths. Herbage allotted.

Finance Partly by sale of parts of the allotments to the prebendary of Heytesbury, prebendary of Swallowcliffe, and dean of Salisbury and partly by rates levied on other allottees as specified in the award.

Maps (1) Parish north of river Wylye. (2) Parish south of River Wylye and Tytherington. (3) Village. Whole parish and village shown.

Schedules (1) Premises in (a) Heytesbury; (b) Tytherington liable to pay rent charge in place of tithe. (2) Terrier of lands in Horningsham for which a modus has always been paid to the prebendaries of Horningsham and Tytherington.

Notes The lord of the manor retained his rights of the soil over the lands of his copy and leasehold tenants. Detailed orders for times and methods of watering Broad Mead, Great Oxen Leaze, Little Oxen Leaze, Barn's Close and Shepherd's Mead. Waters to be divided into seven pitches.

105 HIGHWORTH

Broad Blunsdon

Act 22 G.II c.45, to confirm an *agreement* of 18 Dec. 1747 between (1) George Bryan, vicar of Highworth; (2) William Hippisley of Stanton; (3) Henry Southby of Highworth; (4) John Stapler of Broad Blunsdon and others. *Award* 1749, W.R.O. 4. *Commissioners* Henry Oatridge of Lechlade, Glos.; Jonathan Wirdnam of Shrivenham, Berks.; John Withers of Bishopstone; Thomas Justice of Abingdon, Berks.; John Bowls of Abingdon; Benjamin Fuller of Abingdon; James Smart of Long Wittenham, Berks. *Surveyors* Richard Green of Highworth and Edward Smith of Shrivenham (both schoolmasters).

Vicar George Bryan.

Area 986 a. including old inclosures at least 101 a. [885 a.]. North, South, East and West Fields, Cold Harbour Field, Common Meadow.

Allotments 17. Henry Southby 158 a.; Mary and Nathaniel Roberts 120 a.; John Stapler 86 a.; Thomas Hitchman 73 a.; master and governors of Christ's Hospital 81 a.; William Hippisley 145 a.; Francis Pearce 53 a.; Edward Strange 56 a.; Sir Mark Stuart-Pleydell 20 a.; John Wells 18 a.; Mary Hussey 36 a.; Mary Fowler; vicar of Highworth; Thomas Bailey; churchwardens of Broad Blunsdon for repairing the church; assignees of John, Lord St. John; John Oatridge. *Fencing* with allotments.

See also No. 106.

106 HIGHWORTH [10,820 a.]

Eastrop, Westrop, and Hampton tithings

Act 18 G.III c.21. *Award* 27 Feb. 1779 (enrolled *coram rege* Hilary Term 20 G.III), W.R.O. Acc 7/22 (solicitor's office copy). *Commissioners* Richard Richardson the younger of Ashton Keynes (replacing Thomas Weston of Warwick, refused); John Watts of Sulgrave, Northants.; Thomas Browne of Sevenhampton, Glos. *Surveyor* Thomas Webb of Harford, Warws.

Rector and Prebendary, James Benson of Gloucester; *lessee* William Hussey. *Vicar* Edward Clark.

Area 3,226 a. [3,177 a.] Eastrop North and South Field, Westrop Upper and Lower Field, East Mead, Coleshill Meadow, Cow Common.

Allotments 30. Public: 4 gravel pits 2 a. Prebendary of Highworth 769 a. (including lease and copy, William Hussey 769 a.); vicar of Highworth 99a. (including 96 a. for tithes and 3 a. for a load of hay); John Croft 263 a.; Walter Long 149 a.; William Hussey 647 a.; Robert Craggs Nugent, Earl Nugent, and Edward Eliot 953 a. (including leases, Thomas Belcher, 39 a.: Francis Thatcher 25 a.; John Parker 119 a.; Cordelia Woodbridge

46 a.; Honor Humphris 25 a.; William Billing 18 a.; Henry Merewether 68 a.; Oliver Carter 119 a.; Susannah Selman; Henry Winning; John Gorton; Richard Kempster; Henry Angel; Henry Kinneir); Richard Blofield 70 a.; Daniel Clutterbuck 49 a.; Joseph Cope 45 a.; William Saunders 31 a.; Francis Thatcher; John Weston; Thomas Marsh; John Potts; John Anns; Richard Stephens; Walter Brind; John Lifely; Thomas Coombs; Hannah Reason; William Saunders; churchwardens of Highworth; Richard Humphris; Thomas Sharp; Edward Green; Thomas Selman; Jacob Pleydell-Bouverie, earl of Radnor; William Pinnegar; Richard Kempster. *Fencing* with allotments, and on map.

Tithes commuted by allotments, tithe rent-charge on old inclosures assessed.

Roads 9 public roads, 23 private roads, 2 private roads and public footpaths, 7 public footpaths, 2 private footpaths. Herbage allotted.

Finance £1,623 5*s.* 4*d.* Prebendary's share paid by a deduction from his allotment of 98 a. sold to William Hussey.

Map Allotments numbered. William Hussey's lands coloured, freehold red, leasehold yellow, copyhold blue. Village shown, but Sevenhampton excluded.

Schedules (1) Old inclosures in Eastrop, Westrop, and Hampton discharged from tithes. (2) Old inclosures in Westrop whose owners have insufficient lands to compensate for tithes and which will pay a tithe rent-charge instead. (3) Receipts and payments for inclosure. (4) List of sums charged on tenants of Earl Nugent and Edward Eliot as increase of rent consequent upon the landlords paying their share of expenses.

See also No. 105.

107 BROAD HINTON AND CLYFFE PYPARD [Broad Hinton 3,726 a., Clyffe Pypard 4,040 a.]

Broad Town manor in Broad Hinton and Thornhill in Clyffe Pypard

Act 2 G.IV c.22 (Private). *Award* 30 Oct. 1822 (enrolled 15 April 1823), W.R.O. 120. *Commissioners* John Hayward of West Lavington; William Phelps of Puckrup, Glos.

Lord of Manor of Broad Town, trustees of Broad Town Charity; of Thornhill, principal and scholars of Brasenose College, Oxford.

Area 330 a. [390 a.; Clyffe Pypard 270 a., Broad Hinton 120 a.] The Cliff, Middle, East and West Fields.

Allotments 9. Trustees Broad Town charity 134 a. (104 a. in C.P., 30 a. in B.H.); Brasenose College 134 a. (all in C.P. including leases, Richard Welford 40 a.; Isaac Archer 50 a.; Rev. Edward Goddard 43 a.); Rev. Edward Goddard 32 a.; Robert Codrington 33 a.; Isaac Tuck 32 a. Elizabeth Pye Benet 18 a.; John Brown; executors of William Coleman; Robert Smith. *Fencing* in award and on map.

Roads 1 public road, 1 public bridle way, 2 public footpaths, 3 private roads, 1 private driftway. Herbage allotted.

Finance shown as proportion of £1 that each allottee has to pay.

Map George Hayward of Devizes. Two detached old inclosures shown.

Allotments in Clyffe Pypard outlined in red, those in Broad Hinton in green. Village not shown.

Schedule Expenses in making private roads shown as proportion of £5 payable by each allottee.

See also No. 206.

108 HOMINGTON [1,270 a.]

Act 23 G.III c.36 (Odstock, Homington, West Harnham, and Netherhampton). *Award* 1 June 1787 (enrolled 17 Sept. 1787), W.R.O. 26. *Commissioners* Benjamin Pryce of Wilton; Richard Bloxham of Winterslow; Richard Richardson of Devizes. *Surveyor* Francis Webb late of Stow, Glos., now of Salisbury.

Lord of Manor Jacob Pleydell-Bouverie, earl of Radnor; of the East End lands, provost and scholars of King's College, Cambridge.

Rector dean and chapter of Salisbury; *lessee* Ambrose Harwood.

Area 1,094 a. including roads [1,062 a.] East and West Mead, East, West and Middle Field, Homington Down, Burcombe Down, Minny Marsh, West Mead.

Allotments 6. Dean and chapter of Salisbury 173 a. (including 149 a. for glebe and tithe; lease, Ambrose Harwood 20 a.; Sarah Harwood); earl of Radnor 247 a.; Sir James Harris 142 a. (including lease, William Goodfellow); Samuel Mitchell 145 a.; provost and scholars of King's College, Cambridge, 309 a. (including leases, Samuel Mitchell 256 a.; Elizabeth Bodenham 27 a.; John Barber 26 a.); rector of Stratford Tony 46 a. for tithes of open lands at East End. *Fencing* general with special provisions for West Mead and East Meadow.

Tithes both great and small (except some tithes on the East End) commuted by allotments and a rent-charge.

Roads 8 public roads, 7 private roads. Herbage allotted.

Map Francis Webb of Salisbury 1787. Whole parish including the village and East End lands. Inclosures coloured on map; those exchanged red, those remaining tithable yellow; those subject to tithe rent-charge green.

See also Nos. 64 and 148.

Note Rights of watering meadows and of placing and drawing hatches determined.

109 IDMISTON [5,616 a.]

Act 34 G.III c.32 (Keevil, Idmiston, Fittleton, and Chisenbury de la Folly). *Award* 30 April 1795, W.R.O. 39. *Commissioners* Robert Verry of Netheravon; Richard Davis of Lewknor, Oxon.; Francis Webb of Salisbury. *Surveyors* John Verry of Bristol and William Church of Lewknor, Oxon.

Lord of Manor Michael Hicks Beach.

Rector dean and chapter of Salisbury; *lessees* John Blake and Edward Bowle. *Vicar* Edward Moore.

Area [1,178 a.] Church Hill, Harford Field, Harford Down, Brownberry Field, West Common Field, Hail Field, Turpit Hill, Cow Common, Wiltway Field, Hay Hill Field.

Allotments 3. Dean and chapter of Salisbury 124 a. (including lease, John Blake and Edward Bowle 124 a.); Michael Hicks Beach 1,054 a. (including leases, Martha Case and Mary Jacob 36 a.; Henry Bowle 17 a.; Thomas and Henry Whitmarsh 17 a.; Elizabeth Wristbridge 55 a.; John Dear 127 a.; copy, Thomas Sims 138 a.; Stephen King; John King; Edward Towsey; John Bowle; Mrs. Jane Turner); surveyors of highways.

Roads 14 public roads, 1 public bridle way, 2 private roads. Herbage allotted to lord of manor in place of his rights of the soil.

Map Robert Verry 1794 and 1795. Whole of parish west of the river shown, but only the south part east of the river. Village shown.

See also No. 110.

110 IDMISTON

Porton tithing

Agreement 30 August 1842. *Award* 12 June 1850 (enrolled 2 July 1850), W.R.O. V 170. *Commissioners* Francis Attwood of Salisbury; Thomas Waters of Stratford sub Castle. *Surveyor* James Combes of Fonthill.

Area 902 a. [887 a.]

Allotments 3. Devisees of John Bowle 342 a.; Frederick Butt 417 a.; trustees of marriage of William and Louisa Bonaker 128 a.

Roads 7 public roads. Herbage allotted.

Map James Combes junior of Fonthill. Only the tithing shown, including village.

See also No. 109.

111 KEEVIL

Keevil without Bulkington [2,063 a.]

Act 34 G.III c.32 (Keevil, Idmiston, Fittleton, and Chisenbury de la Folly). *Award* 20 Aug. 1796 (enrolled 10 July 1799), W.R.O. 46. *Commissioners* Thomas Bruges of Melksham; Thomas Sheppard D.D. of Basingstoke, Hants; John Gale of Stert (replacing Robert Verry, retired through ill-health). *Surveyor* John Verry.

Lord of Manor Michael Hicks Beach.

Rector dean and chapter of Winchester; *lessee* Sir William Heathcote Bt.

Area [462 a.] West Moor, North Field, Couple Church Field, Keevil Field, Ham Mead, Evills Mead, Everalds Mead, Pinkney's Field, Week Field.

Allotments 20. Michael Hicks Beach 218 a. (including lease, Jacob Taylor 19 a.; Sarah Beach; Anne Lewden; copy, Mary Watts; John Stileman; Ambrose Turner); Ann and Mary Brown 25 a.; Christopher Matthews 24 a.; Anne Dare 19 a.; dean and chapter of Winchester 20 a.; Walter Long 22 a.; Richard Long 15 a.; Rev. Thomas Leir 19 a.; Anne Mortimer 41 a.; Mary Whitaker; Stephen Watts; Thomas Watts; Thomas Talboy; trustees of charity school of Steeple Ashton; Joseph Bailey; Thomas Bruges; Daniel Capel; John Gaisford; representatives of George Gilbert; Edward Mortimer. *Fencing* general.

Tithes commuted into corn rents.

Roads 3 public roads, 13 private roads, 1 private footpath, 2 public footpaths. Herbage on Drove Lane, Burzley Lane, and Torridge Lane to Michael Hicks Beach.

Map John Verry 1795. Shows manor of Keevil and the village. Fencing duties outlined in yellow.

Schedules (1) Exchanges. (2) Tithe rent-charges.

Note Owner of certain closes able to divert the water running between Keevil and Pinkney.

112 KILMINGTON [2,876 a.]

Act 54 G.III c.93. *Award* 25 Sept. 1821, Somerset R.O. (photostat in W.R.O. V 194). *Commissioners* Thomas Davis; John Charlton.

Lord of Manor Sir Richard Colt Hoare Bt.

Vicar Hon. and Rev. Charles Strangways.

Area [166 a.] Kilmington Common.

Allotments 20 (excluding 6 sale allotments). Sir Richard Colt Hoare Bt. 95 a. (including leases, Christian Brickle; Joseph Bird; William Brimson; Elizabeth Cooper; William Coward; William Case; churchwardens of Kilmington; representatives of Grace Coombes; Charles Edwards; Charles Farr; Edward Gilbert; Dorothy Hartgill; Hugh Lush; Joseph Lush; William Lapham; Joseph Marsh; William Newton; James Newberry; Thomas Ryall; Thomas Smart; Mary Smart; William Savage; representatives of Hugh Shoard; Elizabeth Smith; William Whitaker; John Ward; Mary White); earl of Ilchester 39 a.; James Coombes; Frederick Coombes; John Cross; George Howell; Joseph Lush; Hugh Lush; Hon. and Rev. Charles Strangways; surveyors of highways; George Turner; trustees of — Maidment; George Matthews; John Matthews; Elizabeth Pitman; Richard Ring; Christopher Rose; Robert Tite; Stephen White; Stephen Willis. *Fencing* general.

Roads 3 public roads, 4 private roads.

Finance Sale allotments (22 a.).

Map Allottees and acreages. 6 detached pieces.

Schedule Kilmington Common, rate for repair of private roads.

Note Kilmington was at the time in Somerset, being transferred to Wiltshire in 1896.

113 WEST KINGTON [2,446 a.]

Act 49 G.III c.93 (not printed). *Award* 4 Jan. 1811 (enrolled 14 Jan. 1812), W.R.O. 84. *Commissioners* Richard Richardson of London; Robert Wright Hall of Cirencester, Glos.

Lord of Manor Christopher Codrington.

Rector James John Hume.

Area 950 a. (Act) [1,087 a.] North, South and West Fields, Mill Leaze, Ivey Grove, Harcomb, The Down, Upper and Lower Ham, Six Acres, Handstaffs, Marshes Mead, The Kite, Wick Green, King's Hill, Marshfield Stile, Prior's Ham.

Allotments 12. Public: 7 allotments for gravel pits 2 a. Christopher Codrington 94 a.; Sarah Terrill 157 a.; Mary Tyler 166 a.; Richard Bennett 195 a.;

Sarah Nowell 64 a.; Francis Holborrow 54 a.; Joseph Baldwin 275 a. [it is not possible to determine the tenure of all the above: Christopher Codrington, Mary Tyler, Richard Bennett and 113 a. of Sarah Terrill's holdings were certainly freehold, the rest were lease or copyhold and may have been part of the Codrington estate]; rector of West Kington 47 a.; Stephen King 27 a.; Isaac Hall; Elver Newman. *Fencing* with the allotments, in one place to be walls 4 feet high or quickset.

Roads 5 public roads, 10 private roads.

Map Richard Hall of Cirencester. Whole parish shown including village. Allotments coloured according to proprietor.

Schedule Shows proprietors, acreage allotted and not allotted, and number on map.

114 KNOOK [1,520 a.]

Act 32 G.III c.16. *Award* 13 Dec. 1798 (enrolled 11 Dec. 1797), W.R.O. 57. *Commissioners* Richard Richardson of Devizes; Francis Webb of Salisbury (replacing Richard Bloxham of West Dean, dead); William Jennings of Puddletown, Dorset (replacing Thomas Fricker of Longbridge Deverill, dead). *Surveyor* William Tubb of Fisherton Anger.

Lord of Manor Edward Adolphus Seymour, duke of Somerset (succeeding Webb Seymour, duke of Somerset).

Rector and prebendary of Knook in collegiate church of Heytesbury, dean of Salisbury; *lessee* William Pierce Ashe à Court.

Area 1,466 a. including roads 16 a. [1,450 a.] Horsehill Down, Cow Down, Garden Down, Great Barrow, Stoney Hill, Upper and Lower Garston, Great Mead, South Field, Broad Linch, West Hill, Dunscomb, Gangham Mead, Field under Chitterne Way.

Allotments 8. Prebendary of Knook 320 a. (including 311 a. for tithes); duke of Somerset 1,063 a. (including leases, Thomas Everett 164 a.; John Brewer and Sarah Lewis 38 a.; executors of Thomas Biggs 31 a.); Thomas Everett 16 a.; Thomas Flower and Mary Flower 20 a.; John Gale Everett; Brouncker Thring; Giles Beamister; Edmund Lambert. *Fencing* general.

Tithes Exonerated by allotment of lands. Those with insufficient lands to pay a tithe rent-charge according to a schedule incorporated in the award.

Roads 3 public footpaths, 9 private roads. Herbage allotted.

Finance £656. Allotment deducted from lands awarded to the prebendary of Knook and his lessee to pay their share of expenses and for fencing. Rest paid by allottees and the amounts are specified in the award.

Map William Tubb of Salisbury, 1794. Whole parish and village shown. Boundaries of old inclosures shaded green, of new allotments red. Allottees and acreages shown.

Notes Old inclosures of less than twenty years included. Very full reiteration of the Act in the Award. Fee of 1*s*. to be paid for permission to see the award. Turnpike roads to remain at 40 feet width. Directions for watering Gangham Mead and the Marsh and times for use of water set out. Pond on Garden Down for owners of Knook Farm. Duke of Somerset received an allotment for his rights of the soil, excluding those rights on his leasehold property.

115 EAST KNOYLE [5,564 a. excl. Pertwood]

Act 38 G.III c.22. *Award* 8 Aug. 1799 (enrolled 12 March 1800), supplementary award 25 March 1800 for one allotment omitted in the previous award, W.R.O. 60. *Commissioners* Francis Webb of Salisbury; Thomas Davis of Horningsham; Christopher Ingram of Amesbury. *Surveyors* William Tubb of Fisherton Anger and Thomas Davis junior of Horningsham.

Rector John Savile Ogle.

Area 820 a. (Act), 881 a. (Award) [839 a.] Upton Hadden Common, Milton Hadden Common, Upton Common, Milton Common, Upton Tenantry Down, Milton Tenantry Down, Milton Middle Field, Penning Field, Upton East Field, Milton Holden Field, Upton Middle Field, Little Sand, Drayslot Field, Grammer's Linch, Great Sand, Brookland.

Allotments 15. Bishop of Winchester 350 a. (including copy, Sarah Bye 39 a. Edward Carey 20 a.; William Chisman 120 a.; Rev. Peter Cornwall 23 a.; Peard Jillard 42 a.; William Perry 20 a.; James Still 44 a.; Anthony Burbidge 15 a.; Jane Burbidge; John Huntly; Joel Perman; James Rickets; John Shepherd; James Wyer); Elizabeth Oborne 53 a.; Charles Williams 121 a.; warden and scholars of Winchester College 144 a. (including lease, Rev. George Ashby and others 144 a.); president and scholars of Corpus Christi College, Oxford, 65 a. (including lease, executor of John Russ 65 a.); William Perry 17 a.; rector of East Knoyle 47 a.; William Beckford; John Kellow Bracher; trustees of Robert Compton's charity; executors of John Russ; Elizabeth Sanger; executors of John Sanger; John Shepherd; James Charles Still. *Fencing* general and in award.

Roads 3 public roads, 7 private roads, 3 public footpaths.

Finance Rate (excl. bishop of Winchester, Corpus Christi College, and the rector).

Schedule Number of sheep which the several proprietors are to feed in the commonable places of Upton and Milton, viz. Upton and Milton Hadden, Upton and Milton Commons, Milton Tenants Down, Upton Tenants Down.

See also No. 116.

116 EAST KNOYLE

Act General, 8 & 9 Vic c.118. *Award* 10 Aug. 1867 (enrolled 7 Sept. 1867), W.R.O. 191. *Valuer* James Rawlence of Bulbridge, Wilton.

Rector Robert Newman Milford.

Area [365 a.] Small Eye Gate, Summerleaze, Middle Field.

Allotments 4. Jane Seymour 339 a.; Vere Fane Bennett; president and scholars of Corpus Christi College, Oxford; Rev. Robert Milford. *Fencing* general and with allotments and on map.

Roads 3 private roads, repair duties set out. 3 public footpaths.

Map John Waters of Salisbury. Inclosed areas only, village indicated. Fencing shown and allotments numbered.

See also No. 115.

Note 3 footpaths stopped up.

117 LANDFORD [1,720 a.]

Act General, 8 & 9 Vic. c. 118. *Award* 14 Sept. 1860 (enrolled 13 Oct. 1860), W.R.O. 180. *Valuer* Francis Attwood.

Lord of Manor Frances Nelson, dowager Countess Nelson.

Area [56 a.] Landford Wood.

Allotments 6. Countess Nelson 49 a.; John Harcourt Powell; Hon. John Fox-Strangways; Henry Thomas; James Butcher; Rev. Henry Girdlestone. *Fencing* with allotments.

Roads 1 private road.

Map 1860. Allotments numbered. Landford Wood only.

See also No. 118.

118 LANDFORD

Act General, 8 & 9 Vic. c.118. *Award* 24 Aug. 1861 (enrolled 22 Nov. 1861), W.R.O. L 182. *Valuer* Francis Attwood.

Lord of Manor Frances Nelson, dowager Countess Nelson.

Rector Henry Girdlestone.

Area [740 a.] Landford Common.

Allotments 10. Public: 1 stone and gravel pit 1 a.; exercise and recreation 4 a. Countess Nelson 640 a. (including leases, James Noble; Daniel Moody); Rev. Henry Girdlestone 56 a.; Hon. George Fox-Strangways 27 a.; James Futcher; Thomas Harcourt Powell; Hon. Amelia Fox-Strangways; Henry Thomas; representatives of Mary Webb.

Roads 4 public roads, 3 private roads, 1 public footpath.

Map John Waters of Salisbury 1858. Landford Common and one detached portion.

See also No. 117.

Note Boundary between Landford Common and Dayell Wood straightened.

119 STEEPLE LANGFORD [4,018 a.]

Hanging Langford tithing

Act 3 W.IV c.1 (Private). *Award* 26 July 1836 (enrolled 26 Oct. 1858), W.R.O. V 153. *Commissioners* John Baverstock Knight of Piddlehinton, Dorset; Oliver Stubbs of Hinton St. George, Som. *Surveyor* John Martin of Evershot.

Lord of Manor provost and fellows of Eton College and William Wyndham.

Area 1,000 a. (Act) [1,000 a. including 30 a. sale allotments] Lot Mead, East and West Fields, East and West Tenantry Down, Hooklands, Netherlands, Rough Marsh, Hill Meadow, West Close, West Bake, Farm Bake, Pigs Marsh.

Allotments 4. Provost and fellows of Eton College 357 a. (including copy,

Jane James 15 a.; representatives of Henry Swayne 146 a.; Francis Dew; George Giles; lease, William Wyndham 158 a.); William Wyndham 611 a. (including representatives of Henry Swayne 22 a.); William Rowden; surveyors of highways. *Fencing* on map.

Roads 8 public roads, 3 private roads, 2 public footpaths. Herbage allotted.

Finance 3 sale allotments to William Wyndham (30 a.) £2,000.

Map J. Martin of Evershot 1836. Hanging Langford tithing only. Allottees and acreages.

Schedule Responsibility for repair of private roads, total £5.

See also No. 120.

Notes Inclosures made within the last twenty years included. Expenses of exchanges to be paid by those exchanging.

120 STEEPLE LANGFORD

Act General, 8 & 9 Vic. c.118. *Award* 7 May 1866 (enrolled 16 July 1866), W.R.O. L 186. *Valuer* James Rawlence of Bulbridge, Wilton.

Lord of Manor Francis Baring, Lord Ashburton.

Rector Michael Harrison.

Area [985 a.] Cow Down, Tenantry Down, Great Meadow.

Allotments 6. Public: labouring poor 3 a. Lord Ashburton 862 a. (including lease, John Swayne); William Blake and John Marshall 67 a.; rector of Steeple Langford 53 a.; parish clerk; John Swayne. *Fencing* with allotments.

Roads 2 private roads, 2 public footpaths, 1 private footpath; 3 roads stopped up.

Map John Waters of Salisbury 1863. Whole parish except Hanging Langford and Bathampton. Village shown. Allotments numbered.

See also No. 119.

Notes 36 old inclosures included in the award but not in this abstract. Allotment to labouring poor included a rent-charge based on price of wheat, barley, and oats. Chalk pit on map but not in award.

121 LANGLEY BURRELL [1,704 a.]

Agreement 17 June 1837 (enrolled 19 March 1838), W.R.O. 151. *Commissioners* Robert Hughes of Woodford; Thomas Little of Biddestone.

Lord of Manor Robert Ashe.

Rector Robert Ashe.

Area 114 a. [113 a.] Langley Common (84 a.), Birds Marsh (30 a.).

Allotments 6. Robert Ashe 92 a.; George Knight; John Matthews; Mary Maillard; John Nicholls; John Eddolls. *Fencing* in award.

Roads 2 public roads, 10 private roads.

Finance Proportion payable by each allottee set out in award.

Map Allotments coloured and numbered, and allottees shown.

Schedule Numbers of beast-leases originally held by allottees: Robert Ashe 87, rector 6, Mary Millard 8, John Nicholls 10, John Eddolls 6, George Knight 2, John Matthews 2.

See also Nos. 47 and 48.

122 LATTON AND EISEY [1,826 a.]

Act 41 G.III c.101 (Private and Personal, not printed) (Down Ampney, Glos., Latton, and Eisey). *Award* 23 May 1805, Glos. R.O. (photocopy in W.R.O.). *Commissioner* John Gale of Stert (with Henry Hoyte to assist him). *Surveyor* Edward Webb (replacing Daniel Mumford, incapable).

Lord of Manor John Eliot, Lord Eliot.

Rector (lay) Lord Eliot.

Vicar of Latton, John Lyne.

Area Latton 944 a. [936 a.], Eisey 138 a. [138 a.], Latton West Field, Home Field, Weymoor, Peasebridge Field, Muddleford Field, Little Mead, Washford Green, Sidnell Meadow, Wickmoors, Mere Leaze, Charlham, Mowsdowns, Hill Ground, Marlborough Meadow, Court Field, Cow Leaze, Southam Meadow, Mereleaze, Abbey Croft Field. Eisey: Eisey Meadow.

Allotments 2. Lord Eliot 808 a. (including 96 a. for tithes; leases, Thomas Ware 36 a.; William Roberts 30 a.; executors of late Fitchew 22 a.; James Habgood; Charles Lomax; Ann Hill and Isaac Gleed; Edward Habgood; Susanna Trinder; Edmund King; William Waine; Martha Large; copy, Elizabeth Fitchew; William Ware; Mary Cook); vicar of Latton 127 a. (including 6 a. glebe and the rest re-allotted to Lord Eliot: see below). *Fencing* on map.

Tithes Two allotments (121 a.) to vicar of Latton in place of all vicarial tithes, and later allotted to Lord Eliot who agreed to pay the vicar annually £160 13*s.* 8*d.*; vicar to pay land tax of £7 0*s.* 5*d.* at rate of 4*s.* in £.

Roads Latton, 2 public roads, 1 public bridle way, 9 public footpaths, 1 private road; Eisey, 1 public bridle way. Herbage allotted to new neighbouring allottees.

Maps (1) Down Ampney and Eisey Mead. (2) Latton. Village of Latton shown and Thames and Severn canal. Allotments shown, but not acreages.

Schedule Proprietors with insufficient lands exonerated from payment of tithes by an annual rent-charge payable to Lord Eliot.

Notes Stream which formed the boundary between Latton and Cricklade St. Sampson straightened by the commissioner with the agreement of holders of lands in Cricklade (trustees of Yellow School in Cirencester and William Saunders) and consequent transfer of small pieces of land between Latton and Cricklade St. Sampson. Likewise the Warlake Ditch between Latton and Eisey.

123 LAVERSTOCK [1,625 a.]

Laverstock and Ford tithing

Act 58 G.III c.3 (Private). *Award* 5 July 1820, W.R.O. 114. *Commissioners* William Jennings of Evershot, Dorset; Thomas Davis of Horningsham; Elias Saph of Salisbury. *Surveyor* John Tubb of Fisherton Anger.

Lord of Manor of Laverstock and Ford, Henry Vassall, Lord Holland.

Area 1,211 a. (Act) [1,261 a.] Lower Dean, Robin Hood's Butts, Bush Field, Castle Field, Gravelly Hill Field, Anbarrow Field, Middle Field, Ford

Down, Bridge Field, Cockey Down, South Field, St. Thomas' Bridge Field, Little Down.

Allotments 15. Public: 1 gravel pit; 1 watering place. Lord Holland 142 a. (including leases, Samuel Whitchurch 127 a.; Richard and John Cooe); Sir James Burrough 227 a.; Samuel Whitchurch 176 a.; Edward Baker 128 a.; Thomas Blake 212 a.; priory of St. John at Wilton 70 a. (including lease, Thomas Blake 70 a.); Wadham Wyndham 160 a.; bishop of Salisbury 101 a. (including lease, Thomas Blake 101 a.); Henry Fox-Strangways, earl of Ilchester 18 a.; Peter Templeman; precentor and vicars of cathedral church of Salisbury; Richard and John Cooe; William Windsor.

Roads 7 public roads, 2 private roads and public bridle way, 6 private roads, 3 public footpaths.

Finance £2,275 16*s.* 0*d.* By schedule said to be attached to award but missing, and by 2 sale allotments to Thomas Blake (9a.) £273 2*s.*

Maps John Tubb 1820. (1) Laverstock. (2) Ford. Acreages, allottees, and fencing duties shown. Various detached pieces of Stratford and Milford shown.

Schedule Responsibilities for repair of roads at (1) Laverstock; (2) Ford.

Note Exchanges incorporated in the allotments; there is some difficulty in assigning them but an attempt has been made above to give the original allottees.

124 MARKET LAVINGTON [3,806 a.]

Act 17 G.III c.76. *Award* 12 July 1781 (enrolled 1 Jan. 1782), W.R.O. 18. *Commissioners* Daniel Tanner of Urchfont; Thomas Fricker of Longbridge Deverill; Charles Millerd of Stanton St. Quintin; William Butcher of Little Cheverell; William Gale of All Cannings. *Surveyor* William Simpson of Bath.

Lord of Manor of Lavington Dauntsey and Lavington Rectory, Jacob Pleydell-Bouverie, earl of Radnor.

Rector dean and chapter of Christ Church, Oxford; *lessee* John Wadman. *Vicar* John Dobson.

Area 2,076 a. excl. roads 56 a. [1,995 a.] West Park, East and West Home Field, Lodge Common, West Clay Field, Middle and Farther West Field, Farm Down, Farm Summer Down, Upper West Clay, West Fore Hill, Rowless Common, The Ham, Wish Mead, Freemans Down, Freemans Summer Down, Middle and Farther East Field, Rough Down, Parsonage Ball, The Slay, Great Sands.

Allotments 22. Earl of Radnor 973 a. (including copy, Richard Keil 30 a.; Richard Leg 18 a.; John Smith 23 a.; leases, John Shorter 47 a.; copy and lease, William Sainsbury 23 a.; James Baker; Thomas Macie; John Sainsbury; Rev. John Salmon; Benjamin Sanders; Edward Sharp; John Smith the fisherman; John Street; Henry Chivers Vince); William Sainsbury and John Gawen 84 a.; Richard Leg 396 a.; Rev. Joseph Leg 384 a.; John Still Slade 93 a.; dean and chapter of Oxford 67 a.; vicar of Market Lavington 31 a.; James Locke 16 a.; William Sainsbury; Thomas Smith; Robert Turner; Francis Smith; John Wadman; Thomas à Beckett;

Amram Edwards; Thomas Godwin; William Hobbs; Samuel Mabbett; William Macie; R. C. Shergold; John Sainsbury.

Roads 13 public roads, 11 public footpaths, 5 private roads. Herbage on road from West Park to Moor Mead allotted partly to vicar and partly to earl of Radnor, rest to neighbouring allottees.

Finance £1,169 9*s*. 3*d*. by rate levied on allottees.

Map (No map with award, but one in W.R.O. Acc 836). 1778. Schedule with acreages and numbered allotments. Downs, common, and marsh light green, arable yellow. Fiddington not included. Map rather indistinct in places.

See also No. 125.

Note Well to be dug on Rev. Joseph Leg's land for his use, to be paid for by allottees.

125 MARKET LAVINGTON

Easterton manor and tithing [1,653 a.]

Act 37 G.III c.85. *Award* 18 April 1798 (enrolled 5 Jan. 1799), W.R.O. 55. *Commissioners* Daniel Tanner of Urchfont; Benjamin Haynes of Salisbury; Christopher Ingram of Amesbury. *Surveyor* William Tubb of Fisherton Anger.

Lord of Manor William Hunt Grubbe.

Area 1,352 a. [1,320 a.] Garland Down, Pond Bottom, Frenchman's Ball, Clay Field, Great Trolly, Easterton Bushes, Goose Hill, East and West Land Field, Forehill, Bishop's Coppice, Great and Little Cliff.

Allotments 24. William Hunt Grubbe 261 a. (including leases, James Giles; Thomas Smith); Jacob Giddings 355 a.; Thomas Willoughby 144 a.; John Garratt 185 a.; William Cully 54 a.; John Dowse 133 a.; Harriet Willoughby 33 a.; Andrew and Joan Burbage 44 a.; William Grant 16 a.; John Hobbs; Peter Saunders; Richard Rutt; William Dowse; John Bartley; William Norris; guardians of John Townsend Wadman; Francis Draper; Benjamin Draper; Thomas Dowse; John Matthews; Samuel Neate; William Ford; Ann Calley; William Smith. *Fencing* duties shown in separate schedule.

Roads 7 public roads, 2 public bridle ways, 9 private roads, 2 public footpaths. Herbage allotted.

Map (No map with award, but one in W.R.O. 248/159). Francis Webb and W. Tubb of Salisbury 1797. In three strips, whole parish including the village. Exchanges shown, fencing duties, old inclosures coloured green. Allotments and acreages.

See also No. 124.

Note Right to use Easterton Pond granted to 6 allottees, and pond to be fenced on all sides, except the turnpike road side, by William Hunt Grubbe.

126 WEST LAVINGTON [6,567 a.]

Act General, 6 & 7 W.IV c.115. *Award* 20 March 1840 (enrolled 3 July 1840), W.R.O. 155. *Commissioners* Francis Attwood of Salisbury; Charles Robert Henderson of West Lavington. *Surveyor* Frederick James Kelsey.

Lord of Manor bishop of Salisbury; *lessee* Almeric Spencer, Baron Churchill.
Vicar Robert Clarke Caswall.
Area 4,249 a. [4,183 a.] Lord's Mead, West Field, Stanford Mead, Vaux Hill Field, Ridgeway, Ramscliff, Newlham Pond, Gore Cross, Coppice Field, East Field Clay, Home Field Clay, Warren Clay, Hare Warren, The Cradles, Stibbs Field, East Hill Field, Penning Field, Great Farm Down, Newgate Down, Bower Hill Field.
Allotments 5. Public: 1 watering place (Gore Cross Pond). Lord Churchill 1,352 a.; bishop of Salisbury 2,773 a. (including copy and lease, Lord Churchill 2,768 a.; lease, John Giles); James Tilby 51 a.; vicar of West Lavington. *Fencing* with allotments.
Roads 7 public roads, 5 private roads, 3 public footpaths. Herbage allotted.
Maps (1) Whole parish excl. Littleton and manor of Gore (Market Lavington). (2) Old inclosures exchanged.
Schedule Exchanges.

127 LEA AND CLEVERTON [1,779 a.]
Act 45 G.III c.21 (not printed). *Award* 19 Dec. 1806 (enrolled 8 April 1807), W.R.O. 70. *Commissioners* Richard Richardson of London; John Wilkins of Rowde; John Spackman of Compton Bassett. *Surveyor* Jeremiah Cruse of Bath.
Lord of Manor Richard Fitzwilliam, Viscount Fitzwilliam.
Vicar William Lewis.
Area 192 a. [174 a. including sale allotments 66 a.] Lot Mead, Knowle Hill, Woodbridge Green, Cleverton Common, Lea Upper and Lower Commons, Whitehill Green, Cleverton Down.
Allotments 44. Viscount Fitzwilliam 43 a.; Thomas Handy 18 a.; Henry Cawson; John Heath; Jacob Sampson; overseers of poor of Lea; Richard Reeve; Henry Reeve; Charles Jordan; Edmund Lyne; James Smith; William Smith; Isaac Woodward; Betty Woodward; trustees of estate called the Lea living; Sir Robert Buxton Bt.; William Baker; William Brokenbrow; Jasper Collingborne; Rev. Charles Dewell; Edmund Estcourt Gale; William Hayter; Francis Hill; John and William Jones; William Keen; John Cobb Methuen; John S. Ody; earl of Radnor; John Reynolds; Richard Reeve; William Stevens; James Adey; William Baker; Francis Merewether; William Hill; William Hart; George Woodward; vicar of Lea; John Stockholm; Henry Lee Warner; William Weeks; Daniel Young; trustees of the poor; William Woodward. *Fencing* to be carried out by proprietors.
Roads 7 public roads, 15 private roads, 2 public footpaths.
Finance Sale allotments by auction (66 a.) £2,169 1*s*.
Map Jeremiah Cruse 1806. Allottees and acreages shown. Chiefly roads and verges, village only very sketchily. Workhouse shown.
Notes John and William Reeve of Lea to make the public roads for £33 12*s*. Award delayed by dispute over boundary with Little Somerford and also by objection by earl of Radnor to sale of certain lands to defray expenses.

Lot Mead dealt with separately, viz. allotment to Viscount Fitzwilliam 4 a.; and following allotments for rights of first vesture: trustees of Lea living 2 a.; Rev. Charles Dewell 1 a.; Edmund Estcourt Gale 1 a.; Francis Hill 1a.

128 LIDDINGTON [2,865 a.]

Liddington and Medbourne hamlet

Act 16 G.III c.20. *Award* 27 Feb. 1777 (enrolled 2 May 1777), W.R.O. 8. *Commissioners* Francis Burton of Aynho, Northants.; Hill Haggard of Swindon; James Shipton of Marlborough. *Surveyor* Robert Weston of Brackley, Northants.; (William Gale of All Cannings and Daniel Tanner of Collingbourne valuers for tithes).

Rector (lay) and lessee of prebend, George Spencer-Churchill, duke of Marlborough;

Vicar William Rich Stock.

Area [1,002 a.] Upper and Lower East Field, Upper Middle Field, Little Field, Lower Field, The Breach, Liddington Common, South Down, Upper and Lower West Field.

Allotments 10. Vicar of Liddington 52 a.; duke of Marlborough 869 a.; Margaret Stamp and John Eldridge 15 a.; William Morse 20 a.; Theodora Morse; Thomas Herring; Susannah Drury; executors of John Seymour; Thomas Hatt; John Hatt. *Fencing* with allotments and in Schedule 2.

Tithes exonerated by grants of land to vicar and lay impropriator; 193 a. of old inclosures exonerated from tithes, see Schedule 1. Tithes on prebendal estates dealt with later by Tithe Award of 1841.

Roads 7 public roads, 1 public bridle way. Herbage allotted.

Finance £770 1*s.* 2*d.* including £61 16*s.* 3*d.* for old inclosures.

Schedules (1) Old inclosures exonerated from payment of great and small tithes under the award; (2) Proprietors charged with sums towards the making of fences round the vicar's allotment; (3) Rate for (a) grass seed, (b) survey of old inclosures, (c) expenses of inclosing open fields.

Note Allotment to vicar in place of glebe rights as well as vicarial tithes. Allotment to the duke of Marlborough in place of great tithes and 36 a. of glebe, at rate of 1*s.* 7*d.* an acre for tithes of arable lands and 1*s.* 9*d.* for meadow and pasture out of which tithes were paid.

129 LITTLETON DREW (or Littleton St. Andrew) [980 a.]

Act General, 41 G.III c.109. *Award* 4 March 1847 (enrolled 21 Feb. 1848), W.R.O. V 168. *Commissioner* William Tayler of Doddington, Glos. *Surveyor* Robert Davis Little.

Lord of Manor Henry Somerset, duke of Beaufort.

Rector Anthony Austin (succeeding John Colmer, d. 1843).

Area 364 a. [366 a.] East and West Fields, Barrow Field, Marsh Mead, Lower Mead, Withy Mead, Camp Mead, Hill Mead, Upper Mead.

Allotments 7. Duke of Beaufort 134 a.; rector of Littleton Drew 36 a.; Joseph Neeld 124 a.; trustee of Gabriel Greenman 20 a.; William Coates 28 a.; John Edwards 23 a.; Sarah Brown. *Fencing* in award.

Roads 2 private roads and public bridle ways, 1 private road. Responsibilities for repair set out. Herbage allotted. Six public footpaths, 7 private roads, 1 private road and public bridle way closed; 2 footpaths diverted.

Finance Deduction from rector's allotments and sale to pay his share of expenses.

Maps R. D. Little of Chippenham. (1) Before inclosure (shows strips); (2) After inclosure. Whole parish and village shown. Allotments and old inclosures coloured according to owner.

Schedules (1) Pre-inclosure lands ; (2) Old inclosures; (3) Allotments and old inclosures shown under proprietors.

Note Award complicated by various deaths.

130 LUDGERSHALL [1,789 a.]

Act General, 8 & 9 Vic. c.118, and annual inclosure Act (1851). *Award* 22 April 1853 (enrolled 18 May 1853), W.R.O. 172. *Valuer* Francis Attwood.

Lord of Manor trustee of late William Maund.

Area [87 a.] Spary Leaze, No Man's Ball.

Allotments 11. Public: 1 stone pit; 1 allotment for exercise and recreation; 1 allotment for labouring poor. Trustee of William Maund 39 a.; Joseph Everett 20 a.; Richard Hungerford Pollen; William and Caroline Fishwick; Henry Hunt; Sarah Hunt; William Hutchins; Jane Hutchins. *Fencing* with award.

Roads 1 public footpath; 2 roads stopped up.

Map John Waters of Salisbury 1852. Allotments numbered, fencing shown, inclosed areas only shown.

Notes Exchanges include lands in Kimpton, Hants. Rent-charge for labouring poor divided between trustee of William Maund and Joseph Hague Everett. Allotment for labouring poor valued against price of wheat, barley, and oats.

131 MADDINGTON [3,968 a.]

Act General, 8 & 9 Vic. c.118. *Award* 24 Nov. 1853 (enrolled 3 Dec. 1853), W.R.O. L 173. *Valuer* Thomas Waters of Stratford sub Castle.

Lord of Manor John Sawbridge Erle Drax and trustees of Leonard Pitt Maton.

Area [997 a.].

Allotments 5. Lords of the manor 417 a.; J. S. Erle Drax 576 a.; William Maslen; John Pierce; 'the owner'. *Fencing* in award.

Roads 1 private road. 1 public road stopped up.

Map John Waters of Salisbury 1853. Allotments numbered only. Inclosed area only.

See also No. 132.

132 MADDINGTON

Homanton Fields

Act General, 8 & 9 Vic. c.118. *Award* 17 Jan. 1855 (enrolled 31 Jan. 1855),

W.R.O. 176. *Valuer* John Waters of Salisbury (replacing in 1854 Thomas Waters of Stratford-sub-Castle).

Lords of Manor of Homanton, dean and chapter of Salisbury.

Area [555 a.].

Allotments 2. Trustees of Sarah Erle Drax Burton and Augustus Burton 155 a.; dean and chapter Salisbury 400 a. (including copy, Rebecca Cripps and Charles Wansborough 129 a.; Charles Wansborough 271 a.). *Fencing* general.

Roads 2 private roads.

Map 1853. Allotments numbered only. Inclosed area only.

See also No. 131.

133 MALMESBURY (including land in Foxley) [5,333 a.]

Act 1 & 2 G.IV c.34 (Private). *Award* 18 June 1832 (enrolled 16 Oct. 1832), W.R.O. 142. *Commissioner* Richard Peers Player of Malmesbury. *Surveyor* Jolhn Wilkins of Malmesbury.

Lord of Manor of Foxley, Henry Vassall, Lord Holland.

Rector of Foxley, Philip Shuttleworth.

Area 500 a. (Act), 512 a. (Award) [278 a.] King's Heath, Bridge Yatton.

Allotments 5. Trustees of King's Heath 261 a.; Lord Holland 15 a.; rector of Foxley; Richard and Mary Blackford; corporation of Malmesbury. *Fencing* with allotments.

Roads 1 public road, 1 private road and public bridle way, 9 private roads; 11 ditches determined and size laid down.

Map John Wilkins of Malmesbury 1825. Allotments numbered and acreages shown.

See also No. 171.

Notes One stone bridge to be built opposite Burnt Heath estate. Residue after Lord Holland and the rector and others had claimed their rights to be allotted to trustees and divided into 280 parts being the then number of capital burgesses, assistant burgesses, landholders, and commoners (85 being capital and assistant burgesses). Drains to be constructed out of moneys raised for the inclosure, but to be kept in repair by the burgesses.

134 MANNINGFORD BRUCE [1,113 a.]

Act 41 G.III c.37. *Award* 22 Aug. 1812 (enrolled 17 March 1813), W.R.O. 86. *Commissioners* Richard Richardson of London; John Gale of Stert; John Butcher of Easton. *Surveyor* Thomas Crass of Salisbury.

Lord of Manor James Sutton now deceased; lordship vested in Eleanor wife of Thomas Grimston Estcourt and Sarah Sutton her sister now married to James Matthews.

Rector George Wells.

Area [734 a.] Powell's Ground, Starveall, Ten Acres, Barn Ground, Lains, Hill Piece, Lower Field, Gurmoor, Hatchett Ground, Stone Ground Picked Ground, Ash Bed, Alder Bed, Hundred Acres, Long Mead Coppice Horse Leaze.

Allotments 4. T. G. Estcourt 499 a.; Charles Alexander 78 a.; John Grant 114 a.; rector of Manningford Bruce 43 a.

Roads 4 public roads, 7 public footpaths. Herbage to neighbouring allottees only.

Finance Expenses already paid by respective owners and not therefore included in the award.

Maps (1) Village and north part of parish. (2) South part of parish and downs. All fields numbered and coloured according to allottees.

Schedule gives map number, proprietor, land allotted, and land not allotted.

135 MARSTON MEYSEY [1,334 a.]

Act General, 8 & 9 Vic. c.118. *Award* 23 Jan. 1866 (enrolled 13 April 1866), W.R.O. 184. *Valuer* John Bravender of Cirencester.

Rector of Meysey Hampton, John Wilson.

Area [94 a.] Marston Mead.

Allotments 13. John Archer 39 a.; William Lane 21 a.; William Crouch; James Bainge; Ambrose Willis; W. E. Boyes and Elizabeth his wife; Charles and Diana Pitt; Edward Akers; Robert Kilmister; John Hewer; rector of Meysey Hampton; James and Ann Harding; Thomas Jenner. *Fencing* general and with allotments.

Map Bravender and Son of Cirencester. Marston Mead only.

136 MELKSHAM AND SEEND

Act 53 G.III c.31. *Award* 19 Nov. 1814 (enrolled 29 Dec. 1814), W.R.O. V 93. *Commissioner* Richard Richardson of London; *Surveyor* Young Sturge.

MELKSHAM [8,363 a.]

Lord of Manor of Beanacre and Melsksham Lowells, Paul Cobb Methuen; of Blackmore, George Thicknesse-Touchet, Lord Audley; of Melksham, Richard Godolphin Long, John Long, and Daniel Jones (succeeding Katherine Long).

Rector dean and chapter of Salisbury; *lessee* John Awdry. *Vicar* Joseph Smith.

Area 480 a. (Act), 522 a. including roads (Award) [429 a.] Blackmore or Melksham Common, Whitley Upper and Lower Common, Shaw Hill Common, Westnolls, Beanacre Upper and Lower Green, Bower Hill, Gooseham.

Allotments 81. Paul Cobb Methuen 56 a.; sale allotments 66 a.; John Awdry 32 a.; Mary Thresher 16 a.; representatives of James Beaven; Thomas Bruges; Thomas Beaven; James Bull; Aaron Breach; William Crook; representatives of Charles Collingbourne; John Crew; Hugh and John Dowland; William Eyles; William Fox; John Fox; Thomas Flower; Robert Fowler; Sophia Green; Elizabeth Gaisford; Jacob Hayward; Benjamin Harris; John Harris; Samuel Heathcote; Robert Hunter; Pitt Hampton; Samuel Hancock; William Hazeland; James Johnson; Thomas Jefferys; Anne Jenkyns; Mary Lier; Abraham Ludlow; Lord Audley;

Sarah Awdry; James Arnold; John Beak; Rev. Mr. Brown; Thomas Bourne; John Long; Wadham Locke; representatives of Margaret Locke; John Little; Benjamin Moxham; — Martin; Robert Manning; Henry Moore; William Miles; James Marshman; George Moule; Melksham poor; James Norris; Sir Harry Neale; William Northey; Mary Newman; James Oatley; John Panting; Sarah Poulsham; Mary Palmer; Edward Phillips; William Ramsey; Thomas Redman; poor of Steeple Ashton; Rev. and Hon. Edward Seymour; duke of Somerset; Joseph Smith; Joseph Spragg; Isaac Springford; James Shaul; Robert Taylor; William Taylor; Joseph Taylor; Davenport Talbot; Daniel Wyatt; James Watson; trustees of Catherine Watson; John Watson; David Williams; James Webb; Mary Webb; William Winstone; Joseph Yerbury; Ann Young.

SEEND [2,578 a.]

Lord of Manor of Seend Rew, Ambrose Awdry.

Area [32 a.] Sells Green, Inmarsh, Upper and Lower Green.

Allotments 19. Ambrose Awdry; Thomas Bourne; Thomas Bruges; George Biggs; John Barnes; George Hayward; Roger Hellier; Jeremiah Hellier; George Holland; Samuel Jeffreys; John Little; Wadham Locke; William Porter; John Redman; Henry Scott; duke of Somerset; John Jones; Edward Slade; Richard Godolphin Long and others were allotted the herbage on Roosty Lane in lieu of soil rights.

Roads 10 public roads, 2 public bridle ways, 29 public footpaths, 18 private roads and public bridle ways, 15 private roads and public footpaths, 71 private roads (including 12 in Seend).

Finance Sale allotments.

Maps (1) Melksham Common and North Mead (detached). (2) Whitley Upper and Lower Commons. (3) Detached portions, Cann Meadow, Islay, and roadside verges. (4) Craysmarsh and Redstocks (Seend). (5) Seend Cleeve (Seend). (6) Seend Upper and Lower Green, Sells Green, Inmarsh, Martinslade (Seend). Schedule of roads and allotments with each map.

Schedules Blackmore road rate, Woodrow road rate, Whitley and Shaw road rate, Town tithing road rate, Woolmore road rate, Seend road rate.

137 MERE [7,650 a.]

Mere and Zeals

Act 47 G.III Sess. 1 c.42. *Award* 26 Oct. 1821 (enrolled 1 Jan. 1822), W.R.O. V 116. *Commissioners* John Field of Shepton Montague, Som. (replacing Thomas Davis, d. 10 Nov. 1807); Richard Webb of Salisbury; George Barnes of Andover, Hants (replacing John Gatehouse, declined). *Surveyors* Thomas Davis of Horningsham and John Charlton of Stourton.

Lord of Manor of Mere, George, prince of Wales and duke of Cornwall; of Zeals Clevedon, Thomas Grove; of Zeals Aylesbury, Wyndham Gooden.

Rector dean of Salisbury.

Area [2,977 a.] Little Marsh Common, North Field, Castle Hill, Widenham, Bushays Common, West Hill, Boar's Knap, Great Bottom, Mere Down, Whitehill Common, Mapledore Common, Knowle Common, Burton Down, Burton Field, Middle Hill, Southbrook, Bishop's Corner, Westcombe, Beast Gaston, Ridge Common, Lyemarsh Common, Highcroft, Whatley Mead, Limper's Hill, Rook Street Common, Mere Mead, Lord's Mead, The Broom, Great Mead, Bottom Mead, Ridge Common, Mere Down, Ark Common, Innocks, Great Sand, Whitemarsh.

Allotments 49. Public: 4 stone pits 5 a. Prince of Wales 1,587 a. (all leased by Thomas Schutz and sublet by him to 49 sub-lessees) ; dean of Salisbury 132 a. (including leases, Aaron Dewdney 15 a.; representatives of William Grove 98 a.; Thomas Butt; Elizabeth Butt; Mary Beckett; Thomas Maidment; William Moors; John Pittman; Tryon Still; Ann Wadlow); representatives of William Grove 660 a. (including leases, Rev. John Butt; Edward Evered; William Forward; the Misses Fangoin); duke of Somerset 108 a. (including leases, Nathaniel Dalton 59 a.; executors of William Slade 16 a.; Rev. Joseph Good 33 a.); Rev. William Meyrick 267 a. (including leases, William Harding 43 a.; Robert Cross 16 a.; James Forward; Isaiah Maggs; Grace Moore; Stephen Sly; John Welch; Sir Richard Colt Hoare Bt.; John Lyons); vicar and churchwardens of Mere 20 a.; Edmund Ford 18 a.; Sir Richard Colt Hoare Bt. 43 a.; Thomas Grove and Wyndham Gooden; James Allen; Mary Burfitt; John Coward; James Coward; Richard Coleman; Robert Cross; Stephen Doble; James Dowding; William White; William Forward; James Fry; Shiner Glover; William Glover; William Harding; John White; devisees of James Jukes; churchwardens of Kingston Deverill; Thomas Latimer; James Lander; John Lander; marquess of Bath; Isaiah Maggs; Thomas Moore; Elizabeth Morris; John Merryweather; John Perman; Joel Perman; Stephen Sly; Francis Seymour; devisees of Sir Francis Sykes; William Toogood; Henry Toogood; Richard Taylor; Thomas Taylor; Hannah Usher; Mary Whitaker; John White; William Wilton; George West. *Fencing* for some of the allotments in the award.

Roads 18 public roads, 15 public footpaths, 42 private roads. Herbage allotted.

Finance 9 sale allotments (35 a.) £2,242.

Maps (1) South part of parish, villages of Mere and Zeals shown. (2) Burton, Whitemarsh, and SE. of Mere. (3) North of Wincanton road. Allotments numbered with acreages and allottees, the rest numbered only. Arable land apparently coloured yellow and pasture green.

Schedule Rate for repair of private roads.

Notes Encroachments of less than twenty years included. Allotment of rights to 34 allottees in place of 57 rights of common. Directions for stocking.

138 MILDENHALL [4,177 a.]

Act 19 G.III c.68, to confirm an *agreement* of 24 June 1776. *Award* 10 Sept.

1776, W.R.O. Sav. *Referees* John Pococke of Fawley, Berks.; William Gale of All Cannings; Daniel Tanner of Collingbourne Kingston. *Surveyor* John Clements of Avebury.

Lord of Manor Thomas Bruce, earl of Ailesbury.

Rector Richard Pococke.

Area 476 a. [478 a.] The Deane, Rabley Field, Thickett Field, Small Gains.

Allotments 3. Earl of Ailesbury 251 a. (including copy, William Pearce 51 a.; Jane Looker; Mary Chisman; representatives of Sarah Franklyn); Thomas Calcraft 165 a.; rector of Mildenhall 62 a. *Fencing* with allotments.

Tithes To be paid in kind on sainfoin. If allotments remain under grass (except sainfoin) for more than two years, the rector is to be compensated by 3*s*. 6*d*. an acre per annum in place of corn tithes; this compensation not to extend to land under Rabley Coppice and Poulton Field because of the poverty and barrenness thereof.

Roads 4 private roads; 1 public footpath diverted.

Finance £110 10*s*. 6*d*. as in a schedule which is missing.

Map rough plan with allottees and acreages.

See also No. 32.

139 MILTON LILBORNE [3,588 a.]

Milton Abbots and Milton Havering

Act 14 G.III c.77. *Award* 23 Oct. 1781 (enrolled 27 May 1782), W.R.O. 20. *Commissioners* John Barnes of Collingbourne Kingston; Edward Andrews of Collingbourne Ducis; Thomas Noyes of Westover, Hants (replacing James Poore of East Woodhay, Berks., dead; William Wapshare of New Sarum, refused; and Thomas South of Donhead St. Andrew, refused). *Surveyor* Smart Pyke.

Area 446 a. [468 a.] Hackham Bottom, Great and Little Hill, East and West Hill, East and West Clay. Hitching piece excluded from the award except for fencing duties to be determined by the commissioners and to be inclosed and allotted to its present owners. Also excluded, Parsonage Down (Philip Pulse) and Several Downs (Francis Dugdale Astley).

Allotments 17. Francis Dugdale Astley 131 a.; Philip Pulse 79 a.; trustees of Froxfield almshouse 75 a.; heirs of Dr. George Duke 65 a.; John Richmond Webb 22 a.; John Whitehart Stevens 35 a.; Michael Ewen 40 a.; Richard Tilley; William Naish; Frances Andrews; Charles Cozens; John Smith; Edward Batt; John Batt; William Winter; Thomas Cooper; Peter Wheeler. *Fencing* with allotments.

Roads 1 private bridle way, 2 private roads.

Map (No map with award, but three draft maps, two before and one after inclosure, in W.R.O. Acc 68).

See also No. 96.

140 MINETY [3,778 a.]

Act 51 G.III c.191. *Award* 1813, W.R.O. Acc 374/16 (solicitor's office copy).

Commissioners John Edmonds of Welford, Glos.; Robert Wright Hall of Gloucester.

Lord of Manor Joseph Pitt.

Vicar Thomas Watkins.

Area [728 a.] South Moor, Great Common, Sawyer's Hill, Lower Moor, The Stank, Little Common, Forty Foot Lane, Flistridge Lane, Tickling Corner.

Allotments 53. Public: 1 gravel pit 1 a. Joseph Pitt 174 a. (including copy, John Brown 34 a.; Edward Cripps 21 a.; John Gleed; Henry Howell; William Keene; Joseph Keene; William Telling; Rev. Mr. Young); William Keene 64 a.; Joseph Keene 58 a.; William Maskelyne 82 a.; Paul Methuen 18 a.; Lord Holland 16 a.; John Brown 18 a.; John Pepole 40 a.; Charles Stevens 25 a.; William Telling 23 a.; — Adams; John Alland; Maurice Maskelyne Bennett; Thomas Bedford; Jane Bedford; manor of South Cerney; Samuel Bowly; James Brain; Christopher Cole; Edmund Elliston; John Earl; William Ely; Richard Fry; Charles Granger; John Hawkins; — Hiscock; Thomas Hughes; Henry Howell; William Hindon; Joseph Hiscock; Richard Laurence; Richard Kinneir; Joseph Large; Daniel Malland; trustees of Minety second poor [i.e. the poor not relieved out of the rates]; churchwardens of Minety; Robert Nicholas; Thomas Pope; John Packer; Harry Pepole; John Read; John Sadler; John York Sheldon; Jacob Scuse; John Telling; Robert Timbrell; Philip Timbrell; John Taylor; Joshua Taylor; John Wall; vicar of Minety; Rev. John Cole Young. *Fencing* with allotments.

Roads 9 public roads, 14 private roads.

Map Allotments numbered, village shown and schedule showing lands allotted and not allotted.

Notes An office copy of the award. Inclosures within the last twenty years included.

141 NETHERAVON [4,492 a. including Chisenbury de la Folly]

Act 28 G.III c.36. *Award* 27 Feb. 1790 (enrolled 16 April 1790), W.R.O. 31. *Commissioners* Richard Richardson of West Dean; Benjamin Pryce of Salisbury; Thomas Fricker of Longbridge Deverill; John Grant of Manningford. *Surveyor* Robert Verry of Long Ashton, Som.

Lord of Manor of Netheravon Lamberts and of Cornayles, William Beach.

Rector and Prebendary John Honeywood (succeeding Edward Innes, dead); *lessee* William Beach. *Vicar* Ralph Smith.

Area [3,320 a.] North, Middle and South Home Field, North, Middle and Deadman Summerfield, Outland and Inland Down, Corfe Meadow, West Barn Ground, Church Mead, Long Draught.

Allotments 15. John Howe, Lord Chedworth 672 a. (including leases, William Beach 665 a.; Daniel Compton; James Compton; Anne Ring); Prebendary of Netheravon 164 a. (including William Beach 164 a.); William Beach 2,093 a. (including leases, Henry Tayler 24 a.; Jane Croucher 63 a.; George Griffin Pearce 50 a.; William Spratt); James Compton 151 a.; Daniel Compton 155 a.; Thomas Herne 28 a.; Mary Haines 27 a.; George Griffin

Pearce; Anne Ring; William Spratt; George Maton; Robert Kemm; Sarah Oram; Jane Silverthorne; William Sutton.

Tithes Commuted into rent-charge £373 14*s*. 8*d*.

Roads 12 public roads, 3 bridle ways, 4 private roads, 1 private footpath. Herbage allotted.

Map Whole parish including the village.

Schedule shows owner, acreage, and tithe charge to prebendary and vicar.

See also No. 142.

Note Waterman to be elected yearly on 29 Sept. at 11.0 in the parish church (or on following day if a Sunday) by a majority of occupiers of water-meadow lands, 'to distribute the water equitably and fairly over the said meadow and to be paid by owners in proportion to their lands'.

142 NETHERAVON

Chisenbury de la Folly [966 a.]

Act 34 G.III c.32 (Keevil, Idmiston, Fittleton, and Chisenbury de la Folly). *Award* 20 Aug. 1796 (enrolled 10 July 1799), W.R.O. 44. *Commissioners* Thomas Sheppard D.D. of Basingstoke; Francis Webb of Salisbury; John Gale of Stert (replacing John Verry of Bristol, declined through ill health). *Surveyor* John Verry.

Lord of Manor of Chisenbury de la Folly, Michael Hicks Beach.

Rector Prebendary of Netheravon, John Honeywood.

Area [966 a.] Chisenbury Down, Lavington Way Down.

Allotments 1. Michael Hicks Beach 966 a.

Tithes commuted to rent-charge to rector £105, to vicar £15. Tithes to be paid at Rectorial or Prebendal House in Netheravon. Disagreement over the tithe between Robert Verry and Thomas Sheppard settled by the umpire Francis Webb.

Roads 8 public roads, 3 public bridle ways, 1 public footpath. Herbage to lord of manor.

Map John Verry 1794 and 1795. Manor of Chisenbury de la Folly.

Schedule shows proprietor, acreage, value in wheat, tithe rent to rector and vicar.

See also No. 141.

Note Chisenbury de la Folly, in Netheravon at the time of the award, was transferred to Enford in 1885.

143 NETHERHAMPTON [778 a.]

Act 23 G.III c.36 (Odstock, Homington, West Harnham, and Netherhampton). *Award* 17 March 1787 (enrolled 17 Sept. 1787), W.R.O. 29. *Commissioners* Benjamin Pryce of Wilton; Richard Bloxham of Winterslow; Richard Richardson of Devizes. *Surveyor* William Corfield of Salisbury.

Lord of Manor Henry Herbert, earl of Pembroke.

Vicar John Hawes.

Area 541 a. including roads 16 a. [512 a.] East Field, West Field, Middle Field, The Down.

Allotments 2. Earl of Pembroke 507 a.; vicar of Netherhampton 5 a. Allotment of a chalk pit to earl of Pembroke and his lessees and copyholders to raise chalk to improve their lands and repair roads.

Roads 4 public roads, 5 private roads, 1 public footpath, 1 private road to be made by earl of Pembroke, and disturbed tenants to be compensated at 40*s*. an acre per annum. Herbage allotted.

See also No. 195.

Note Allotments to be separated by 18in. linches or landshards and to continue to be cultivated in the course of three fields, one for wheat, one for lenten grains, and one for summer feed. Down allotments to be depastured in common. Regulations might be altered by application of 12 out of the 17 yardlanders at the court baron and with consent of the earl of Pembroke.

144 NETTLETON [1,971 a.]

Act 52 G.III c.2 (not printed). *Award* 19 Feb. 1814 (enrolled 20 Dec. 1814), W.R.O. 92. *Commissioners* Robert Wright Hall of Cirencester, Glos.; Young Sturge of Bristol (a Quaker who affirmed). *Surveyor* John Hayward of Devizes.

Lord of Manor Andrew Carrick.

Rector Henry Frederick Bythesea.

Area 535 a. [530 a.] West and East Field, Three Stone Field, Shrub Green, Villee Green, Horse Down, Great Marsh, Little Marsh, Brottenhill, Burton Hill.

Allotments 10. Public: 3 allotments for stone quarries. Andrew Carrick 483 a. (including leases, Thomas and William Comely 46 a.; Joseph Buckle 35 a.; Joseph Wood 96 a.; executors of Elizabeth Watson 96 a.; Isaac Millar 23 a.; William Coates; John Hall; Daniel Hall; Zachariah Huggins; Henry West); rector of Nettleton; George Yeeles; John Goulter; Thomas Shapland; William Coates; John Marsh; Isaac Hall; Jasper Hulbert. *Fencing* on map and in award.

Roads 21 private roads, 2 public bridle ways, 3 public footpaths.

Map with schedule of allotments. Commonable land allotted, red. Old inclosures exchanged, blue. Allottees and acreages shown. Whole parish shown but large areas in outline only.

Schedule Sums to be paid by proprietors for making and repairing roads.

145 NORTH NEWNTON [1,146 a.]

Act General, 6 & 7 W.IV c.115. *Award* 8 July 1840 (enrolled 25 Aug. 1840), W.R.O. 156. *Commissioners* John Hayward of Devizes; Richard Stratton of Upavon. *Umpire* Thomas Davis of Portway, Warminster. *Surveyor* William Bryan Wood of Barnbridge near Chippenham.

Area [205 a.] Catsbrain Way.

Allotments 6. William Jesse 81 a.; trustees of Thomas Falkner 58 a.; Henry Herbert, earl of Pembroke 15 a.; George Fowle 46 a.; Thomas Chandler Hayward; earl of Normanton. *Fencing* general.

Roads 2 public roads, 1 public bridle way, 1 private road.

Map W. Bryan Wood 1839. Excludes Hilcot tithing. Allotments numbered and coloured according to allottees.

Schedule Allotments and old inclosures.

146 NORTON BAVANT [2,221 a.]

Act 45 G.III c.74 (not printed). *Award* 24 April 1809 (enrolled 23 April 1810), W.R.O. 80. *Commissioners* George Barnes of Andover, Hants; John Charlton of Stourton; John Gatehouse of Buckhorn Weston, Dorset.

Lord of Manor of Norton Bavant, John Benett; of Little Sutton, marquess of Bath; of Heytesbury, Sir William Pierce Ashe à Court; of Bishopstrow, Mrs. Sarah Temple; of Edington, Joshua Smith.

Vicar George Smith.

Area [1,348 a.] Banham Mead, Scratchbury Down, Cotley Down, Eight Acres, Heathfield.

Allotments 3. John Benett 1,275 a. (including 39 a. for rectorial glebe); vicar of Norton Bavant 39 a.; John Knight 33 a.

Roads 3 public roads, 3 private roads, 1 private bridle way, 1 public footpath.

Map Allottees and acreages. Parish shown without Middleton but including the village.

See also No. 21.

Note Boundaries between Norton Bavant and Sutton Veny as fixed by the Sutton Veny Commissioners taken as being correct.

147 OAKSEY [1,924 a.]

Act 42 G.III c.39 (Private and Personal, not printed). *Award* 21 July 1802, P.R.O. C 54/7764 (photocopy in W.R.O.). *Commissioner* Thomas Davis of Horningsham.

Lord of Manor Francis Webb.

Rector Ralph Smith.

Area [94 a.] Oaksey Common.

Allotments 3. Francis Webb 92 a.; rector of Oaksey; Rev. William Howell. *Fencing* general.

Roads 1 public road, 1 private road and bridle way.

Finance Sale allotment (12 a.) £270.

148 ODSTOCK [1,295 a.]

Act 23 G.III c.36 (Homington, West Harnham, Netherhampton and Odstock). *Award* 15 June 1787 (enrolled 17 Sept. 1787), W.R.O. 28. *Commissioners* Benjamin Pryce of Wilton; Richard Bloxham of Winterslow; Richard Richardson of Devizes. *Surveyor* Francis Webb late of Stow, Glos., now of Salisbury.

Lord of Manor Jacob Pleydell-Bouverie, earl of Radnor.

Rector John Bedwell.

Area 528 a. including roads [473 a.] Tenantry Field and Down, Upper and Lower Common Meadow, Further Yew Bushes Down, Midsummer Marsh.

Allotments 3. John Bedwell 243 a.; earl of Radnor 191 a.; Tristram Huddle-

stone Jervoise 39 a. *Fencing* none except for one fence in the meadows.
Tithes Commuted by allotment of land.
Roads 4 public roads, 1 public footpath. Herbage allotted.
Map Francis Webb of Salisbury 1787. Whole parish and village.
Notes Agreement between the earl of Radnor and Tristram Jervoise for watering Lombard's Meads; detailed instructions as to days on which hatches were to be drawn. Orders made concerning the East Meadow in Homington Inclosure Award to be binding on parties in Odstock.

149 OGBOURNE ST. ANDREW [5,386 a.]
Act 18 G.III c.37. *Award* 19 Dec. 1780 (enrolled 13 March 1781), W.R.O. 14. *Commissioners* Solomon Hughes; John Pocock of Fawley, Berks.; Daniel Tanner of Urchfont. *Surveyor* John Clements of Avebury.
Lord of Manor provost and scholars of King's College, Cambridge.
Area 1,292 a. [1,286 a.] Maplegate Field, Hamsden Field, Foxlinch Field, Whatley Bridge Field, Woodway Field, Hitchin Field, Cow Down, Sheep Down.
Allotments 5. Public: 5 a. furze on Sheep Down. King's College, Cambridge 354 a. (including copy, Drusilla Richens 65 a.; Samuel Hawkes 46 a.; Daniel Appleford); Samuel Hawkes 895 a.; Hannah Woodroffe 25 a.; Gilbert and Sarah Hatfield.
Roads 5 public roads. Herbage allotted.

150 OGBOURNE ST. GEORGE [3,572 a.]
Act 32 G.III c.26. *Award* 27 May 1796 (enrolled 24 May 1797), W.R.O. 42. *Commissioners* Richard Richardson of Devizes; William Jennings of Puddletown, Dorset (replacing Richard Bloxham, refused); James Pepler of Calne.
Lord of Manor provost and scholars of King's College, Cambridge.
Area 1,624 a. [1,609 a.] Swinghill, Boarlands, Redlands Field, The Down, Buslade, Whitehill, Macehill, West Field, West Halve, Garston Ends, Bitham Down.
Allotments 33. Public: 2 furze allotments 20 a. John Woolldredge 254 a.; John Richens 79 a.; Catherine Pain 50 a.; Elizabeth Woolldredge 70 a.; John Griffin 103 a.; James Kemm 64 a.; Elizabeth Brunsden 56 a.; King's College, Cambridge, 80 a. (including copy, John Woolldredge 26 a.; William Goddard 31 a.; Elizabeth Woolldredge; William Crook; Drucilla Richens); Job Matthew 128 a.; John Crook 62 a.; James Smith 133 a.; trustees of John Braithwaite 150 a.; Philip Pearce 74 a.; Thomas Chance 70 a.; William Goddard 17 a.; John Reynolds 49 a.; James Higham 15 a.; Richard Kemm 21 a.; John Winter 24 a.; William Paine; Timothy Castle; William Bennett; Edward Titcomb; James Titcomb; Moore Goddard; Jane Mortimer; Thomas Ryder; Thomas Potter; Charles and Elizabeth Masters; William Liddiard; Sarah Manning; John Cole. *Fencing* with allotments.
Roads 9 public roads, 7 public footpaths, 11 private roads.
Maps 1794. (1) Parish west of Swindon–Marlborough road. (2) Parish east

of Swindon–Marlborough road. North part of parish including Whitefield Farm not shown. Allottees and acreages and the village shown.

151 WEST OVERTON

West Overton [4,248 a.], Overton Heath [124 a.], and Clatford Park [310 a.]

Agreement 25 March 1802. *Award* 7 July 1802, W.R.O. 61. *Commissioners* John Seagrim of Wilton; Stephen King of Overton. *Surveyor* John Charlton of Stourton.

Lord of Manor George Herbert, earl of Pembroke.

Area [551 a.].

Allotments 11. Earl of Pembroke 204 a. (including Edward Pumphrey 131 a.; William Cook 73 a.); John Cook 88 a.; Lettice Sweetapple 64 a.; Jane Cook 40 a.; John Cook of Manton 32 a.; Michael Cook 16 a.; Ann Brown 18 a.; Edward Brown 39 a.; Hannah Martin 35 a.; John Lewis; John Knight. *Fencing* in schedule.

Tithes not commuted or extinguished, but tithes on certain fields were allotted to the earl of Pembroke and the duke of Marlborough who were entitled to certain parts of the great tithes.

Roads 3 public roads, 3 private roads.

Map John Charlton of Stourton 1802. Includes the village and a detached part of West Overton next to Oare Common. Does not include East Overton.

Schedule (1) Proprietors and allotments. (2) Fencing duties.

See also No. 152.

Notes Allotments in schedule only and not embodied in award. The award was the result of an agreement between the earl of Pembroke, the duke of Marlborough, Robert Ashe, Edward Brown, Ann Brown, Hannah Martin, Lettice Sweetapple, John Cook, Richard Cook, William Cook, Jane Cook, Edward Pumphrey, John Lewis, and John Wright.

152 WEST OVERTON

East and West Overton and Fyfield [1,121 a.]

Act 54 G.III c.148. *Award* 3 Jan. 1821 (enrolled 14 Oct. 1822), W.R.O. 117. *Commissioners* Decimus Godson of London (replacing Stephen Godson, dead); John Gale of Stert. *Umpire* John Davis of Bloxham. *Surveyor* Decimus Godson.

Lord of Manor of East Overton and Lockeridge, George Spencer-Churchill, duke of Marlborough; of Fyfield, John Goodman.

Rector (lay) duke of Marlborough. *Vicar* Charles Hoyle.

Area 2,410 a. [2,691 a.] White Hill, Gore Hill, Lammas Mead, White Barrow Field, East Overton Tenants Down, Dean Coppice, Heath Grounds, Wansditch, Forehill, Hounds Hill, Smallands, New Broke, Rylands Field, Paddle Down, Hackpin Sheep Down, Lockeridge Sheep Down, Lower Field, Henly Wood, Pound Field, Long Meadow, Horse Meadow, Yat Field, Cattenborough, Pickle Dean, Fyfield Down, Rodden Down, Priest Grove Common, Berry Meadow, East Hill.

Allotments 14. Public: 3 stone pits 2 a. Duke of Marlborough 2,177 a.; (including 512 a. for tithes); John Goodman 218 a. (including leases, John Clarke; Edward Vaisey); vicar of Overton 240 a. (including 200 a. for tithes); trustees of Edward Brown 30 a.; Henry Tanner; Stephen King; Edmund Flower; Little and Knight; General F. St. John; Mary Brown; Rosanna Davis; William Clifford; Sarah Clifford.

Tithes extinguished by allotments in lieu and payments by those without lands. Tithes not to be redeemed on Shaw Farm (425 a.). Earl of Pembroke paid £1,380 16*s.* 8*d.* to extinguish his tithes. Richard Matthews paid £387 1*s.* 6*d.*, Stephen King paid £33 17*s.*, and 19 others paid £156 17*s.* 6*d.*

Roads 5 public roads, 1 private road and public bridle way, 4 private roads.

Map Decimus Godson 1815-16. Schedule of allotments attached. Village shown and boundaries of East and West Overton and Fyfield and Lockeridge tithing and Shaw Farm. Acreages shown on allotments only. Stems in the water-meadows shown.

Schedules (1) Proportions payable of the £27 due to the owner of West Overton mill for water for irrigation. (2) Rules for irrigation of water-meadows.

See also No. 151.

Notes Boundaries of Fyfield determined by commissioners. Very detailed description of watercourses with depth, width, and course set out in the award. Proportion of expenses for repair of culverts payable by the duke of Marlborough, vicar of Overton, and Stephen King set out. Expenses for repair of watercourses to be borne by owners through whose lands they flow. Three main courses: 1. Main float south of the Kennet; 2. Main float under the Bath Road with its branches; 3. Water from the Kennet for Custard Meadow, Mill Meadow, and Round Meadow. Edward Pumphrey, owner of West Overton mill, agreed to allow the water to be turned out of the mill dam if necessary for irrigation, between 1 Dec. and 5 April and between 5 May and 1 July in return for £27 payable by those named in Schedule 1. Area to be divided into 7 stems (shown on map) to be watered in succession from December to April and for 2 days and nights to each stem from May to July.

153 PATNEY [884 a.]

Act 18 G.III c.50. *Award* 21 Sept. 1780 (enrolled 1 April 1782), W.R.O. 19. *Commissioners* Charles Millerd of Stanton St. Quintin; Daniel Tanner of Urchfont; William Gale of All Cannings. *Surveyor* William Simpson of Bath.

Lord of Manor Jacob Pleydell-Bouverie, earl of Radnor.

Rector James Foster (succeeding Henry Cookson, dead).

Area 560 a. [527 a.] Clay Field, West Mead, Calves Leaze, Puckland Field, Long Slade Common, Sandfield, Little Field, Broad Mead, Inn Mead, Bell Leaze.

Allotments 12. Rector of Patney 127 a.; earl of Radnor 344 a. (including lease, George Lewis 65 a.; copy, Sarah Amor 27 a.; William Amor 17 a.;

Edward Drewett 15 a.; — Giddings 15 a.; John Hayward 21 a.; Simon Pyle 24 a.; lease and copy, Robert Amor 49 a.; William Pearce); Michael Burrough 24 a.; Rev. J. M. Hazeland 19 a.; Robert Amor; John Bell; Thomas Dicker; Thomas Dykes; John Hayward; Jenny Hayward; Richard Bailey; Joseph Pearce.

Tithes both great and small commuted by allotment, and money payments for those with insufficient lands.

Roads 3 public roads, 7 public footpaths, 9 private roads. Herbage in the Drove to the earl of Radnor.

Finance £519 9*s*. Freeholders to pay the whole of the expenses for their allotment. Copyholders to pay half, the other half being paid by the holders of the reversion, 2 lives to pay $\frac{1}{3}$, reversionaries $\frac{2}{3}$, one life to pay $\frac{1}{6}$, reversionaries $\frac{5}{6}$. Rector excepted.

Note Lord of manor received equivalent of 20*s*. per annum for rights of the soil.

154 PEWSEY [4,784 a.]

Southcott and Kepnal Down, Work Down, and Pewsey Common

Act 15 G.III c.79. *Award* 17 June 1777 (enrolled 15 June 1778), W.R.O. 11. *Commissioners* Daniel Tanner of Collingbourne Kingston; Thomas Noyes of Westover Farm, Hants; William Gale of All Cannings. *Surveyors* Walter Dutton and John Hand.

Rector Joseph Townsend.

Area Pewsey Common 136 a., the rest 1,932 a. [1,387 a.] Pewsey Field, Kepnal Croft, Broom Croft, Southcott Field, Shercott Field, Race Post Piece.

Allotments 38. Francis Dugdale Astley 317 a. (including leases, Jane Cooper 32 a.; Sarah Hooper 23 a.; copy, William Winter 34 a.; Thomas Mannings 39 a.; Thomas Allen 19 a.; Thomas Munday; John Hailstone; Thomas Munday of Chippenham; Ralph Winter; Hester Batchelor; Ann Dunford; Sarah Smith; Catherine Goodman); John Winter 55 a.; John Winter, grocer 85 a.; Edmund Somerset 61 a.; Christopher Deavin 50 a.; Charlotte Finch, countess of Aylesford 317 a.; Richard Pye 38 a.; William Winter 48 a.; John Walker 26 a.; Thomas Pyke 35 a.; Anthony Mills 30 a.; Henry Reeves 19 a.; rector of Pewsey 23 a.; Jane Somerset 23 a.; Peter Smith 39 a.; George Wroughton 29 a.; heirs of Henry Goodman 34 a.; Thomas Glass 44 a.; proprietors of Work Down (Rev. Joseph Townsend and John Winter, grocer) 29 a.; governors of hospital of St. Thomas 32 a. (including — Hayward; John Amor; countess of Aylesford); Henry Fox, Lord Holland; William Maslen; John Allen; Richard Fidler; Sarah Smith; William Kent; Stephen Allen; Robert Hooper; John Oram; Rev. George Gibbs; John Maslen; John Stratton; Thomas Mannings; Thomas Price; James Stevens; Stephen Pyke; John Lee; John Reeves.

Roads 11 private roads, 1 public footpath.

Note Race Post Piece 6a. allotted to proprietor of Pewsey Farm (countess of Aylesford).

155 PEWSEY

Southcott and Kepnal manors

Act 6 G.IV c.3 (Private). *Award* 24 Oct. 1826 (enrolled 6 July 1827), W.R.O. 130. *Commissioners* Michael Festing of Maiden Bradley; Robert Hughes of Salthrop, Wilts. *Surveyor* John Daniell of Warminster.

Lord of Manor of Southcott and Kepnal, Sir John Dugdale Astley Bt.

Rector Hon. and Rev. Frederick Pleydell-Bouverie.

Area 400-500 a. (Act) 425 a. Southcott and Kepnal Down (Award) [428 a.].

Allotments 8. Sir John Dugdale Astley Bt. 243 a. (including copy, William Batchelor); George Winter 64 a.; William Summersett 61 a.; Thomas Pyke 21 a.; devisees of Anthony Mills 20 a.; Stephen Allen; John Reeves; George Barnes. *Fencing* general.

Roads 4 public roads.

Finance £1,263 12*s.* 9*d.* Rate included in award.

Maps John Daniell of Warminster. (1) South end of parish, allotments and acreages. (2–5) Exchanges.

See also No. 154.

156 POTTERNE

Potterne [3,185 a.], Worton [972 a.], and Marston [906 a.]

Act 5 G.IV c.32. *Award* 10 April 1835 (enrolled 13 Nov. 1841), W.R.O. 159. *Commissioner* Richard Webb of Salisbury. *Surveyor* John Hayward of Devizes.

Lord of Manor, bishop of Salisbury; *lessee* Henry Stephen Olivier.

Rector and prebendary, bishop of Salisbury. *Vicar* George Edmonstone.

Area [268 a.] Furzehill Common, Stroud Common, Rushy Common; and in Marston: South Field, East Field, Norney Field.

Allotments 10. Bishop of Salisbury 89 a. (including copy, V. H. Mairis 22 a.; Martha May 23 a.; James Biggs; Richard Rudman; Jonathan Grant; William Hayward; Ann and Louisa Douglas; Mary Horn; Henry Biggen; Thomas Potter); trustees of Simon Watson Taylor 143 a.; William and John Grant; James Biggs; John Parkinson; Thomas Perrett; Thomas Potter; churchwardens of Marston; surveyors of highways; the hayward. *Fencing* general and shown on map.

Tithes Furzehill, Stroud, and Rushy Commons exonerated from tithe so long as they are held by the poor only.

Roads 3 private roads.

Finance 2 sale allotments (10 a. and by deduction from the bishop's allotments) £800.

Maps John Hayward. (1) Arable fields in Marston. (2) Four commons, Rookey, Furze Hill, Stroud, Rushey. Late commonable lands blue, exchanges red.

Schedules (1) Allotments. (2 and 3) Exchanges. (4) Rate for repair of private roads.

Notes Furzehill Common, Stroud Common, and Rushy Common lately inclosed, brought into tillage and used for the poor of Potterne under management of the churchwardens, overseers, and vestry. It was intended to inclose Potterne Field under the Act and a provision was made that more than 3 a. in Potterne Field should not be allotted to any person other than those in possession thereof without consent of such persons. These consents were not obtained and the inclosure of Potterne Field was not proceeded with. Waste lands were declared by the commissioners as unsuitable for inclosure.

157 PURTON [6,465 a.]

Momes Leaze

Act 5 G.II c.31. *Award* 25 Sept. 1733 (enrolled 15 Jan. 1734), W.R.O. Q.S. enrolled deeds 60–61. *Commissioners* Giles Earle; Hawkins Chapman of Ashton Keynes; Thomas Brown of Minety; John Nott of Braydon; James Powell of Rodbourne; Harry Tuckey of Braydon; Robert Carter of Purton; John Ponting of Brinkworth; John Bendry of Christian Malford; William Odey of Christian Malford; John Oram of Lea; John Buckeridge of Garsdon; John Simpkins of Lea.

Vicar Richard Glass.

Area 280 a. [260 a.] Momes Leaze.

Allotments 12. Thomas Boucher 121 a.; Mary Jacob 19 a.; Isaac Sharp 22 a.; John Dowell 21 a.; Winchcomb H. Parker 17 a.; vicar of Purton 18 a.; Anne, Mary, and Elizabeth Jacob; borough of Malmesbury; John Verebee; John Stockham; Thomas Davis; Hon. Laurence Shirley. *Fencing* to be undertaken by each allottee including the vicar.

Tithes Land allotted in place of vicarial tithes only, in Momes Leaze.

Roads Public roads to be 24 feet wide.

Finance £210. Payable by allottees in proportion to their beast leazes.

See also Nos. 158 and 159.

158 PURTON

Great Purton, Purton Keynes, and Purton Pouchers manors

Act 10 G.II c.7. *Award* 11 April 1738, W.R.O. 1 & 2. *Commissioners* Thomas Bennett of Salthrop; Hawkins Chapman of Ashton Keynes; Henry Tuckey of Haydown; Thomas Browne of Minety; Anthony Southby of Marston; Richard Franklin of Wroughton; Richard Waite of Eastcourt; William Maskelyne the younger of Leigh; Harry Oatridge of Lechlade, Glos.

Lord of Manor George Pitt of Stratfield Saye, Hants.

Rector (lay) Anthony Ashley Cooper, earl of Shaftesbury. *Vicar* Richard Glasse.

Area 1,250 a. [1,000 a.] Purton Common, Purton Stoake Common or Shooters Hill, Peaven Hill, Bagbury Green, Little Marsh, Widham, Cow Street.

Allotments 53. Public: 3 common ponds. Executors of George Clarke 73 a.; Nevil Maskelyne 138 a.; earl of Shaftesbury 160 a.; John Herring 54 a.; John Phelps 50 a.; Thomas Batson 22 a.; Thomas Chandler 20 a.; Toby Richmond 26 a.; Richard Pannell 24 a.; Walter Hardwick 34 a.; Anthony Wheeleck 25 a.; Anthony Whitehead 15 a.; Richard Diggs 34 a.; Thomas,

Robert, and John Moulden 32 a.; William Bathe 16 a.; John Barratt; William Waite; Sibell Sloper; James Bayly; John Skinner; Anthony Bathe; Sarah Bathe; William Smith; Edward Smith; Edmund Morgan; Mary Burgess; Stephen Wamen; William Richens; John Say; vicar of Purton; Clifford Martin; Jeremiah Read; Arthur Evans; Richard Goddard; Thomas Richmond; Rachel Restall; executors of Thomas Bray; Richard Plummer; Richard Hardwick; John Jewell; churchwardens of Purton; trustees of poor's ground; William Baker; John Giles; John Harding; Elizabeth Fitchew; Edward Hanson; Robert Carter; trustees of poor of Cricklade and Fairford; trustees of poor of Kemble; trustees of poor of Latton; George Pitt. *Fencing* each to fence his own.

Map (No map attached, but a tracing of a map which refers to the award is in the W.A.S. Library and a photocopy in W.R.O.).

See also Nos. 157 and 159.

Note Lord of manor had no rights of common; he received 5 a. for timber rights only.

159 PURTON

Act 39 G.III c.64. *Award* 30 Nov. 1799 (enrolled 26 Nov. 1800), W.R.O. 58. *Commissioners* Richard Richardson of Bath; John Gale of Stert. *Surveyor* Thomas Crass of Bath.

Area 344 a. excl. roads 6 a. [421 a.] Church Field, Hyde Field, Battle Field, Berk Field, Sparswell Field, Barn Brimnall, Milway Ground, Gossy Mead, Longhams Mead, Millmoor, Woodwards Bridge Mead, Claredown Field, Hurn Mead, Goddard's Mead, Stoke Common Mead, Brook Mead, Stoke Common.

Allotments 33. Anthony Ashley Cooper, earl of Shaftesbury 118 a.; provost and fellows of Worcester College, Oxford, 53 a.; Rev. Nevil Maskelyne D.D. 29 a.; executors of John Bathe 34 a.; Anthony Bathe 26 a.; Richard Watts Read 22 a.; Robert and Margaret Wilson; Sarah Plummer; John Haskins; William Morse; Charles Seymour; Rev. William Bayly; Richard Morgan; Robert Seymour; Joshua Large; John Matthews; Edward Deane; Richard Carter; Edmund Wilkins; Ann Phillips; Stephen Warman; Richard Francome; Henry Hinder; Ann Grymes; John Embury; Thomas Hill; William Large; Mary Evans; executors of Arthur Evans; William Lewis; James Sadler; John Templer; John Watson. *Fencing* with allotments.

Roads 19 private roads, 13 public footpaths.

See also Nos. 157 and 158.

160 RAMSBURY [Ramsbury 9,874 a.; Baydon 2,485 a.]

Ramsbury Town, Park Town, Whittonditch, Eastridge, and Baydon all in manor of Ramsbury

Act 17 G.III c.125. *Award* 18 Sept. 1778, W.R.O. Acc 154/2 & 3. *Commissioners* John Watts of Sulgrave, Northants.; James Shipton of Marlborough; John Stephens of Childrey, Berks. *Surveyor* Francis Webb of Stow on the Wold.

Lord of Manor Sir William Jones Bt. and Dame Elizabeth his wife.

Vicar Richard Garrard.

Area 2,505 a. including roads 75 a. [2,317 a.] Upper and Lower Little Marsh, Hodshill, Costern Field, Royal Ditch, Great Marsh, Middle Field, East, West and North Fields, Lower Field, Upper Marriage Field, Little Field, Field behind the Wood, Elm Down, Marriage Green, Ford Field.

Allotments 68. Sir William Jones Bt. and Elizabeth his wife 626 a. (including leases, Jonathan Moore 32 a.; Thomas Mildenhall 18 a.; Thomas Kimber 28 a.; Robert Shepherd 15 a.; Anthony Stroud 19 a.; lease and copy, William Williams 185 a.; John Finch 40 a.; Thomas Stroud 30 a.; copy, Edward Pearce 24 a.; Henry Blanchard 18 a.; Henry Reade; Roger Spanswick; John Appleford; William Dance; Nathan Atherton; Stephen Adams; Edward Harris; Benjamin Dixon; Elizabeth Keate; Robert Pullen; John Day; William Harris; Simon Appleford; Thomas Chouls); Thomas Shefford 91 a.; Jonathan Moore 53 a.; Thomas Lovegrove 78 a.; Thomas Mildenhall 56 a.; Peter Delme 310 a.; John Goodsalve 142 a.; John Brown 78 a.; John Finch 50 a.; Henry Read 221 a.; vicar of Ramsbury 71 a.; William Williams 101 a.; Robert Walrond 51 a.; Rev. Daniel Borman 28 a.; Elizabeth Batson 33 a.; Sir Edward Ernle 19 a.; Nathan Atherton 24 a.; Roger Spanswick 42 a.; Henry Dawkins 34 a.; Thomas Stroud 41 a.; John Finch junior 35 a.; Thomas Chouls of Lambourn 20 a.; James Alford; Robert Walrond; Thomas Kimber; Henry Blanchard; Francis Popham; Daniel Borman; Joseph Elderton; Elizabeth Francis; Edward Francis; Charles Gibbons; Henry Allen; Robert Pullen; Giles Braxstone; John Day; John Schollar; John Pound; Joseph Pound; Mary White; Elizabeth Keate; Mary Keate; Mary Hinde; Thomas Appleford; Seymour Munday; Benjamin Simmonds; Mary Porter; Anne Popjoy; Mary and Ann Elton; John Harris; John Webb; William Cowley; Edmund Church; Elizabeth Pizzie; Edward Scott; Elizabeth Appleford; Edward Alexander; James Blackman; Mary Carent; Rachel Bacon; Peter Johns; Robert Pullen; John Schollar; Thomas Chouls of Bedwyn; Thomas Beckingham; Richard Adams; Joseph Stroud; John and Sarah Waldron. *Fencing* with allotments.

Tithes commuted allotments.

Roads 16 public roads, 10 public footpaths, 1 public bridle way and private road, 34 private roads, 3 private footpaths. Herbage allotted.

Map (W.R.O. Acc 154/3). Francis Webb of Stow and Tewkesbury, Glos. Allottees and acreages shown. Area round town only, including the town. Appears to be a draft map.

Schedules Old inclosures for the tithes of which lands were allotted. Arranged under copy, lease, and freeholders and under Ramsbury Town, Park Town, Whittonditch, Eastridge, Baydon, and Axford.

Notes Many tithe-owners. Rights of lords of manor in watercourses maintained. Road across marsh from Ramsbury to Hungerford of a width to allow for drains. Fishing rights in brooks not to imply ownership. Bridge for cattle to be erected in Great Marsh within 12 months.

161 ROAD OR RODE

Rode and North Bradley parishes, partly in Wilts., partly in Som.

Act 30 G.III c.23. *Award* March 1792, W.R.O. 32 & 33. *Commissioners* Richard Richardson of Devizes; Thomas Davis of Longleat; John Billingsley of Ashwick, Som.

Lord of Manor of Rode and Langham, Edward Andrews.

Rector Henry Bayntun.

Area 489 a. [472 a.] Vaggs Hill, Rode Common.

Allotments 56. Edward Andrews (now a cornet in 3rd Regiment of Dragoons) 55 a.; Joseph Houlton 62 a.; John Thomas 20 a.; John Brownjohn 17 a.; Joshua Cabell 18 a.; Daniel Clutterbuck 28 a.; John Edwards 21 a.; Samuel Lloyd Harford 34 a.; Jonathan Noad 32 a.; John Pool 33 a.; John Sloper 24 a.; John Greenfield; Mary Ponting; James Roddoway; Thomas Adlam; rector of Rode; James Bethel; Samuel Bowden; John Bond; Thomas, Jane, and Arundell Bunn; Richard Clement; William Collier; James Collins; Daniel Crook; William Dyer; John Fowle; Joseph Greenhill of Beckington; Joseph Greenhill of North Bradley; Robert Hayward; Thomas Hervey; William Higgins; Stephen Hillman; William Holder; Charles James; Samuel Ledford; — Martyn, widow; Paul Methuen; Richard Moger; Robert Moger; John Mortimer; Samuel Normen; Scudamore Perry; James Quance; churchwardens of Rode; Katherine Rose; William Sheppard; Richard Singer; Elizabeth Smith; William Steevens; John Thomas; Edward and Henry Tovey; John Wadman; William Waldron; Sarah West; Mary and Elizabeth Whitaker; William Whitaker. *Fencing* with allotments.

Roads 7 public roads, 5 public bridle ways, 8 private roads, 3 public footpaths.

Finance by sale of part of the lands to be allotted.

See also No. 27.

Note Allotment to Edward Andrews of 1 a. 'where the fair of Rode used to be held'.

162 RODBOURNE CHENEY [2,806 a.]

Haydon, Haydon Wick, and Moredon tithings

Act 59 G.III c.61 (Private, not printed). *Award* 29 Nov. 1820, supplementary award 29 Nov. 1820 with owners' permission for exchanges (enrolled 14 Oct. 1823), W.R.O. V 123. *Commissioner* John Hayward of Rowde. *Surveyor* George Hayward of Devizes.

Area [285 a.] Moredon Field, Haydon Field, Middle Meadow, Woodward's Bridge Meadow, Rye Mead, New Meadow, Stile Yatt, Broken Cross, Dole Meadow, The Folly.

Allotments 15. Rev. Arthur Evans and Henry Evans 121 a.; Margaret Wilson 48 a.; Richard Tuckey 49 a.; John Osborn 20 a.; Edward Francome 18 a.; William Seager; William Halling; Thomas Osborn; William Hiscock; Marty Titcombe; trustees of Wootton Bassett school; John Hitchman;

Latimer and Strange; devisees of Robert Caswell; devisees of William Tayler.

Roads 1 public road, 4 public footpaths.

Map Part of parish only. Commonable lands red, old inclosures exchanged green. Fields numbered only.

Schedules (1) Allotments. (2) Exchanges.

163 RUSHALL [2,204 a.]

Act 43 G.III c.61 (not printed). *Award* 12 Jan. 1804 (enrolled 12 July 1808), W.R.O. 72. *Commissioner* John Gale of Stert. *Surveyor* John Charlton of Stourton.

Lord of Manor Sir John Methuen Poore, Bt.

Rector Henry Whitfield.

Area [103 a.] West and North Field, Hay's Field, Lower House Ground, Twintown Meadow, Man Meadow, Golden Stick Meadow.

Allotments 5. Sir John Poore Bt. 39 a.; rector of Rushall 25 a.; Edward Poore 39 a.; heirs of Stephen Ford; Henry Temple, Viscount Palmerston, for Duck's Acre given by Viscount Palmerston, grandfather of Henry Temple, to the Thrashers of Charlton to celebrate the memory of the Rev. Stephen Duck [the poet, who had been a thresher at Charlton and was commemorated with an annual dinner: *D.N.B.*].

Roads 5 public roads, 1 private road, 2 public bridle ways, 5 public footpaths.

Maps 1803. (1) Village and north-east end of down. (2) South-west part of down. Whole parish and village, allotments coloured according to allottees.

164 SEAGRY AND CHRISTIAN MALFORD [Seagry 1,082 a.]

Act General, 6 & 7 W.IV c.115; 3 & 4 Vic. c.31. *Award* 11 May 1883 (enrolled 21 May 1883), W.R.O. 193. *Commissioner* Henry Herbert Smith.

Area [124 a.] Seagry Lower Mead, Hungerdown Mead.

Allotments 6. Trustees of late earl of Mornington 84 a.; heirs of Henry Bayliffe 21 a.; heirs of John Bayliffe; James Godwin; Eleanor Large; Elizabeth Sevier. *Fencing* with award.

Roads 1 private road.

Map Alexander Chalmers of Chippenham. Allotted lands green, old inclosures outlined.

See also Nos. 28 and 54.

165 SHALBOURNE AND OXENWOOD

Act 39 & 40 G.III c.32. *Award* 6 Dec. 1805 (enrolled 21 Sept. 1808), W.R.O. 73. *Commissioners* John Gale of Stert; Richard Davis of Lewknor, Oxon. *Surveyor* Benjamin Haynes.

Vicar William Masters.

SHALBOURNE [3,809 a.]

Area [1,153 a.] Little Field, New Field, Great Field, North Field, Denville

Corner, Crook's Field, East End Field, Putt Mead, Cudden Hill Field, King's Mead, East Field, Shalbourne Down, Heath Bottom, Kite's Hill, Five Acre Field, Twenty Acre Field.

Allotments 18. Thomas Bruce, earl of Ailesbury 801 a. (including copy, John Barns 213 a.; Hannah Dance 47 a.; Rev. Thomas Stockwell 63 a.; Richard Burford 22 a.; John Marcott; Francis French; John French; Thomas Gale; Edward Nutley; Thomas Batt); Elizabeth Worgan 146 a.; Thomas Rendall 77 a.; Benjamin Worgan 47 a.; John Barns 20 a.; William Eldridge and Martha Vice 16 a.; Elizabeth Knight; John Piper; William Orum; Ann King; Anthony Kingston; David Hutchins; churchwardens of Shalbourne; vicar of Shalbourne; William Blandy; John Palmer; dean and canons of Windsor; churchwardens of Great Bedwyn.

Tithes exchanged but not commuted. 'John Barns is seised in fee simple of the chapel and chapelry of Shalbourne and of the great and small tithes on certain fields lying dispersedly' (151 a.). Complicated exchange of tithes between the earl of Ailesbury as lessee under the dean and canons of Windsor, and the vicar of Shalbourne. Free chapel with chapel and yard allotted to the earl of Ailesbury, and tithes arising from 7 parcels of land exchanged for two of the earl's allotments (37 a.).

Roads 12 public roads, 1 public bridle way, 4 public footpaths, 4 private roads. Herbage allotted to neighbouring allottees only.

Note Regulations for cleaning the watercourse and drain from Ropewynd along the Ham road set out.

OXENWOOD [1,798 a.]

Area [311 a.] Great and Little Fields, Beacon's Farm Field, Oxenwood Green, Heigh Down.

Allotments 4. Thomas Rendall 199 a.; John Barns 70 a.; earl of Ailesbury 76 a. (including copy and lease John Barns 76 a.); Rev. William Churchill 42 a.

Note Freeholders in Oxenwood to have access to pond in road from Oxenwood to Beacon's Farm.

Maps Benjamin Hodges. (1) General map showing areas covered by maps 2–5. Lands in Berkshire coloured green, in Wiltshire white. (2) North part of the parish including Bagshot. (3) Shalbourne village. (4) South part of parish including Rivar. (5) Oxenwood. (6) Exchange of tithes. Ownership of all fields shown and allotments with allottees and acreages. County boundary determined by the commissioners.

166 SHERRINGTON [1,315 a.]

Agreement 2 April 1794 between Edmund Lambert of Boyton, the rector of Sherrington, guardians of Thomas Mussell, Sarah Viney, Mary Lambert, Elizabeth Patient, Wiliam Imber the younger, Thomas Alford, Thomas Feltham, and William Stockwell. *Award* 1796 (enrolled 1 Jan. 1797),

W.R.O. 41. *Referees* Christopher Ingram of Amesbury; Thomas Davis of Longleat.

Lord of Manor Edmund Lambert of Boyton.

Rector Thomas Davies.

Area [711 a.] Hitchland, Hooklands Field, East and West Mead, Low Field, Smoak Acre Furlong, Coneygar Field, Down Field, Mill Mead, Tenantry Down.

Allotments 7. Public: 1 common watering place at East Sheep pond. Edmund Lambert 626 a. (including copy, Mary Lambert 30 a.; Sarah Viney 36 a.; Richard Imber); guardians of Thomas Mussell the younger 61 a.; rector of Sherrington 20 a.; William Stockwell; Henry Fox-Strangways, earl of Ilchester; Thomas Alford.

Roads 7 public roads, 1 public footpath, 4 private roads.

Finance £171 13*s*. 10*d*., amounts detailed in award.

Map Village and whole parish except Cow Down and the Woods. Common plot between Stockton and Sherrington shown.

Notes Edmund Lambert had his allotments on the boundary of Boyton. Low Field, Down Field, and Coneygar Field to be sown, stocked, and fed in common by the rector and six allottees. Common sheep down of 145 a. Allotments in watered meadow called the East Meadow to four allottees to be watered as before and fed in the early spring by their own flock of sheep in common, and after the hay is mown by the owner.

167 SHERSTON MAGNA [3,758 a.]

Act 14 G.II c.13. *Award* 24 June 1743 (enrolled 12 July 1743), W.R.O. 3 (Q.S. enrolled documents 78). *Commissioners* Henry Wightwick of Tetbury, Glos.; Thomas Heather of Didmarton, Glos.; William Robbins of Didmarton, Glos.; William Tugwell of Beverstone, Glos.; John Peach of Norton; William Guest of Norton; and 19 additional commissioners. *Surveyor* William Briston of Norton.

Lord of Manor Thomas Estcourt Cresswell.

Rector dean and chapter of Gloucester; *lessee* T. E. Cresswell. *Vicar* Jeremiah Butt.

Area 1,042 a. [1,317 a.] Sherston North and South Field, Wilsley North Field, Wind Mill Field, Austen's Mead, Short Mead, South Moor.

Allotments 30. T. E. Cresswell 704 a.; dean and chapter of Gloucester 242 a.; Richard Goodenough 70 a.; Anne Hillier 63 a.; Elizabeth Watts 19 a.; Robert Ambidge 19 a.; Charles Gale 30 a.; Walter Watts 20 a.; Elizabeth Watts 25 a.; Thomas Hort 31 a.; and Jane Weeksy; James Wood; Thomas Chapman; John Chapman; Thomas Holborow; John Gostlett; Jane Hort; Samuel Hill; assignees of — Manning; Samuel Bryan; vicar of Sherston; Rebecca Hall; Robert Holford; Dame Martha Long; John Goodenough; Thomas Gore; David Rice; William Mannings; Samuel Bryan; Dorothy Power. *Fencing* with allotments.

Tithes Great tithes extinguished by lands deducted from allotments. Vicarial tithes not commuted.

Finance £290 11*s.* 5*d.* by rate levied proportionately on allottees.
See also No. 168.
Note Any quorum of commissioners must contain two of the eight nominees of dean and chapter of Gloucester.

168 SHERSTON PARVA (or Pinkney) [966 a.]
Act General, 6 & 7 W.IV c.115; 3 & 4 Vic. c. 31. *Award* 27 June 1844 (enrolled 3 March 1845), W.R.O. 165. *Commissioner* Richard Hall of Gloucester.
Area [84 a.] Pinkney Field.
Allotments 3. Robert Holford 57 a.; trustees of Captain Day's charity 24 a.; William and James Tyler.
Roads 2 private roads.
Map 1844. Allottees and acreages shown, coloured according to allottees. Schedule with allotments.
See also No. 167.

169 SHREWTON [2,203 a.]
Act 38 G.III c.51. *Award* 17 March 1801 (enrolled 3 Feb. 1802), W.R.O. 59. *Commissioners* Benjamin Haynes of Salisbury (replacing Christopher Ingram of Amesbury, refused); Thomas Davis of Horningsham; John Gale of Stert. *Surveyor* William Tubb of Fisherton Anger.
Vicar John Skinner D.D.
Area 2,147 a. [2,112 a.] Windmill Hill, Upper Bale, Peck's Hill, Windmill Linch, Upper Ball, Shrewton Lower Meadow, Nett Field, Home Field, Nett Down, Frogg Meadow, Nett meadow, Breach Field, Hill Field, Dean Bottom, Shrewton Down.
Allotments 32. Sir Nathaniel Holland Bt. 143 a. (including 29 a. for tithes; leases, Robert Gennings 29 a.; James Mundy 27 a.; Ann Blewden 15 a.; John Hooper; William Bennett; James Mills); Charles Howard Wansborough 258 a. (including tithes; William Moore; William Pearce; Ann Blewden; Richard Thring); John Wansborough 441 a. (including tithes); Sarah Goddard 457 a. (including tithes); Jane Folliott 287 a. (including tithes; lease, Christiana Munday); Robert Gennings 246 a. (including tithes); Mary Warren 45 a.; Mary Cripps 48 a.; George Mills 17 a.; James Munday 26 a.; Jane Whitehorn 26 a.; John Hooper 20 a.; vicar of Shrewton 28 a.; John Petty; trustees of charity lands; William Smith; Ann Blewden (all the foregoing have allotments for tithes); trustees of church lands; Ann Fiander; William Moore; Abraham Munday; Ann Petty; John Mogg; George Baker; Simon Pain; John Garrat; Richard Grosvenor (including lease, C. H. Wansborough); John Newberry; Elizabeth Long; William Watts; Wadham Locke; John Howe, Lord Chedworth.
Tithes rectorial tithes in the hands of 17 persons all of whom received allotments in lieu.
Roads 3 public roads, 10 private roads, 1 public bridle way, 2 public bridle ways and private roads. Herbage allotted.
Maps William Tubb 1800. (1) North part of parish, 'The Downs'. (2) 'The

Fields'. Whole parish shown including 3 detached areas of water-meadows. Acreages and allottees shown. 'Nathaniel Dance shown on these maps is since created a baronet by the name of Sir Nathaniel Holland.'

Note Shrewton-Orcheston boundary rationalized by commissioners.

170 GREAT SOMERFORD [1,660 a.]

Act 46 G.III c.63 (not printed). *Award* 6 Aug. 1809 (enrolled 30 July 1816), W.R.O. 98. *Commissioners* John Davis of Bloxham, Oxon.; Francis Webb of Salisbury; Thomas Davis of Horningsham.

Rector Stephen Demainbray.

Area 1,649 a. including heath 48 a., old inclosures 700 a. [1,147 a.] Startley Common, Seagry Heath, Goose Green, Rodmead, Down Field, Broad Field, West Field, South Mead, Broad Mead, Nythe, New Leaze, The Moor, Horsham, 4 acre Field, Lower Marsh.

Allotments 21. Public: 1 gravel pit 1 a. William Smith 269 a.; rector of Great Somerford 332 a. (including 302 a. for tithes); Thomas Pyke 207 a.; William Randell 52 a.; John Parsloe 89 a.; Thomas Thynne, marquess of Bath, 81 a.; Mary Randell 19 a.; feoffees of Week's Charity 25 a.; William Sealy; Catherine Tylney Long; Elizabeth Hungerford; heirs of Mary Riley; Ruth Leonard; John Leonard; Richard Leonard; Jacob Smith; Jacob Barnes; Ann Turtle; Ann Hopkins; Thomas Fry. *Fencing* with allotments

Tithes extinguished by allotment to rector.

Roads 4 public roads, 5 public footpaths, 10 private roads, 2 private footpaths.

Finance See Schedule 3.

Maps 1809. Whole parish and village shown. Old inclosures grey, common meadow and pastures green, common arable yellow. Boundary with Dauntsey shown in red.

Schedules (1) Responsibilities for repair of private roads. (2) Compensation payable by those without sufficient lands to permit grant in place of tithes to rector, £223 16*s*. (3) Expenses of obtaining award: general expenses £2,189 2*s*. 9*d*., road rate £995 0*s*. ½*d*.

Notes Boundary with Dauntsey fixed by commissioners. Site of and responsibility for hatches set out. Three drains to be made and size and course laid down. Fourteen allotments of waste to rector and churchwardens for the owners of ancient cottages.

171 LITTLE SOMERFORD (including parts of Malmesbury and Brinkworth) [1,435 a. including Somerford Common]

Whychurch, Milbourne, and Little Somerford manors

Act 30 G.III c.43. *Award* 18 Dec. 1792, W.R.O. 34 & 35. *Commissioners* Richard Bloxham of Winterslow; Ralph Whitehart of Salperton, Glos. (replacing Thomas Carter of Foxley, refused); Richard Richardson of Devizes. *Surveyor* William Tubb of Salisbury.

Lords of Manor of Whychurch and Milbourne, Jacob Pleydell-Bouverie, earl of Radnor; of Little Somerford, Susannah Earle.

Rector of Little Somerford, William Jones; of Brinkworth, John Penton.

Area 381 a. excluding roads [374 a.] Wallow Marsh 12 a.; Whychurch Marsh 44 a.; Millbourne Common 105 a.; Little Somerford 204 a.; Lot Mead 15 a.; Crabb Mead.

Allotments 19. Earl of Radnor 126 a.; Mrs. Susannah Earle 54 a.; Thomas Powys 77 a.; Richard Keinneir 22 a.; rector of Brinkworth 26 a.; John Godwin; Henry Pockeridge; Sir John Rushout; John Howard, earl of Suffolk; Sarah Gale; John Beak; Robert Stump; Mary Player; Thomas Rice and Richard Brooke ; Mary Saunders; — Jones, widow; Thomas Gauntlett; rector of Little Somerford; Lucy Heath. *Fencing* with allotments.

Roads 6 public roads, 5 private roads. Herbage allotted.

Finance £734 11*s*. by general rate, book of expenses to be deposited in the parish church of Malmesbury.

Maps (1) Wallow and Whychurch marshes (Malmesbury). (2) Lot Mead (Malmesbury). (3) Milbourne and Little Somerford Common (detached in Brinkworth).

Schedule State of property of proprietors in each of four areas.

See also No. 133.

Note Penalties for failure to repair fences and private roads.

172 STANTON ST. QUINTIN [1,807 a.]

Act 22 G.III c.26. *Award* 18 June 1783 (enrolled 8 Dec. 1783), W.R.O. 24 and Acc. 490/1019. *Commissioners* Thomas Fricker of Longbridge Deverill; Richard Richardson of Devizes; Daniel Tanner of Urchfont; Thomas Brown of Sevenhampton (refused). *Surveyor* Francis Webb of Stow, Glos.

Lord of Manor Jacob Pleydell-Bouverie, earl of Radnor.

Rector Samuel Smith.

Area 347 a. including roads [331 a.] Upper Field, Lower Field, Hawkes' Field, Behind Town Field.

Allotments 3. Rector of Stanton St. Quintin 130 a. (excluding 77 a. of old inclosures allotted to the rector); earl of Radnor 198 a. (including leases, Charles Beak 42 a.; Isaac Cottle 28 a.; Isaac Beak, Humphrey Beak, and William Summers 26 a.; Richard Jones; John Beak and Humphrey Beak; John Beak; Humphrey Beak; Charles Miller); churchwardens of Stanton St. Quintin. *Fencing* with allotments.

Tithes Allotment to rector for all tithes both great and small, and certain rent-charges.

Roads 3 public roads, 1 public bridle way and footpath, 5 private roads and public bridle ways, 2 private roads, 2 public footpaths. Herbage allotted.

Map Francis Webb of Stow 1783. Whole parish including village, allottees and acreages shown.

Schedule shows proprietors, lifeholders under the earl of Radnor, and other estates. Exchanges marked and areas remaining to the rectory.

173 STAPLEFORD [2,084 a.]

Act 50 G.III c.58 (not printed) (Stapleford and Winterbourne Stoke). *Award* 28 April 1812 (enrolled 22 Jan. 1818), W.R.O. 103. *Commissioner* Richard Richardson of London. *Surveyor* Thomas Crass of London.

Lord of Manor Alexander Baring and Henry Seymour.

Area 1,913 a. [2,019 a.] Uphampton Field, Cow Down, Cote Mead, Stapleford Down, Parsonage Croft, Southington Field, The Butts, Gooseham, West and East Meadow, Little Marsh, Pitlands Field, Burnbak Field, Callonhay Field, Overstreet Down, Church Street Down.

Allotments 13. Alexander Baring 790 a. (including leases, Solomon Dredge 37 a.; George Saph and others 40 a.; executors of Richard Coombs 41 a.; Charles Saph 32 a.; Henry Cornish 26 a.; copy, George Saph 38 a.; Phoebe Coombs 43 a.; executors of George Pavie; Frances Ball); John Saph 125 a.; Henry Seymour 758 a. (including leases, executors of John Coombs 56 a.; Thomas and William Barnett 19 a.; George Baker 34 a.; Martha and Elizabeth Tanner 35 a.; Thomas Hayter 26 a.; lease and copy, John Saph 45 a.; and Henry Cornish; executors of George Pavie; John Brown); dean and canons of Windsor 116 a. (including lease, Martha and Elizabeth Tanner 116 a.); James Harris, earl of Malmesbury 193 a.; Martha and Elizabeth Tanner 21 a.; churchwardens of Stapleford; James Roles; John Brown; Charles Saph; Sir E. Knatchbull Bt.; John Jarett; Solomon Dredge. *Fencing* in the award.

Roads 8 public roads, 3 public bridle ways, 4 public footpaths, 14 private roads, 1 private footpath, 1 sheep drove.

Finance paid by Alexander Baring and Henry Seymour who are to be reimbursed by their tenants at 5 per cent interest according to a rate set out in the award.

174 STOCKTON [2,122 a.]

Act 49 G.III c.110. *Award* 8 Sept. 1815 (enrolled 3 May 1821), W.R.O. 112 & 113. *Commissioners* Richard Webb of Salisbury; Thomas Davis of Horningsham. *Umpire* John Gale of Stert. *Surveyor* William Tubb of Salisbury.

Lord of Manor Harry Biggs.

Rector Henry Good.

Area 1,500 a. [1,732 a.] Burnbake, Oxen Marsh, Black Mead, Old Lands, Farley's Mead, East and West Fields, Lime Pits Field, Coneygree Field, Tenantry Down, Pillis Common, Southlands Field, Oat Close.

Allotments 4. Rector of Stockton 623 a.; John Pinchard 190 a.; Harry Biggs 916 a. (including leases, John Pinchard 70 a.; Thomas Humphries); bishop of Winchester and William Beckford his lessee receive an allotment in lieu of the first shear in Stockton belonging to Fonthill Bishop farm.

Tithes exonerated by allotment in lieu.

Roads 3 public roads, 3 private roads, turnpike roads mentioned separately.

Map William Tubb and Son 1815. Allottees and acreages shown in the whole parish. Village shown.

Schedules (1) Rate for repair of private roads. (2) Additional rent-charges on cottages to compensate landlord for extinguishing tithes.
Note System of watering meadows to continue.

175 STRATFORD SUB CASTLE AND MILFORD
Act 39 G.III c.76. *Award* 4 Dec. 1800 (enrolled 30 Sept. 1808), W.R.O. 74. *Commissioners* Richard Richardson of Bath; Francis Webb of Salisbury; Richard Davis of Lewknor, Oxon. *Surveyor* William Tubb.

STRATFORD SUB CASTLE [1,501 a.]
Lord of Manor of Stratford Dean, dean of Salisbury; *lessee* Thomas Pitt, Lord Camelford.
Prebendary of Stratford St. Lawrence, dean of Winchester; *lessee* Rev. Edward Cooper.
Area Stratford 1,073 a. including roads 32 a. [1,042 a.] Crab Tree Ham, Upper Meadow, The Pennings, Upper Field, North Hill Field, Home Field, The Down, Cheynhams Meadow, Goose Mead, Mill Mead, South Field, Middle Field, Great and Little Home Field, Great Field, St. John's Field, Town Meadows, Hill Park, Bridge Meadow, Paul's Dean.
Allotments 13. Dean of Salisbury 292 a. (including lease, Lord Camelford 292 a.); dean and chapter of Salisbury 290 a. (including lease, Lord Camelford 290 a.); succentor of Salisbury 123 a. (including lease, Lord Camelford 123 a.); prebendary of Stratford St. Lawrence 156 a. (including leases, Rev. Edward Cooper 147 a.; John Whitchurch; Stephen Hutchins); John Blake 61 a.; chancellor of Salisbury 16 a.; Rev. Edward Cooper 32 a.; Lord Camelford 43 a.; George Herbert, earl of Pembroke; Thomas Ogden; Nicholas Elliot; William Child; churchwardens of Stratford.
Roads 5 public roads, 2 public bridle ways and private roads; 4 public footpaths, 5 private roads.
Finance £704 9*s.* 1*d.*

MILFORD [1,388 a.]
Lord of Manor bishop of Salisbury; *lessee* (Lord Farmer) William Beckford.
Area 423 a. (including roads 18 a.) [409 a.] Bishop's Down Farm, Milford Hill, Weeping Cross, Greencroft, Horse House Field.
Allotments 6. Bishop of Salisbury 400 a. (including leases, William Beckford 289 a.; John Geary 38 a.; John Merris 29 a.; copy and lease Samuel Whitchurch 15 a.; copy William Goldwyer 15 a.; William Hayter; John Edgar); John P. Geary; John Merris; Samuel Whitchurch; H. P. Wyndham; James Coombs. *Fencing* banks two feet high to be made and maintained against the highways.
Roads 5 public roads, 6 private roads, 6 public footpaths.
Finance Sale allotments £430 11*s.* 9*d.*

Map Rather worn, does not show the whole of either parish. Allottees and acreages, Old Sarum, and the river Avon shown. Schedules of small allotments in (1) Stratford; (2) Milford.

Note Very detailed description of the process of raising the money to pay the expenses of inclosure by deduction of allotments from those liable to pay the expenses and sale of these allotments to persons who will pay the expenses.

See also No. 123.

176 STRATTON ST. MARGARET [3.055 a.]

Act 35 G.III c.105. *Award* 19 Sept. 1796 (enrolled 19 June 1798), W.R.O. 49. *Commissioners* Richard Richardson of Bath; Francis Webb of Salisbury; Richard Davis of Lewknor, Oxon. *Surveyor* William Tubb of Fisherton Anger.

Lord of Manor of Stratton, Ambrose Goddard; of Corsham, Paul Cobb Methuen.

Rector warden and scholars of Merton College, Oxford. *Vicar* James Hare.

Area [1,836 a.] Upper, Middle and Long Field, Redlands Field, Ryall Farm, Stratton Marsh, Cow Common, Flaxlands, Hatmoor Pond, Clay Field, Stanhill Field, The Barrow, Blindmore Field, Great and Little Sturry Field, Shiplands Field, Little Peaks, Hay Field, Catsbrain, Dunge Furlong.

Allotments 64. Public: 6 allotments for roads. Warden and scholars of Merton College, Oxford, 482 a. (including lease, William Croome 482 a. for glebe and tithes); Paul Cobb Methuen 180 a. (including copy, William Croome 77 a.; Edward Byrchall 24 a.; Lucy Gray 42 a.; Richard Read; John Kempster; Thomas North; Richard Looker; Benjamin Richardson; James White; Richard Kempster); John Hitchman 50 a.; Sarah Haggard 136 a.; Benjamin Richardson 127 a. (including 1a. for fencing the allotment of the vicar of Chiseldon, William Stock); John Blandy 97 a.; John Bradburne 53 a.; Catherine Evans 93 a.; Lucy Gray 52 a.; William Maskelyne 25 a.; William Tomkins 42 a.; vicar of Chiseldon 17 a.; James White 26 a.; Richard Kempster 16 a.; Philip and Robert Hyatt 17 a.; Thomas Garrett 48 a.; John Herring 26 a.; Martha Jones 25 a.; Richard Watts Read 40 a.; Edward Byrchall 40 a.; Jane Carpenter 29 a.; Elizabeth Evans 43 a.; Ambrose Goddard; John Hatt; John Reason; John Stone; Gilbert Turner; Sarah Ouchterlony; John Grymes; William Gay; William Jones; Sarah Watts; Henry Shewry; Gabriel Hyde; Richard Woolford; churchwardens of Stratton; John Osborne; William Tomkins junior; John Jordan; William Savory; trustees of Hannington poor; William Pewsey; Mary Kemble; John Munday; John Beckingsale; John Day; John Panting; John Kemble; Joseph Cooper; Thomas Bizley; Richard Panting; Joshua Hyde; James Lee; Mary and Ann Lee; Richard Looker; feoffees of lands in Swindon; John Adams; Fanny Godwyn; John Wells; John King; William Pickett; John Blandy; John Day. *Fencing* with allotments and on map.

Tithes commuted for corn-rents.

Roads 3 public roads, 2 public bridle ways and private roads, 15 private roads, 24 public bridle ways, 4 private roads and public footpaths, 14 public footpaths. Herbage allotted.

Map whole parish including village, new allotments edged in green, old inclosures in yellow, old inclosures charged with payments in place of tithe in red.

Schedule Yearly corn-rents to be paid instead of great and small tithes, under headings, viz. acreage; corn-rent in place of great tithes; wheat equal in value to corn-rents; corn-rent in place of small tithes; wheat equal to corn-rents.

Notes Parts of Stratton were within Corsham manor. Surveyors of highways appointed by commissioners. Corn-rents could be reviewed after 14 years.

177 SUTTON MANDEVILLE [1,326 a.]

Act 54 G.III c.74, to confirm an *agreement* of 6 Dec. 1811 between William Wyndham, Rev. James Hibberd, and ten others. *Award* 15 Nov. 1813 (enrolled 26 January 1814), W.R.O. 90. *Commissioner* John Seagrim of Wilton.

Lord of Manor William Wyndham.

Rector James Hibberd.

Area 533 a. (Award), 375 a. and Down 170 a. [664 a.] Two Oaks, Adlam's Close, Glasses Lane Field, Ivers Field, Middle Field, Hill Ground, Hut Field, Mann Mead, Middle Hill.

Allotments 9. Public: 1 chalk pit 1 a. William Wyndham 527 a. (including leases, Thomas King 19 a.; Robert Larkham 43 a.; copy and lease, Thomas Talbot 49 a.; Henry Goodfellow 38 a.; John Cross; John King; Samuel Cross; James Richardson); Rev. James Hibberd 16 a.; Edward Jukes Bracher 16 a.; Edward Bracher 36 a.; Henry Larkham 49 a.; Mary Snook; Thomas Talbot; John King. *Fencing* with allotments.

Roads 1 public road, 1 private road. Herbage allotted.

Maps 1812. Village and allottees and acreages shown. (1) Commonable lands south of the Salisbury–Shaftesbury road. (2) Old inclosures and exchanges, north part of parish and village.

Schedule proportion of cost to be paid by allottees.

Notes Very confusing terminology in this award. Wild's Mead to be watered as before.

178 SUTTON VENY [3,822 a.]

Act 38 G.III c.75. *Award* 19 May 1804 (enrolled 15 May 1805), W.R.O. 62. *Commissioners* Richard Richardson of Bath; John Gale of Stert; Christopher Ingram of Amesbury. *Surveyor* William Tubb of Fisherton Anger.

Lord of Manor of Little Sutton, Thomas Thynne, marquess of Bath.

Rector Brouncker Thring D.D.

Area [2,876 a.] Little Sutton Down, Bussage Common, Woodcomb, Butt's Common, Leaze Common, Minument Meadow, Rack Ham, Dummock's Lane Ground, Lord's Wood, West Heath Common, Upend, Culverland, Eastleigh Wood, Sand Field, Broad Mead, Vale House Meadow, West Meadow, Upper and Lower Blacket, Henford's Meadow, Lower Field, Odd Mead, North and South Field, Eastleigh Common, Wheaten Hill, Coomb Coppice, Woodcroft's Common, Hawcomb, Lake Meadow.

Allottees 27. Rector of Sutton Veny 830 a. (including glebe and tithes); Francis Dugdale Astley 856 a. (including 22 a. for tithes; leases, Richard

Collier; Stephen Noke; William Hughes; Stephen Best; Robert Whatley; Thomas Brown; William Barter; Francis Musselwhite; Mary Musselwhite); Walter Long 295 a.; marquess of Bath 307 a. (including leases, Christiana Long 38 a.; John Randall 26 a.; Giles Halliday 180 a.; Samuel Long; John Gale Everett; Sarah Randall; William Hinton); William Hinton 123 a. (including lease, Thomas Marsh); Samuel Long 199 a.; William Long 60 a.; John Bennett 40 a.; Richard Collier 26 a.; Susannah Swepson 32 a.; Mary Long 31 a.; Sir William Ashe à Court 21 a.; John Hinton; Samuel Long; William Carter; Thomas Warren; Betty Whitteridge; Thomas Imber; George Long; Richard Harman; William Long; Stephen Best; James Brown; Edward Imber; Richard Long; Benjamin Rebbeck; churchwardens of Sutton Veny.

Tithes allotment to rector for all tithes great and small except those called the 'thirties', for which half-yearly rents were established.

Roads 8 public roads, 4 public footpaths, 2 public bridle ways, 20 private roads, 1 private bridle way. Herbage allotted.

Finance Proportion of expenses to be borne by each allottee (except the rector) shown in the award.

Maps (1) South part of parish. (2) Central part with village. (3) West part. Whole parish shown.

See also Nos. 21 and 104.

Notes Watercourse in the Old Meadow called Pigeon House Cut allotted to W. P. Ashe à Court; watercourse called the Upper Cut to owners and occupiers of lands in Sutton Veny and Heytesbury; regulations for cleaning the half of the river in Sutton Veny set out. Surveyor of roads appointed.

179 SWALLOWCLIFFE [1,350 a.]

Act 25 G.III c.56 (Fovant, Swallowcliffe, Broad Chalke, Ebbesborne Wake, Bower Chalke, Alvediston, Bishopstone, Fifield Bavant). *Award* 3 Jan. 1792 (enrolled 17 Nov. 1794), W.R.O. V 38. *Commissioners* Richard Bloxham of West Dean; Richard Richardson of Devizes; Francis Webb (replacing William Corfield of Salisbury, d. 1787). *Surveyor* Benjamin Haynes (replacing William Corfield).

Lord of Manor Henry Herbert, earl of Pembroke.

Prebendary of Swallowcliffe, Thomas Osborne.

Curate and officiating clergyman, William Easton.

Area [625 a.] Gold Hill, The Down, Bucklesbury Field, East, West and Middle Fields.

Allotments 8. Public: for the poor 3 a. Earl of Pembroke 478 a. (including lease, Adam Powell 21 a.; copy and lease, Francis Best 20 a.; Edward Jerrard; Elizabeth White; John Fitz); Henry Jerrard 109 a.; prebendary of Swallowcliffe 18 a. (including lease, Arundell Frome 18 a.); master of St. John's Hospital near Wilton 16 a. (including lease, John Fily 16 a.); and John Wright; churchwardens of Swallowcliffe. London Pond by London Elm allotted to all the proprietors and occupiers.

Roads 9 public roads, 1 public bridle way, 1 public footpath. Herbage allotted.

Finance Not detailed, except that the prebendary's expenses were paid for by sale, for £12 9*s*. 7*d*. of 2 r. 39 p. out of his allotment, to Henry Jerrard and by sale for £8 2*s*. of 2 r. 3 p. from allotment to St. John's hospital to Henry Jerrard, the rest to be paid by allottees.

Map Part south of and including the village only. Allotments and exchanges shown.

Schedules (1) Lifeholders under the earl of Pembroke who are to pay interest to the reverseionary who has paid their expenses. (2) Charges assessed by the commissioners on various lifeholders under the earl of Pembroke.

Note The Charity Commissioners' report of 1902 mentions an earlier inclosure by decree of Court of Chancery 4 Nov. 15 c. II.

180 TIDCOMBE [2,473 a.]

Act 14 G.III c.68. *Award* 2 July 1782, P.R.O. K.B. 122/471 (photocopy in W.R.O.). *Commissioners* William Wapshare of Salisbury; Richard Bloxham of West Dean; Benjamin Pryce of Wilton (replacing James Poore of East Woodhay, Hants, and William Sweetapple of Andover, both dead).

Lord of Manor John Tanner.

Area 867 a. [811 a.] East, West and North Fields and uninclosed arable called Mouseholes between Tidcombe and Wexcombe.

Allotments 5. Public: Coomb Pond. Thomas Rendall 90 a.; John Tanner 686 a. (including copy, Thomas Pike 591 a.; Mary White and others 51 a.); dean and canons of Windsor 27 a. (including lease, Hon. James Arundell and Ann his wife 27 a.); Benjamin Hopkins. *Fencing* with allotments, size of hedges and ditches set out.

Roads 8 public roads, 2 private roads, 3 public footpaths. Herbage allotted. Duties for repair of private roads set out.

Note 230 a. to be kept annually in tillage and sown with wheat, barley, oats, beans, or pease by executors of Edward Tanner (206 a.) and Thomas Rendell (24 a.).

181 TILSHEAD [3,883 a.]

Act 51 G.III c.177. *Award* 20 May 1814 (enrolled 2 Jan. 1827), W.R.O. 127. *Commissioners* Richard Richardson of London; Thomas Davis of Horningsham; William Jennings of Evershot (replacing John Billingsley of Ashwick Grove, Som., dead). *Surveyor* George Barnes of Andover.

Lord of Manor of Tilshead South Side, Katharine Long as lady of the manor of Steeple Ashton; of Tilshead North Side, Rev. Charles Gore, Daniel Clutterbuck, Charles Blagrave, Philip Hayward, and Edward Sampson.

Rector (lay) Gorges Lowther; *lessee* Thomas and Mary Lawes. *Vicar* David Williams.

Area 3,832 a. [3,632 a.] Bompwell Field, Wheton Hill Down, South Down, West Horse Down, Gilton Down, East Hill Field, Cow Down, East Baked Down, Great Lynch Field, Horton Down, Wateridge Field, Long Half Field, Dog Bottom Field, Bonywell, Bennett's Lynch Field, Windmill Field, Sand Pit Field.

Allotments 15. Public: 1 chalk pit 1 a. Lords of manor of Tilshead North

Side 801 a.; Gorges Lowther 1,026 a. (including 296 a. as lay rector); Thomas Lawes and Mary his wife 87 a. (as lessees of the tithes); vicar of Tilshead 238 a. (for tithes); dean and chapter of Salisbury 94 a. (including lease, Leonard Lawes 94 a.); R. E. D. Grosvenor 152 a.; Richard Norris 844 a.; William Slade 221 a.; William Alsop Lawes 151 a.; Catherine Baker; Elizabeth Palmer; Laurence Kite; Jane Hussey; Katharine Long.

Tithes extinguished by allotments in lieu.

Roads 17 public roads, 6 private roads. Herbage allotted.

Finance Sale allotments (7 a.) £630.

Map George Barnes of Andover. Whole parish, and village on inset map. North Side blue, South Side yellow. Allottees and acreages.

Schedule of allotments with the map.

Note Agreement by the Crown as patrons to exchanges affecting the vicar.

182 TISBURY [East Tisbury 2,803 a., West Tisbury 2,718 a.,
Tisbury and Wardour Wardour 2,015 a.]

Act 4 & 5 W.IV c.2 (Private). *Award* 9 May 1836 (enrolled 21 May 1836), W.R.O. V 149. *Commissioners* James Combes of Tisbury; Oliver Stubbs of Hinton St. George, Som.; Francis Burridge of Shaftesbury, Dorset (replacing John Jefferys of Donhead St. Andrew, refused).

Lord of Manor of Tisbury, James Henry Arundell, Lord Arundell of Wardour; of West Hatch, Sir Hyde Parker Bt.; of Tisbury Parsonage, dean and chapter of Bristol.

Area [1 a.] Tisbury Common, Twiners Mead, Tucking Mill Mead.

Allotments 4. Lord Arundell of Wardour; dean and chapter of Bristol; John Fraser and James Mortimer; William Wyndham. *Fencing* general and in award.

Roads 1 public road.

Maps 1836. (1) East Tisbury. (2) West Tisbury. (3) Wardour.

Notes The main purpose of the award was to divide Tisbury into three parishes, West Tisbury, East Tisbury, and Wardour. This took effect from 25 March 1835 but did not affect the ecclesiastical parish or the election of churchwardens. The boundaries were fixed and the maps certified by the Speaker of the House of Commons. Commissioners decided what portion of the poor rate was chargeable to each parish and what proportion of debt. Tisbury, Staple, Chicksgrove, and Hatch tithings.

183 TROWBRIDGE AND HILPERTON

Act 55 G.III c.28 (Private). *Award* 8 Nov. 1816 (enrolled 1 April 1817), W.R.O. 101 & 102. *Commissioner* Young Sturge of Bristol (a Quaker who affirmed). *Surveyor* Jacob Player Sturge.

TROWBRIDGE [2,400 a.]

Lord of Manor of Trowbridge, Thomas Timbrell; of Trowbridge Dauntsey, Charles Pierrepont, Earl Manvers.

Area [98 a.] Studley Green, Quar Lane, Silver Street, Andrew's Lane, Holbrook Lane, Drynam Lane, Choxalls Lane.

Allotments 38. Thomas Timbrell; Earl Manvers; Richard Godby; Sarah Herne; Kennet and Avon canal; representatives of John Little; Abraham Ludlow (including the herbage of Silver Street); Thomas Merriman; Elizabeth Alner; executors of Joseph Amer; Joachim Bell; James Bird and others; Sarah and Ann Bissey; John Bythesea; trustees of Samuel Bythesea; James Caswell (including herbage of Andrew's Lane); James Chapman; John Clark; John Cook; George Crabbe; William Culverhouse; William Dalmer; George Drinkwater; William Edgell; James Elton; Elizabeth Eyre; Edward Horlock Mortimer (including herbage in Quar Lane); Elizabeth Mortimer; Charles Mortimer; Sarah Ann Page; Ann Raynor; Edward Sheppard; Joseph Smith; Thomas Stillman; John Taunton; Sarah Taylor; Trowbridge poor; Harriet Walker. *Fencing* general.

Roads Staverton, 3 private roads, 1 public footpath; Studley, 4 private roads and public bridle ways, 9 private roads, 3 public footpaths, 3 private roads and public footpaths, 1 private footpath. Responsibility for repair of private roads set out.

Finance 18 sale allotments (5 a.].

Map See Hilperton.

Schedule shows proprietor, allotment, and road rate. Staverton road £5 1*s.*; Studley road £3 7*s.* 9*d.*

See also No. 24.

HILPERTON [965 a. excl. part of Whaddon]

Lord of Manor Richard Godolphin Long, John Long, and Daniel Jones Long.

Rector George Innes.

Area [92 a.] Hilperton Marsh.

Allotments 18. Lords of the manor 34 a. (including leases, Wyatt Cottle; William Culverhouse; George Feltham; Samuel Ferris; Sarah Hallett; James Marven; William Pead; Anthony Rogers; and herbage of Whaddon Lane); Earl Manvers; rector of Hilperton; Robert Long; representatives of John Matthews; Edward Besser; James Bethell; Robert Clement; John Edwards; Hannah Richman; Anthony Rogers; James Selfe; Richard Shrapnell; John Slade; Joseph Slade; Henry Slade; Trowbridge poor; James Watts. *Fencing* general.

Roads 3 private roads and public footpaths, 7 private roads, 3 private roads and public bridle ways, 3 public footpaths.

Finance 18 sale allotments (5 a.).

Map Waste, commons, and marsh in Hilperton, Staverton, and Studley. Allotments numbered only.

Schedule Proprietor, allotment, and road rate. Hilperton road £10 5*s.* 3*d.*

Note Boundary between Hilperton and Trowbridge determined by commissioner.

184 UPAVON [3,352 a.]

Act 42 G.III c.82 (Private and Personal, not printed). *Award* 3 Dec. 1804 enrolled 17 July 1806), W.R.O. 66. *Commissioners* Richard Richardson of Lincoln's Inn Fields, Mdx.; John Gale of Stert; George Barnes of Andover, Hants. *Surveyor* John Charlton of Stourton.

Lord of Manor William Wyndham of Dinton.

Rector (lay) provost and scholars of King's College, Cambridge. *Vicar* Sampson White.

Area 3,108 a. including old inclosures [2,380 a.] Fair Ground, Great and Little Hay Mead, Little Hook, Great and Little Dock Mead, Alexander's Dock Mead, Workman's Dock Mead, Beggar's Bush Field, Hocombe Field, Chisenbury Field, Flower Ditch, Slay Hill, Middle Hams, Catterly Banks, West Field, Broad Mead, North Field, Ham Field, Rich Field, Cow Down, Whiteheadge Mead.

Allotments 18. William Wyndham 1,734 a. (including lease, Stephen Buckland 109 a.; Thomas Jarvis 86 a.; copy, Thomas Hunt 153 a.; lease and copy, John Workman 139 a.; Thomas Alexander 94 a.; Thomas Compton; Samuel Newman; John Lloyd; John Smith; Roger Benner; Samuel Marchment; William Bruges; James Biffin; Sarah Coster; Levi Lampard); Thomas Alexander 92 a.; Charles Gibbs and John Adcock 175 a.; Michael Hicks Beach 45 a.; provost and scholars of King's College, Cambridge, 276 a.; Sir John Methuen Poore 31 a.; surveyors of highways; Thomas Maton; Edward Wells; Joseph Benner; churchwardens of Upavon; vicar of Upavon; overseers of Upavon; Sarah Coster; Henry Hunt; James Davidge; — Coles; Levi Lampard.

Tithes 'Those lands which paid tithe to continue to do so and those that are free to continue so'.

Roads 9 public roads, 2 public bridle ways, 13 private roads, 6 public footpaths, 2 private bridle ways.

Maps (1) Central part of parish. (2) West part and Widdington farm. (3) East part and Farm Down. Whole parish with village and allotments and acreages.

185 UPTON LOVEL [1,424 a.]

Act 55 G.III c.50 (Private). *Award* 15 April 1825 (enrolled 9 Sept. 1829), W.R.O. 139 & 140. *Commissioners* Ambrose Patient of Boyton; John Hayward of West Lavington; Joseph Phelps of Norton Bavant (replacing John Rogers of Burcombe, d. May 1820). *Surveyor* George Hayward of Devizes.

Lord of Manor John Gale Everett (succeeding William Clare).

Rector William Roles.

Area 1,500 a. (Act) [1,307 a.] Upton Marsh, Marsh Field, King Meadow, West Meadow, Nether Meadow, Cross Field, West Hill, Long Dole Meadow, East Hill.

Allotments 6. Public: 1 gravel pit 1 a. J. G. Everett 538 a. (including copy, Christopher Ingram 5 a.); devisees of Christopher Ingram 290 a.; John

Raxworthy 456 a.; rector of Upton Lovel 21 a.; Thomas Mogg.

Roads 2 public roads, 3 public driftways, 1 public bridle way, 3 private roads. Herbage allotted.

Map T. Tilbrook of Horningsham. Coloured according to allottees. Whole parish and village.

186 UPTON SCUDAMORE [2,538 a.]

Act 43 G.III c.75 (not printed). *Award* 25 Oct. 1805 (enrolled 21 Oct. 1806), W.R.O. 67. *Commissioners* Richard Richardson of Lincoln's Inn Fields, Mdx.; John Gale of Stert. *Surveyor* Thomas Crass of Lincoln's Inn Fields, Mdx.

Lord of Manor of Norridge, Thomas Thynne, marquess of Bath.

Rector Thomas Owen.

Area [1,892 a.] Norridge Hill, Norridge Common, Norridge Wood, Bourne Ditch Field, One Barrow Field, Two Barrow Field, Hay Furlong Field, Upper East Field, White Way Down, Ramscomb, Tenantry Down, Ridgeway Down, Broad Mead, Goose Nest, Court Field, Woeberry Piece, Forward Cow Down, Backward Cow Down, Cold Castle Field, Thoulston Field, Great and Little Moat Ground, Rye Bottom, Behind Town Field, Garston.

Allotments 26. Public: 1 stone pit 5 a. Marquess of Bath 308 a. (including leases, John Barter 69 a.; Robert Turner 18 a.; William Miller; John Withey); Heytesbury almshouse 91 a. (including leases, Jane Somerville and Mary Seaman 90 a.; Robert Butt); trustees of Anthony Kington 136 a. (including an allotment for glebe of Norridge parsonage); Jane Somerville and Mary Seaman 452 a.; William Temple 379 a.; Thomas Hollway 94 a.; John Pearce 183 a.; James Bayly 59 a.; Lady Hester Seymour 50 a.; Louisa Barton 44 a.; Andrew Pearce 16 a.; rector of Upton Scudamore 20 a.; Thomas Hickman; Samuel Provis; Edmund Miles; Thomas Payne; Robert Baker; John Turner; churchwardens of Upton Scudamore; Charles Lewis Phipps; John, Susannah, and Elizabeth Coope; Nathaniel Barton; John Moore; John Coward; John Eyres (the last five for estates in Corsley).

Tithes Certain rearrangements effected.

Roads 7 public roads, 3 public footpaths, 1 public bridle way, 10 private roads.

Maps Thomas Crass. (1) West part of parish. (2) East part. Whole parish and village. Allottees and acreages shown.

Schedules (1) Lands allotted, exchanged, or awarded. (2) Lands not allotted.

See also No. 189.

Notes Trustees of Anthony Kington claimed tithes (123 a.) and glebe (19 a.) belonging to the free chapel of Norridge. Marquess of Bath claimed great tithes on 67 a. belonging to the prebendary of Luxfield in Wells Cathedral and on 41 a. held under the dean and chapter of Salisbury. As these lands had been reallotted the commissioners attached the tithes to other allotments and declared certain lands to be tithe free.

187 URCHFONT AND BEECHINGSTOKE

Act 29 G.III c.18. *Award* 13 Nov. 1793 (enrolled 1 Nov. 1794), W.R.O. 37. Commissioners Richard Richardson of Devizes; John Gale of Stert; Richard Bloxham of Winterslow. *Surveyors* Benjamin Pryce and Benjamin Haynes of Salisbury.

URCHFONT [6,285 a.]

Lord of Manor William Salmon.

Rector dean and canons of Windsor. *Vicar* Henry Kent D.D.

Area 1,623 a. [1,576 a.] Wedhampton West and North Fields, Wedhampton Plain, Corset Field, North Grove, Foxley Hook, Foxley Coppice, Wickham Green, Wedhampton Down, Urchfont Green, Fore Down, Summer Down, Green Hill, Eastcott Green and Heath.

Allotments 23. Public: 1 watering place. William Salmon 695 a. (including leases, William Keetch 112 a.; copy, John Alexander 21 a.; Edward Edwards 16 a.; Stephen Powell 22 a.; Sarah Pile 26 a.; Jane Giddings 66 a.; Sarah Powell of Devizes 16 a.; Sarah Powell of Quidhampton 23 a.; John Sainsbury 20 a.; Mary Pierce 20 a.; copy and lease, Rev. Charles Gibbs 26 a.; Rev. James Rouquet 25 a.; Samuel Chapman; Elizabeth Davis; John Dean; Thomas Edwards; William Tyler; Richard Alexander; John Butcher; John Crook; Priscilla Durnford; Naomi Pile; Charles Giddings; Charles Giddings of Uphill; Roger Giddings of Cannings; Roger Giddings of Foxley; Alexander Giddings; Lucy Noyes; Ephraim Pierce; executors of Robert Pierce; Mary Pierce; John Giddings; executors of James Pierce; executors of Sarah Giddings; Sarah Pennock; Robert Sainsbury; Henry Snooke; Sarah Snooke; Elizabeth Hazell; Humphrey Giddings; Thomas Dowse; William Smith); Jacob Pleydell-Bouverie, earl of Radnor 97 a.; Teresa Titchborne 108 a. (including lease, John Jones); Richard Erle Drax Grosvenor 188 a. (including leases, Charles Giddings 22 a.; George Giddings 15 a.; Humphrey Giddings; William Macey; William Keetch; William White); Vincent Snook 64 a.; Jacob Giddings 234 a.; William Pierce 16 a.; Thomas Attwater 20 a.; John Garnett 21 a.; Thomas Lewis 22 a.; Anne Tinker 48 a.; and John Hazell; James Rouquet; executors of Seymour Wroughton; Gifford Warriner; William Crook; Elizabeth Prickter; Henry Snook; Thomas Dowse; John Sainsbury; executors of Judith Compton; dean and canons of Windsor.

Roads 12 public roads, 7 public footpaths, 24 private roads.

Maps (1) East part of parish including Wedhampton, Corset, and Yardland fields. (2) Eastcott and Eastcott Urchfont north-west of Ridgeway. (3) Eastcott and Eastcott Urchfont south-west of Ridgeway, and Wedhampton Down and Plain. Allotments distinguished by allottees' initials.

Schedule Lands and tenements in Urchfont held under William Salmon, and amount of interest or other payment to be made to William Salmon.

Notes List of allotments still tithable to the vicar; the rest to be still tithable to the rector but subject to exchanges between the two. Filk Mead (26 a.) still commonable.

BEECHINGSTOKE [891 a.]

Rector Charles Mayo.

Area 286 a. [274 a.] Gold Hill, North and Middle Fields, Drove Furlong.

Allotments 4. Dean and chapter of Winchester 161 a. (including copy, Richard Hayward 80 a.; Anne Howes 37 a.; Thomas Sawyer 34 a.; Thomas Amor); president and scholars of Corpus Christi College, Oxford, 85 a. (including lease, Joseph Gilbert 85 a.); rector of Beechingstoke 21 a.; John Walker Heneage.

Roads 4 public roads, 1 public bridle way, 1 private road, 1 public footpath.

Finance Deduction from allotments to Corpus Christi College to pay for share of expenses.

Map Village not shown.

188 WANBOROUGH [4,514 a.]

Act 19 G.III c.75. *Award* 2 June 1780 (enrolled 18 May 1781), W.R.O. 15. *Commissioners* Richard Richardson of Devizes; Rev. Thomas Shepperd D.D. of Amport, Hants; Richard Bloxham of Winterslow; Thomas Browne of Sevenhampton, Glos.; James Shipton of Marlborough. *Surveyor* Thomas Webb of Halford, Warws.

Lord of Manor of Wanborough, Samuel Pocklington; of Wardinage, president and scholars of Magdalen College, Oxford.

Rector dean and chapter of Winchester; *lessee* Samuel Pocklington. *Vicar* Christopher Fox.

Area 3,862 a. [3,715 a.]

Allotments 59. Public: 4 stone and gravel pits. Dean and chapter of Winchester 463 a.; vicar of Wanborough 165 a. (including tithes); Samuel Pocklington 636 a. (including leases, John Lawrence 39 a.; Sarah Hatt 20 a.; John Bowles 33 a.; William Warman and others 24 a.; Dorothy Edwards 47 a.; John Kent of Bourton 18 a.; Thomas Edwards 18 a.; Daniel Porter 18 a.; Robert Harding 17 a.; John Brunsdon 27 a.; John Coventry 48 a.; William Choules; John Simmonds; Benjamin Kent; John Kent of Wanborough; Charles Kent; Charles Avenell; Ralph May; copy, William Brind); Thomas Edwards 51 a.; Henry Langford 153 a.; Elizabeth Wells 204 a.; Robert Harding 66 a.; Elizabeth Smith 77 a.; John Goodinge 54 a.; William Fuidge 61 a.; Ambrose Goddard 216 a.; Peregrine Furie 222 a.; Hill Haggard 527 a.; president and scholars of Magdalen College, Oxford, 265 a. (including copy, Stephen Wells 45 a.; John Smith 19 a.; Elizabeth Smith 52 a.; Ann Sharps 23 a.; William Lea 47 a.; William Howell 15 a.; John Brind 20 a.; Ralph May; John Simmonds; Thomas Edwards; William Stout; Henry Avenell; John Eyles; Robert Harding; Edward Smith senior; Edward Smith junior; Henry Eyles; Jeremiah May); Bartholemey Tombs 33 a.; Peckham Williams 18 a.; William Stout 31 a.; trustees for Warman's children 42 a.; Thomas Nash 32 a.; Henry Avenell 32 a.; Wallinger Goodwin 27 a.; Matthew Dick 46 a.; William Smith 39 a.; John Simmonds; Michael Tombs; Henry Eyles; John Eyles; Robert Sharp; James Bendry; Mary Brind; Ann Pready; Edward Smith; Daniel Porter; John Coventry; Elizabeth Ballard; Joshua Gray; Edne Witts;

Mark Brown; John Stratton; Thomas Honeybone; Nathaniel May; George Lea; Thomas Webb; John Thorne; Richard Farmer; Edward Southby; Francis Herring; John Brind; Joseph Heath; James Goodman; Samuel Comeline; trustees of poor; Jonathan Westall; Ralph Thorn; Thomas Thorn; George Thorn; Robert Dunn; Nathaniel May. *Fencing* with allotments.

Tithes extinguished by allotments in lieu.

Roads 6 public roads, 2 public bridle ways and private roads, 23 private roads, 1 private bridle way, 11 public footpaths.

Finance £2,563 11*s.* 10¼*d.* set out in Schedule 2.

Schedules (1) Messuages, cottages, and ancient inclosures now exempt from tithes due to dean and chapter of Winchester and vicar of Wanborough by allocation of lands in lieu. (2) Proportion of the costs of inclosure and of fencing payable by each allottee.

Note Water rights set out.

189 WARMINSTER AND CORSLEY [Warminster 6,564 a., Corsley 2,785 a.]

Act 20 G.III c.36. *Award* 22 Nov. 1783, W.R.O. 23. *Commissioners* Richard Richardson of Devizes; Thomas Fricker of Longbridge Deverill; Richard Bloxham of West Dean. *Surveyor* Thomas Webb late of Halford, Warws.

Lord of Manor of Warminster, Corsley, Huntenhull, Whitbourne, and Bugley, Thomas Thynne, Viscount Weymouth; of Furnax, president and scholars of Corpus Christi College, Oxford, and guardians of the Free School of Bruton.

Rector of Warminster, dean and chapter of Salisbury; *lessee* Thomas Walter Younge. *Vicar* Millington Massey. *Rector* of Corsley, Thomas Huntingford (succeeding William Slade, dead).

Area 5,016 a. [4,668 a.] Warminster Field, West Field, Bickenham Field, Chedlanger Field, Warminster Down, Warminster Common, Clay Hill Field, Woodman Field, Boreham Field, Corsley Wood, Arn Hill Down, Norridge Wood, Henfords Marsh, Pauletts Meadow, Bugley Over and Lower Leys, Spurt Mead, Hound's Mead, Bright Mead.

Allotments 16. Rector of Warminster 783 a. (including lease, Thomas Walter Younge 783 a.); rector of Corsley 56 a.; Viscount Weymouth 1,864 a. (including leases, John Barton 27 a.; William Everett 299 a.; Jarvis House 37 a.; Solomon Hughes 39 a.; Thomas Morgan 51 a.; William Randall 236 a.; James Smith 36 a.; John Whittock 25 a.; Edward Wilton 82 a.; Charles Aldridge; Richard Aldridge; Margery Adlam; Elizabeth Ayres; William Bailey; John Lambe; Thomas Barter; John Barter; William Brock; Mary Bleak; William Younge; John Curtis; John Provis; Mary Butler; John Buckler; Thomas Cornish; John Carpenter; Mary Cary; George Cary; Richard Collins; Anne Elcott; Henry Ferris; John Ferris; Mary Halliday; Mary Hawkins; James Hancock; William Holder; James Hayes; Anne Hillier; John Hughes; John Humphry; John Knight; John Laune; John Langley; Edward Larkham; Jane Love; George Markes;

Thomas Maskelyn; George Marvin; John Maskelyn; Edward Middlecott; Solomon Mifflen; William Mussell; William Prior; William Peters; Jane Prince; Jacob Smith; John Seagram; Roger Shrapnell; Robert Turner; Henry Chivers Vince; William Walker; John Walter; William Wansboro; Pitman Warren; Joseph Webb; John Withey; Mary Webb; Robert Woodyear; Richard Wyche; William Young); prebendary of Luxfield in Wells Cathedral 225 a. (including lease, Viscount Weymouth 225 a.); vicar of Warminster 138 a.; prebendary of Warminster in Salisbury Cathedral 184 a. (including lease, Benjamin and James Ludlow 184 a.); John Coope and Elizabeth Jesser 62 a.; Edward Middlecott 358 a. (including Mary Bleek; John Goodfellow; Benjamin Harrington; Lewis Rogers; William Wilton; John Lambe; Edward Miles); William Slade 98 a.; Pitman Warren 115 a.; William Buckler 631 a. (including Robert Ford; William Hinton; John Haines; Jane Lawrence; Jane Love; Sarah Minety; William Bailey; John Lambe; John Curtis; John Provis; Lewis Rogers; George Wansey; William Wansey; John Skinner; John Barter); president and scholars of Corpus Christi College, Oxford, and guardians of the Free School of Bruton 122 a. (including John Wansy 102 a.; John Langley; Mary Marsh; Edward Middlecott; John Seagram; William Slade; John Slade; Edward Wilton; William Wilton); prior and brethren of St. John's Hospital, Wilton; feoffees of St. Lawrence's chapel; president and scholars of Eton College. Allotment to all owners of common rights in Norridge Wood of 21 a. (in Norridge Wood). *Fencing* to be erected by allottees; vicar of Warminster's and rector of Corsley's to be at general expense.

Tithes Allotments in place of rectorial and vicarial tithes, and rent-charge for those with insufficient lands.

Roads 12 public roads, 1 public bridle way and private road, 56 private roads. Herbage allotted.

Finance by sale of lands deducted from allotments to dean and chapter of Salisbury and the prebendary of Luxfield, and the rest by rate.

Maps Thomas Webb of Warminster. (1) Corsley area. (2) Norridge Wood and east part of Corsley. (3) Area south of map 2 and stretching to county boundary between Longleat and detached part of Norton Bavant. (4) Sambourne and Warminster Common. (5) Boreham and Battlesbury. (6) Warminster Field. (7) Warminster Down. (8) Pit Mead and Moothill Farm. (9) Warminster Town. Tithable inclosures coloured green, allotments outlined in grey. Whole parish and town with a few minor exceptions shown.

Schedules (1) 13 schedules of proportions payable for repair of private roads. (2) Old inclosures exonerated from payment of tithes by deduction of lands from allotments. (3) Old inclosures exonerated by money payment. (4) Old inclosures remaining tithable. (5) Houses and gardens in the town not included in foregoing schedules. (6) Lands tithe-free by prescription.

See also Nos. 21 and 186.

Notes Allotments in place of lands formerly in Upton Scudamore to be in Upton Scudamore in future. Rights of drowning and duties of repair of hatches in the steam from Warminster to Smallbrook Mill determined.

190 WESTBURY AND BRATTON AND DILTON

Act 42 G.III c.79. *Award* 29 July 1808 (enrolled 15 Aug. 1809), W.R.O. V 76. *Commissioners* Richard Richardson of London; Jacob Sturge of Westbury on Trym, Bristol; Thomas Singer of Berkley, Som. *Surveyor* Thomas Davis the younger of Horningsham.

WESTBURY AND DILTON [11,900 a.]

Lord of Manor of Westbury, Montagu Bertie, earl of Abingdon [but see *V.C.H. Wiltshire*, viii. 148].

Vicar Robert Denison.

Area [3,790 a.] Allmarsh, Stone Acre, Low Field, Middle Mead, Coney Knoll, Lot Mead, Red Pit Common, Great and Little Court Field, Brook Common, Ham Field, North Leys Common, Dilton Lower Marsh Common, Neates Grove, Chalford Sands, Madbrook Field, Lower Marsh, Shallow Wagon Mead, Heywood Common, West Woods, Black Dog Woods, High Trees, Hawkridge Common, Westbury Common, Stormers Green, Middle Grip Tyning, Grass Acres, Pound Knap, The Gallery, Westbury East Field, Forehead Lands, Charcoal Bushes, Five Lords Common, Row Moor Common, Four Hundred Down, Thirteen Hundred Down, Bayly's Hollow, Wood Lane Common, Venn Common, Sandy Field, Biss Hill, Westbury Leigh Upper Field, Hysomley Field, Titford Field, Bremeridge Common.

Allotments 154. Public: 5 watering places 5 a.; 2 stone pits 11 a. Earl of Abingdon 244 a. (including lease, Ebenezer Smith 20 a.; Richard Bourne; James Humphries; William Hughes; Abraham Ludlow; John Matravers; Elizabeth Matravers; William Vine); Abraham Ludlow 599 a. (including leases, Henry Melhuish 40 a.; Thomas Henry Hele Phipps; earl of Abingdon; Joseph and Jane Gawen; Mary Hales; 76 a. sale allotments); Messrs. White and Gale 180 a. (including leases, executors of Samuel Bourne; James Singer; copy, William Austin; Sarah Eden; John Rolf; Ebenezer Smith; Sarah Withers); John Matravers 183 a. (including leases, Nathaniel Everett 114 a.; Robert Abraham; Drew Townsend); Thomas Thynne, marquess of Bath 361 a. (including leases, John Barter; Christopher Dunning; Thomas Glass; William Reeves; James Silcox; devisees of Mary Warren); executors of William Burgess 137 a.; Thomas Peckham Phipps 113 a. (including lease, Joseph Wheeler); Charles Lewis Phipps 384 a. (including lease, James Phipps); James Harris 60 a.; Simon Hiscocks 71 a.; John Hooper 80 a. (including lease, Joseph and Jane Gawen 80 a.); Joseph and Jane Gawen 67 a.; Thomas Henry Hele Phipps 80 a. (including leases, John Mills; Mary Bartlett; William Grant); Edward Moore 87 a. (including lease, William Paviour; copy, Abraham Ludlow 27 a.; Richard Bourne 21 a.; Joseph and Jane Gawen 17 a.; Susannah Haynes; John Grant; Joanna Ferris); Joseph Ford 152 a.; John Whittaker 203 a. (including 91 a. sale allotments); Stephen Applegate 30 a.; Richard Bourne 34 a.; Gilbert Turner 25 a.; executors of Richard Kebby 41 a.; Susanna Haynes 24 a.; Thomas Meech 19 a.; executors of Henry Blatch 22 a.; Edward Frowd Seagram 19 a.; vicar of Westbury 24 a.; Sarah Woodyear 35 a.; churchwardens of Westbury 25 a.; Samuel Provis 15 a.; Edmund Hooper 23 a.; William Lanham 15 a.; James Carpenter 19 a.; Daniel Clutterbuck 15 a.; William Vine 15 a.; William Austin; James Applegate; William Ball; John Barter; Thomas Barter; Philip Blatch; Henry Blatch; Roger Townsend; William Wilkins; John Pearce; Hannah Pearce; Elizabeth Patient; Arthur Paviour; George Pearce; John Paviour; Nicholas Parsons; John Parsons; David Quant; Thomas Burges; James Phipps; William Phipps; Elizabeth Phipps; Whatley Paviour; executors of William Wansey; Ann Randall; James Rymell; Benjamin Roberts; William Smith; James Shawl; executors of Robert Tucker; James Humphries; John Hall; Richard Harris; Rev. Thomas Cripps; William Hughes; Cottle House; John Harris; Thomas Hall; John Hooper; Isaac Hillman; widow Hewitt; Joel Hague; Henrietta Hawkins; John Hayter; William Vine; Thomas Jefferies; John Kebby; devisees of Abraham Ludlow of Bristol; William Fripp; June Fricker; George Fisher; James Glover; William Gerrish; Samuel Greenhill; George Golding; John Grant; William Grant; Thomas Glass; executors of Robert Tucker; executors of John Turner; Henry Wansey; William Hooper; William Hooper of Dilton; James Lanfear; William Matravers; Nathaniel Everett; Edward Moore; James Mines; George Marvin; Henry Blatch; Thomas Lewis; Thomas Lowe; Elizabeth Millard; trustees of old meeting house in Westbury; trustees of Baptist meeting house in Leigh; trustees of old meeting house in Chapmanslade; Stephen Nokes; Henry Newman; Thomas Tregonwell Napier; William Open; William Smith; John Crosby; Mr. Coles and others; John Currier; Nicholas Cockell; Mrs. Cockell; Elizabeth Cowdall; Shadrach Cook; Robert Carpenter; George Compton; Mary Drewitt; George Dyer; Nathaniel Davies; Abraham Dew; Samuel Enly; Bryan Edwards; William Bristow; John Barnes; executors of Samuel Bourne; Joseph Ball; William Baily; George Bigwood; Stephen Brown; Hannah Chapman; Samuel Stafford; John Stafford; James Singer; Isaac Tucker; Cornelius Townsend; Joseph Wheeler; Martha Willis; John Wilkins; Rev. John Watts; Joseph Watts; Mary Wereat; John Watts; William Wilkins; John Waldron; Daniel Webb. *Fencing* to be at expense of proprietors, and boundary watercourses to be scoured by them also.

Roads 10 public roads, 114 private footpaths, 17 public footpaths.

Finance 109 sale allotments to 73 persons, £7,061 12*s.* 2*d.*

Maps (1) Dilton, Dilton Marsh, and west part of parish. (2) Chalford, Hawkeridge, Storridge. (3) South part of parish. (4) Town map and Dilton Marsh. Schedule attached to each map with allotment number, proprietor, field names, and acreage. Arable outlined in red, meadow and pasture in blue, downs commons and woody wastes in green.

Schedule (1) Name of road and number on map. (2) Superintendent for collection of money. (3) Number of allotment chargeable with repairs. (4) Person to whom allotment is awarded. (5) Share each person is to contribute. (6) Road schedule with contributory shares for (a) Westbury, (b) Bratton.

Note Commoners' feeding rights in Black Dog woods bought out by marquess of Bath for £914 14*s.*

BRATTON [3,791 a.]

Lord of Manor marquess of Bath.

Area [2,696 a.] West Meadow, Withey Mead, Sand Field, Cow Down, Hill Field, Langcomb Botton, Low Field, Church Hill.

Allotments 20. Marquess of Bath 615 a. (including leases, executors of Ann Ballard 22 a.; Joseph Flower 36 a.; John Neville 41 a.; Edward Seagram 156 a.; John Smith 16 a.; Thomas Williams 112 a.; Philip Whitaker 44 a.; executors of John Whitaker 152 a.; Caroline Whitaker 16 a.; Philip Blatch; Thomas Brown; Philip Peplar; Sarah Price; Henry Smith; Mary Whitaker); Richard Erle Drax Grosvenor 833 a.; John Neville 76 a.; Charles Lewis Phipps 93 a.; Philip Whitaker 803 a.; Montagu Bertie, earl of Abingdon 130 a.; Joseph Flower 56 a.; Mary Attwater 18 a.; Edward Frowd Seagram 36 a.; William Whitaker 20 a.; Philip Blatch; churchwardens of Bratton; Thomas Dew; Joseph Emm; Joseph Ford; Simon Hiscocks; John Matravers; Charles Mitchell; executors of John Whitaker; Thomas Whitaker.

Roads 3 public footpaths, 15 private roads, 1 public footpath.

Finance See Westbury.

Map with schedule giving allotment number, proprietor, field name, and acreage.

Schedule Bratton private roads with shares of contributors and superintendent to collect moneys.

191 WHITEPARISH [6,427 a.]

Whelpley manor

Act 42 G.III c.85 (Private and Personal, not printed). (Whiteparish and West Grimstead). *Award* 19 Feb. 1805 (enrolled 15 Jan. 1806), W.R.O. 64. *Commissioners* Francis Webb of Salisbury; Thomas Charlton of Stourhead; Richard Richardson of Lincoln's Inn Fields, Mdx. *Surveyor* William Tubb of Fisherton Anger.

Lord of Manor of Whelpley, John Maurice Eyre.

Area 149 a. including roads [146 a.] Royal Field, Triple or Tipple Field Elm or Ellon Field, Southern Field.

Allotments 11. John Maurice Eyre 37 a. (including leases, Stephen Blandford; John Griffin; John Lush; Jane Luffman; Frances Penny); George Yalden Fort 51 a.; Henry Dawkins 26 a.; David Park 16 a.; Robert Bristow; Richard Figes; John Hillier; devisees of Henry Eyre; devisees of Henry Dench; Dorothy White; Moses Welstead. *Fencing* in the award, and to be protected from sheep for twenty years.

Roads 1 public road, 3 public footpaths, 1 private road and public footpath, 3 private roads. Herbage allotted.

Finance £503 10*s*. 11*d*., proportions to be paid said to be in a schedule, which is missing.

Map William Tubb of Salisbury 1804. New allotments only, with allottees and acreages.

See also No. 98.

192 WILCOT [2,668 a.]
Oare tithing and part of Huish
Act 39 G.III c.18. *Award* 3 Dec. 1803, W.R.O. Acc 425/1 (copy made in 1831). *Commissioner* John Gale.
Rector Charles Mayo.
Area [395 a.]. Rainscombe Field, Huish Field, Broom Piece, How Croft, Oare Down, Great Sandy Leaze.
Allotments 10. John Goodman 150 a.; Hester Edmonds 54 a.; Jane Frederick 61 a.; John Pontin 45 a.; John Reeves 35 a.; trustees of Somerset charity at Froxfield 41 a. (including copy, Hester Edmonds 41 a.); George Benger; John Banning; representatives of Richard Edmonds; St. John's College, Cambridge.
Tithes Some exchanges of tithes only. John Pontin also a tithe-holder.
Roads 3 public roads, 1 public bridle way, 4 public footpaths, 7 private roads; 3 footpaths stopped up. Herbage to neighbouring allottees only.
Map 1803. Acreages, allottees, and some field names shown. Footpaths through old inclosures shown. Oare tithing only.

193 WILSFORD (North Wilts.) [1,310 a.]
Manningford Bohun tithing and manor.
Act Private, 42 G.III c.49. *Award* 13 Feb. 1805 (enrolled 24 Jan. 1806), W.R.O. 65. *Commissioners* John Gale of Stert; John Tredgold of Winchester, Hants; George Barnes of Andover, Hants. *Surveyor* George Barnes of Andover.
Lord of Manor William Wyndham.
Area 958 a. including roads 24 a. [934 a.] Lawn Field, Woodbridge Field, Upper and Lower Field, The Down, New Mead, Woodborough Ground, Bottlesford Mead.
Allotments 4. Public: 1 chalk pit 1 a. William Wyndham 899 a. (including lease, John Alexander 41 a.; copy, Elizabeth Alexander 85 a.; John Chandler 48 a.; S. Holloway 33 a.; W. Holloway 47 a.; lease and copy, J. E. Arundell 50 a.; W. Edwards; Stephen Waite; Gratiana Waite; William Dyke); John Alexander 34 a.; surveyors of highways.
Roads 8 public roads, 6 public footpaths, 4 private roads. Herbage allotted.
Finance £1,265 3*s*. 3*d*. by rate on all allottees.
Map with schedule of allotments and allottees distinguishing copy, free, and leasehold.
See also No. 194.
Note Boundary between manor of Manningford Bohun and parish of Manningford Bruce straightened, and consequent exchanges between parishes confirmed.

194 WILSFORD (or Wilsford Dauntsey) (North Wilts.) [1,759 a.]
Act 41 G.III c.113 (Private and Personal, not printed). *Award* 14 Sept. 1808 (enrolled 12 Sept. 1809), W.R.O. 78. *Commissioners* John Gale of Stert;

John Butcher of Easton. *Surveyor* William Tubb of Fisherton Anger.

Lord of Manor Francis Dugdale Astley.

Vicar Edmund Benson.

Area 1,618 a. excl. roads 19 a. [1,602 a] Middle, West and East Sand Field, Farm Field, Neatham, Sheep Street, Cuttenham Mead, Clay Field, The Down, West Meadow, Pookshipton Mead, Northbrook Meadow, Catbane Meadow, Horsepin Common, Oxlease Common.

Allotments 6. Francis Dugdale Astley 1,563 a. (including leases, Thomas Hayter 518 a.; John Langland 24 a.; copy, Mary Jarvis 72 a.; William Chandler 30 a.; Mary Springbatt 20 a.; lease and copy, John Box 66 a.; Edward Tapper; Samuel Strong; Richard Hayward); Mary Springbatt 24 a.; Sir John Poore; Joseph Gilbert; devisees of James Sutton; vicar of Wilsford.

Tithes on two allotments of 9 a. and 1 a. allotted to Charles Mayo rector of Beechingstoke in place of tithes on other fields, which were allotted to vicar of Wilsford. Tithes on three allotments 38 a., 49 a., and 27 a. allotted to George Bissett, rector of Dauntsey, in place of tithes on 103 a. held previously. Tithes on 114 a. belonged to rector of Dauntsey, and the rest to hospital of St. Nicholas, Salisbury.

Roads 5 public roads, 3 public bridle ways, 2 public footpaths, 2 public bridle ways and private roads, 8 private roads (including a private drove 66 feet wide). Herbage to neighbouring allottees only.

Map 1808. Whole parish and village. Allottees shown. Old inclosures green.

See also No. 193.

Note Allotments in place of mowing rights.

195 WILTON, BURCOMBE, FUGGLESTONE, AND NETHERHAMPTON

Act 6 G.IV c.21 (Private). *Award* 16 Jan. 1860 (enrolled 19 Jan. 1860), W.R.O. V 179. *Commissioners* William Robson of Wilton (replacing William Woodcock, d. 1843); Richard Nightingale (replacing Richard Nightingale of Eling, Hants, d. 1847). *Umpire* Thomas Davis.

Lord of Manor of Wilton, Bulbridge, Ditchampton, Burcombe, Netherhampton, and Fugglestone St. Peter, Robert Herbert, earl of Pembroke (succeeding George Herbert, earl of Pembroke, d. 1827).

Rector of Wilton and chapelry of Netherhampton, vicar of Bulbridge, and rector of Ditchampton, Richard Chermside (succeeding Henry Hetley); of Fugglestone, Wellesley Pole Piggott (succeeding William Coxe).

WILTON [1,855 a.]

Area [1,020 a].

Allotments 5. Public: 1 chalk pit 1 a. in Netherhampton. Earl of Pembroke 998 a. (including the deer park); prior, brethren, and sisters of the hospital of St. Giles; prior, brethren, and sisters of hospital of St. John; rector of Wilton. *Fencing* in award and with allotments.

Roads 1 public road, 1 public bridle way, 1 private road.

Map Poole and Newman of Sherborne 1859. Allotments only, enlarged map of Wilton, and detached allotment in Bishopstone.
Notes Lord Pembroke's maps used for the inclosure. Large number of exchanges mostly of old inclosures.

BURCOMBE
North Burcombe tithing [1,448 a.]
Area [409 a.] Chalk Piece, Bake Field, Barnwell Mead, Gray's Mead, West Field, Middle Field.
Allotments 2. Earl of Pembroke 296 a. (including lease, James Rogers 296 a.); master, brethren, and sisters of hospital of St. John 113 a. *Fencing* in award and with allotments.
Roads 1 public bridle way, 3 private roads.
Map Poole and Newman of Sherborne 1859.
Schedule Rate per £ for making and repairing private roads Nos. 2 and 4.

FUGGLESTONE ST. PETER
Area [547 a.].
Allotments 5. Earl of Pembroke 428 a. (including lease, Thomas Thring); dean and chapter of Salisbury 53 a. (including lease, Rev. Thomas Protheroe 53 a.); Rev. Nixon Hooper 27 a.; master, brethren, and sisters of hospital of St. Giles in Wilton 36 a.; rector of Fugglestone.
Roads 3 public roads, 5 private roads, 1 public footpath.
Map Poole and Newman of Sherborne 1859.
Schedule Rate for repairing private roads.
See also No. 97.
Note Six hatches to be kept in repair by owners of meadows irrigated.

NETHERHAMPTON
Area [730 a.].
Allotments 3. Public: chalk pit 1 a. Earl of Pembroke 723 a. (including leases, John Woodcock 692 a.; John Rowden 24 a.; Henry Swayne); rector of Wilton. *Fencing* in award and with allotments.
Roads 3 public roads, 1 private road.
See also No. 143.

196 WINGFIELD [1,389 a.]
Wingfield and Rowley
Act 3. G.IV c. 9 (Private). *Award* 21 Nov. 1823, W.R.O. 124, 125, & 126. *Commissioner* Young Sturge, who affirmed. *Surveyor* Jacob Player Sturge.
Lord of Manor Thomas Timbrell.
Rector Thomas Spencer of Bristol.
Area [76 a.] Upper Common, Lower Common.
Allotments 16. Thomas Timbrell 16 a. (including 2 a. for rights of the soil); Eleazer Pickwick 15 a.; John Guillemard; Thomas Stillman; Henry Shrapnell; Gilbert Rotton; John Coryton; John C. Hobhouse; Thomas Morris; rector of Wingfield; John Bailey; Thomas Bracher; Rev. Benjamin

Richardson; Joseph Silcocks; James Bethell; Edward Lawrence. *Fencing* general.

Roads 1 public road, 9 private roads, 4 private footpaths, 6 private roads and public footpaths, 5 public footpaths.

Finance Sale allotments (11 a.).

Map Several detached pieces, allotments numbered only. Secondary map shows Wingfield–Farleigh boundary, which was determined by the commissioner.

Schedule Road rate, proprietor, allotments, amount of rate.

See also No. 24.

197 WINTERBOURNE DAUNTSEY [1,190 a.]

Act General, 8 & 9 Vic c.118, and annual inclosure Act (1848). *Award* 17 Feb. 1851 (enrolled 1 April 1851), W.R.O. 171. *Valuer* Francis Attwood of Salisbury.

Area [438 a.] South and North Fields, Little Field.

Allotments 5. Miss Mary Skinner 83 a.; John Henry Campbell Wyndham 324 a.; George Burtt; Ecclesiastical Commissioners; churchwardens for the labouring poor. *Fencing* in the award; detailed instructions about the making of fences.

Roads 1 public road; 3 roads stopped up.

Maps (1) Allotments. (2) Common fields with proprietors and acreages. Whole parish shown but not the village.

Note Allotment to the churchwardens for the labouring poor of 5 a. valued against price of wheat, barley, and oats.

198 WINTERBOURNE EARLS [1,720 a.]

Act 35 G.III c.16 (Winterbourne Earls and Allington). *Award* 6 April 1796 (enrolled 4 Dec. 1798), W.R.O. 54. *Commissioners* Richard Richardson of Bath; Francis Webb of Salisbury; John Hodding of Salisbury. *Surveyor* William Tubb of Fisherton Anger.

Lord of Manor of Hurdcott, Henry Penruddocke Wyndham; of Winterbourne Earls [none stated but Nicholas Nicholas had an allotment for rights of the soil in lands which he leased from the bishop of Salisbury].

Prebendary Humphry Sumner; *lessee* Nicholas Elliott.

Area 1,423 a. including roads 35 a. [1388 a.] West and East Side Fields, West and East Side Down, Boney's West Close, Dockey Ham, Hurdicote East and West Side Fields, Broad Mead, Harding's Mead.

Allotments 5. Bishop of Salisbury 514 a. (including lease, Nicholas Nicholas 514 a.); Henry Penruddocke Wyndham 380 a.; Nicholas Nicholas 329 a. (including copy, Nicholas Elliott 154 a.; Frances Tanner 62 a.; H. P. Wyndham 58 a.; Robert Woods 31 a.; Betty Boney; John Mundy; James Combes); prebendary of Winterbourne for glebe 131 a. (including lease, Nicholas Elliott 131 a.); master of hospital of St. John, Wilton 34 a. (including lease, H. P. Wyndham 34 a.).

Roads 10 public roads, 1 public bridle way, 4 private roads. Herbage allotted to (1) H. P. Wyndham and owners of freehold farm in Winterbourne Earls (2) Nicholas Nicholas and owners of Winterbourne Farm and neighbouring allottees.

Notes Various holdings by copy under Nicholas Nicholas who in turn held by lease from the bishop of Salisbury. Directions for watering the meadows set out and days of the week when owners can use the water. In West Side Down, allotments to Frances Turner, Elizabeth Bowles, and Robert Woods to be fed in common and a shepherd appointed and a ram acquired by them.

199 WINTERBOURNE GUNNER [1,530 a.]

Act General, 8 & 9 Vic. c.118. *Award* 19 Nov. 1853 (enrolled 30 Dec. 1853), W.R.O. 175. *Valuer* Francis Attwood of Salisbury.

Lord of Manor Anna Evans wife of Rev. Francis Evans.

Rector Charles John Coleman.

Area [552 a.] Hookland, Great Field, Dunch Plot Field, West Field.

Allotments 6. Trustees of Anna Evans 479 a.; Rev. Francis Evans 60 a.; rector of Winterbourne Gunner; Richard Wilson; John Wyndham; labouring poor 3 a. changed into a rent-charge of £3. *Fencing* with allotments.

Roads 1 public road.

Map West Field and Down. Village shown.

Notes Allotment for labouring poor calculated on price of wheat, barley, and oats. John Wyndham consented that certain lands allotted to him under the Winterbourne Dauntsey award be included in this award and be transferred from Winterbourne Dauntsey to Winterbourne Gunner, and one allotment transferred from Winterbourne Gunner to Winterbourne Dauntsey, thus straightening the boundary.

200 WINTERBOURNE MONKTON [1,879 a.]

Act 53 G.III c.178. *Award* 28 June 1815, P.R.O. C 54/9626 (photocopy in W.R.O.(. *Commissioners* John Davis of Bloxham, Oxon.; Richard Richardson of London. *Surveyor* Thomas Phillips of Andover.

Lord of Manor Edward Leyborne Popham.

Vicar James Mayo.

Area 965 a. (Act) [948 a.] Middle Field, South Field, Long Wor Field, Barwick Side Field.

Allotments 8. Public: 1 chalk pit 2 a. Vicar of Winterbourne Monkton 61 a. (including tithes and glebe); Edward Leyborne Popham 453 a. (including tithes; lease, John Hitchcock 67 a.); Charles Hitchcock 150 a. (including great tithes in Winterbourne Monkton farm 221 a.); John Brown 218 a.; John Hitchcock 50 a.; Stephen Stiles; Sarah Pearce. *Fencing* general and sometimes with allotments.

Tithes Allotments in lieu. Vicar entitled to rectorial tithes on 100 a. and vicarial tithes on whole parish except 640 a. Charles Hitchcock entitled to rectorial [and vicarial?] tithes on 640 a. (Winterbourne Monkton farm). Edward Leyborne Popham entitled to the rest of the [rectorial] tithes. [The arrangements are not absolutely clear.] Vicar entitled also to £10 a year from impropriator of Avebury. Money payments due from homesteads with insufficient land to make an allotment.

Roads 2 public roads, 7 private roads (to be repaired by neighbouring allottees).

Map 1815. Whole parish including the village. Allottees and acreages.

Schedule for repair of private roads. Proprietor and proportion of £14 payable.

201 WINTERBOURNE STOKE [3,572 a.]

Act 50 G.III c.58 (not printed) (Winterbourne Stoke and Stapleford). *Award* 28 April 1812 (enrolled 22 Jan. 1818), W.R.O. 104. *Commissioner* Richard Richardson of London. *Surveyor* Nicholas Webb of Hatherop, Glos.

Lord of Manor Alexander Baring.

Vicar James Eyre.

Area 2,671 a. [2,659 a.] Mill Pond Common, Lammas Mead, Breach Field, Tenantry Sheep Down, Cranham Hill Field, Fore Down, Cow Down, Cheswell Field, Parsonage Field, High Down, North Field, Hyde Field, Westbrook Field, Westbrook Common, Small Mead, Ham Field, Bourton Mead, Woolhams, Two Barrows Field, Long Barrow Field, Horse Down, Ranhams Mead.

Allotments 11. Alexander Baring 2,621 a. (including leases, William Godwin 81 a.; George Kellow the younger 107 a.; George Kellow and Mary Gibbs 135 a.; George Kellow victualler 93 a.; George Griffin Pearce 126 a.; John Richards 100 a.; copy, Rev. Robert Collins Kellow 283 a.; Martha Kellow 80 a.; John Chalk; John Downton; George Dyer; George Grant; John Pearce; James Roles); Henry Biggs 21 a.; churchwardens of Winterbourne Stoke; vicar of Winterbourne Stoke; Hampden Hely; Charles Hibberd; Mary Cripps; churchwardens of Maddington; Jonathan Flower; Elizabeth Godwin; churchwardens of Shrewton. *Fencing* general.

Roads 4 public roads, 2 public footpaths, 1 private road and public bridle way, 9 private roads.

Finance Expenses paid by Alexander Baring whose tenants are to reimburse him at 5 per cent by scheduled amounts to be added to their rents.

Map Late Thomas Crass of London. Whole parish with village. Allottees and acreages shown. Water meadows intermixed with those of Rollestone, Maddington, and Orcheston. Schedule with inclosures.

Notes Chalk pits shown on map but not in the award. Water-meadows to be watered in the usual manner. Certain areas in Tenantry Sheep Down to be fed in common and permitted numbers of sheep are laid down.

202 GREAT WISHFORD [1,679 a.]

Agreement 3 May 1809 between earl of Pembroke and 13 others. *Award* 20 Dec. 1809 (enrolled 14 May 1810), W.R.O. 81. *Commissioners* John Seagrim of Wilton; Christopher Ingram of Amesbury. *Surveyor* John Charlton of Stourton.

Lord of Manor George Herbert, earl of Pembroke.
Rector James Birch.
Area 1,479 a. [1,424 a.] East and West Tenantry Down, Abbey Mead, Mill Mead, Rook Hay Meadow, Priory Mead, Broad Close, Middle Field, King's Mead, West and South Field, Farm Down.
Allotments 4. Sir Edward Knatchbull 413 a. (including lease, George Rowden 413 a.); earl of Pembroke 994 a. (including leases, Solomon Dredge 185 a.; James Randall 389 a.; Mary Hinwood 112 a.; William Dredge 45 a.; John Fitzgerald 31 a.; Mary Eve 15 a.; Hannah Alexander 40 a.; copy, James Birch 29 a.; William Winter 32 a.; George Petty 15 a.; Jane Eve 31 a.; Henry Newman; John Rowden; Alice Trubridge; Ann Turner; Richard Carpenter; Frances Dredge; John Trowbridge; William Scammell; Richard Macklin); rector of Great Wishford 16 a.; vicar and churchwardens. *Fencing* with allotments.
Roads 4 public roads, 2 public footpaths, 3 private roads. Herbage allotted.
Map John Charlton of Stourton 1809. Whole parish shown including village but not including Grovely.
Notes Signatories agreed that their rights in Grovely should be extinguished. Allotments to earl of Pembroke for his farm in South Newton. Directions for watering King's Mead from 1 Nov. to 5 April. Repairs of Stapleford hatches to be borne by allottees in proportion to the yearly value of their allotments.

203 WOOTTON BASSETT [5,126 a.]

Woodshaw, Greenhill, and Nore Marsh tithings.
Act 1 G.IV c.12 (Private). *Award* 24 April 1822 (enrolled 14 Oct. 1822), W.R.O. 118. *Commissioner* Decimus Godson of London.
Lord of Manor Thomas Villiers, earl of Clarendon.
Rector (lay) earl of Clarendon and Robert Hughes of Salthrop. *Vicar* Thomas Hyde Ripley.
Area [72 a.] Greenhill Common, Nore Marsh Common, Dunnington Common, Trickles Lane, Pudding Lane, Woodshaw Common.
Allotments 14. Earl of Clarendon 50 a.; Rev. Robert Ashe; Sir Robert Buxton Bt.; Mary Cruse; Drax Grosvenor; Jasper Maskelyne; William Parham; Joseph Pitt; Jacob Pleydell-Bouverie, earl of Radnor; vicar of Wootton Bassett; Elizabeth Rumboll; Richard Smith; Wadham Wyndham; William Wiggins. *Fencing* with allotments.
Roads 5 public roads, 11 public footpaths, 1 private road and public bridle way, 7 private roads.
Map Decimus Gordon 1821. Allotments numbered, village indicated only.
Notes Commissioner to be paid £3 3*s.* a day. Encroachments within the last twenty years included.

204 WOOTTON RIVERS [1,200 a.]

Act General, 6 & 7 W.IV c.115. *Award* 21 Nov. 1842 (enrolled 17 Oct. 1844), W.R.O. 163. *Commissioners* John Iveson of Shepperton; Richard Stratton of Upavon. *Surveyor* William Stanley of Burbage Wharf.

Lord of Manor master, fellows, and scholars of St. John's College, Cambridge.

Rector Thomas Stone D.D.

Area [135 a.].

Allotments 4. St. John's College, Cambridge, 121 a. (including Philip Neale 73 a.; Thomas Banning 20 a.; Thomas Somerset 26 a.; Samuel Pickett; executors of James Scrivens); trustees of Charles Brudenell-Bruce, marquess of Ailesbury; rector of Wootton Rivers; Edmund Somerset. *Fencing* general.

Roads 3 private roads.

Map 1842. Inclosed area only. Village not shown. Allotments numbered and acreage given.

205 WROUGHTON [6,061 a.]

Wroughton in Elstub hundred

Act 35 G.III c.40. *Award* 6 Oct. 1796 (enrolled 26 March 1798), W.R.O. 47 and Acc 551/114. *Commissioners* John Tredgold of Chilbolton, Hants; Richard Davis of Lewknor, Oxon.; John Gale of Stert. *Surveyors* William Church and Edward Kelsey of Lewknor.

Rector Edmund Ferrers (entitled to the great tithes on that part of the parish in Elstub). *Vicar* James Merrest or Merest. *Lessee* (of both rectory and vicarage) William Codrington.

Area 2,097 a. [2,062 a.] Great and Little Upper Fields, Further and Hither Walley, Crow Bridge, Cow Common, West Field, Prior's Hill, Lot Meadow, Marsh Common, Bodge Field, Market Hill, Brook Lains, Wanshot, Denby's Linches, Ladder Hill Field.

Allotments 37. [There is no reference in the award to the lord of the manor, no allotment for rights of the soil, and although there are references to copy and leasehold tenure there is nothing in the award to say under whom they were held.] Rector of Wroughton 578 a. (glebe and tithes); lease, John Evans 392 a.; copy, Stephen Buckland 64 a.; William Codrington 26 a.; John Martin 44 a.; Morris King 50 a.; William Hill 25 a.; Mary Seymour 21 a.; James Buckner 23 a.; Mary Buckland 25 a.; Daniel Dick 39 a.; Elizabeth Franklin 18 a.; Mary Bendry 19 a.; Elizabeth Phelps 38 a.; Walter Brind 28 a.; copy and free, Jacob Picket 144 a.; John Duck 60 a.; Edward Brown 128 a.; Richard Read 51 a.; Samuel Austin junior 69 a.; John Seymour 45 a.; vicar of Wroughton 29 a.; John Dore Bendry 41 a.; William Austin; John Austin; John Bedford; Joseph Matthews; Samuel Austin senior; Isaac White; George Carpenter; William Sadler; Anne Picket; Richard Austin; John Mills; William Shortland; Merriam Cook; Edward Tarrant; surveyor of highways. *Fencing* by allottees including the rector.

Tithes extinguished by deduction from allotments, the rest chargeable and some still tithable.

Roads 5 public roads, 3 public bridle ways and private roads, 6 private roads, 1 public bridle way, 1 private bridle way, 3 public footpaths, 6 private footpaths.

Map R. Davis of Lewknor 1795 (W.R.O. Acc 551/114). Allotments numbered and allottees shown. Area shown: Wroughton excl. Overtown,

Elcombe, and Westlecot. Village shown and some field names. Schedule with proprietor, freehold, copyhold, total, and exchanges.

See also No. 206.

Notes Trees planted near the roads not to be closer than 50 yards apart. Watercourse from Alexander's Hedge to Duck Pools and Westlecot to be kept scoured by neighbouring allottees.

206 WROUGHTON

Elcombe manor in Wroughton and Uffcott tithing in Broad Hinton

Act 36 G.III c.26. *Award* 27 May 1797 (enrolled 4 May 1798), W.R.O. 48 and Acc 551/115. *Commissioners* John Chamberlain of Cropredy, Oxon.; Richard Davis of Lewknor, Oxon.; John Gale of Stert. *Surveyor* James Jennings of Somerton, Oxon.

Lord of Manor of Elcombe, governors of the Charterhouse.

Rector Edmund Ferrers; *lessee* William Codrington. *Vicar* James Merrest. *Vicar* of Broad Hinton, Thomas Henry Hume.

Area 1,296 a. [1,238 a.] Wroughton: Hackpen Field, The Marsh, Markham, Little South Field, Cotlands, Tithe Acres, Meer Mead, Horsehay, Black Croft, Lammas Meadow, The Linches, Splint Hill, Water Quarry, Hollow Way Acres, Elcombe Down. Uffcott: Crossway Piece, West Field, Uffcott East and Middle Fields, Uffcott Down, Dean Piece, Milk Hill Meadow.

Allotments 13. Rector of Wroughton 129 a. (including lease, William Codrington 128 a.); master of the hospital of St. Nicholas, Salisbury, 97 a. (including lease, Frances Post 97 a.); governors of the Charterhouse 788 a. (including leases, Thomas Richens 79 a.; Anthony Bathe 49 a.; Matthew Vivash 16 a.); chancellor of Salisbury cathedral 58 a. (including lease, John Bedford 58 a.); dean and chapter of Salisbury 61 a. (including lease, James Garrett 61 a.); vicar of Wroughton 18 a.; vicar of Broad Hinton 22 a.; Isaac White 28 a.; William Sadler; Matthew Vivash; Stephen Buckland; Charles Ruddle; provost and college of Eton. *Fencing* with allotments.

Tithes extinguished by deduction from allotments. The tithe-holders in Wroughton were the provost of Eton and his lessee Anthony Bathe, the rector of Wroughton, and the vicar of Wroughton; and in Uffcott, the master of the hospital of St. Nicholas, Salisbury, and his lessee Frances Post and the vicar of Broad Hinton.

Roads 10 public roads, 2 public bridle ways and private roads, 1 private road, 3 public footpaths. Anthony Bathe of Elcombe appointed surveyor of public roads by the commissioners at £10 per annum.

Finance £2,079 2*s*. 11*d*.

Map James Jennings, May 1797 (W.R.O. 551/115). Elcombe only, with three detached pieces. Villages of Elcombe and Uffcott. Allottees and allotments shown; a schedule with allotments and old inclosures.

Schedules (1) Old inclosures exonerated from tithes. (2) Amount of expenses to be paid by copyholders and percentages to be paid in addition to their rents. (3) Amount of money received and paid my Mr. James Bradford, clerk to the commissioners.

See also No. 205.

Notes The governors of the Charterhouse claimed exemption from tithes except for two small moduses. The commissioners upheld the claim, deducting only the equivalent of the two moduses and allotting it to the rector.

207 WYLYE [2,314 a.]

Act General, 6 & 7 W.IV c.115. *Award* 5 Sept. 1861 (enrolled 20 Aug. 1866), W.R.O. V 187. *Commissioners* William Robson of Wilton (replacing William Woodcock, d. 1843); James Poole of Sherborne. *Umpire* William Thring (never called on to act, and died in 1852).

Lord of Manor Robert Herbert, earl of Pembroke.

Rector Joseph Stockwell (succeeding Francis Baker).

Area 1,551 a. [1,352 a.].

Allotments 7. Public: 1 chalk pit for the tenants; 1 watering place 1 a. Earl of Pembroke 1,237 a. (including lease, Thomas Barnes 50 a.; lease and copy, William Perrior 526 a.; Ann and Diana Poticary 86 a.; John Waters junior; William Dowty; John Swayne; Stephen Titt; Joseph Titt; William Thompson); Elizabeth Small 90 a.; John Davis 16 a.; rector of Wylye; John Waters junior. *Fencing* general and on map.

Roads 3 public roads, 7 private roads; 1 road altered.

Map Poole and Newman, Sherborne 1861. Allotments numbered only. Whole parish and village shown and fencing duties.

Schedule Rate for repair of private road expressed as a proportion of £1.

See also No. 91.

Note Sheep bridge to be erected on private road No. 2.

APPENDIX 1

WILTSHIRE INCLOSURE AWARDS AND AGREEMENTS IN THE WILTSHIRE RECORD OFFICE

W.R.O.	
1 & 2	Purton (Great Purton, Purton Keynes, and Purton Pouchers)
3	Sherston Magna
4	Highworth (Broad Blunsdon)
5	Chiseldon (Badbury)
6	Heddington
7	Enford (Compton)
8	Liddington
9 & 10	Bremhill
11	Pewsey (1777)
12	Chiseldon
13	Bishop's Cannings (Coate)
14	Ogbourne St. Andrew
15	Wanborough
16	Charlton St. Peter
17	Kingston Deverill
18	Market Lavington
19	Patney
20	Milton Lilborne
21	Erlestoke
22	Chicklade
23	Warminster and Corsley
24	Stanton St. Quintin
25	Heytesbury
26	Homington
27	West Harnham
28	Odstock
29	Netherhampton
30	Colerne
31	Netheravon
32 & 33	Road or Rode
34 & 35	Little Somerford
36 (& 52)	Durnford (North End and Hungerford Durnford)
37	Urchfont and Beechingstoke
V 38	Alvediston, Bishopstone, Bower Chalke, Broad Chalke, Ebbesborne Wake, Fifield Bavant, Fovant, and Swallowcliffe
39	Idmiston
40	Cricklade (Great and Little Chelworth)

W.R.O.	
41	Sherrington
42	Ogbourne St. George
43	Longbridge Deverill
44	Netheravon (Chisenbury de la Folly)
45	Fittleton
46	Keevil
47	Wroughton
48	Wroughton (Elcombe and Uffcott)
49	Stratton St. Margaret
50	Berwick St. James
51	Berwick St. John
52 (& 36)	Durnford (North End and Hungerford Durnford)
53	Fisherton Anger
54	Winterbourne Earls
55	Market Lavington (Easterton)
56	All Cannings
57	Knook
58	Purton
59	Shrewton
60	East Knoyle (1799)
61	West Overton (West Overton, Overton Heath, and Clatford Park)
62	Sutton Veny
63	Great and Little Cheverell
64	Whiteparish
65	Wilsford (North Wilts.) (Manningford Bohun)
66	Upavon
67	Upton Scudamore
68	Great Bedwyn
V 69	Somerford Keynes (in Glos. since 1896)
70	Lea and Cleverton
71	Fisherton Delamere
72	Rushall
73	Shalbourne and Oxenwood
74	Stratford sub Castle and Milford
75	North Bradley and Southwick

W.R.O.	
V 76	Westbury and Bratton and Dilton
77	Chirton
78	Wilsford (North Wilts.)
79	Enford (Coombe, Fifield, and East Chisenbury)
80	Norton Bavant
81	Great Wishford
82	Fisherton Delamere (Bapton)
83 (& V85)	Downton (Charlton)
84	West Kington
V85 (& 83)	Downton (Charlton)
86	Manningford Bruce
V 87	West Wellow (in Hants since 1894)
88	Biddestone
89	Bishop's Cannings, Chittoe, and Marden
90	Sutton Mandeville
91	Bishopstone (North Wilts.)
92	Nettleton
V 93	Melksham and Seend
V 94	Barford St. Martin
95	Avebury
96	Alderbury
97	Bromham
98	Great Somerford
99	Great Bedwyn (Marten)
100	West Grimstead
101 & 102	Trowbridge and Hilperton
103	Stapleford
104	Wintebourne Stoke
105	Chitterne
106	Coombe Bissett
V 107	Steeple Ashton
V 108	Alderbury (Pitton and Farley)
109	Bishop's Cannings (Bourton, Easton, Horton, Nursteed, and Wick)
V 110	Calne
111	Boyton
112 & 113	Stockton
114	Laverstock
115	Bishopstrow
V 116	Mere
117	West Overton (East and West Overton and Fyfield)
118	Wootton Bassett
119	Froxfield and Milton Lilborne
120	Broad Hinton and Clyffe Pypard
121	Corsham
V 122	Downton
V 123	Rodbourne Cheney
124, 125, & 126	Wingfield
127	Tilshead
128	Burbage, Collingbourne Kingston, and Poulton
129	Cherhill
130	Pewsey (1826)
131	Brinkworth
132	Hankerton
133	Enford (Littlecot)
134	Ham
135 & 136	Codford St. Peter (Ashton Giffard)
137 & 138	Codford St. Peter
139 & 140	Upton Lovel
V 141	Cranborne Chase
142	Malmesbury
143	Cricklade (Great and Little Chelworth and Braydon Forest)
144 & 145	Durrington
146	Poulton (in Glos. since 1844)
147 & 148	Durnford (South End and Salterton and Newtown)
V 149	Tisbury
V 150	Dinton and Teffont Magna
151	Langley Burrell
152	Compton Bassett
V 153	Steeple Langford (Hanging Langford)
154	Fittleton (Haxton)
155	West Lavington
156	North Newnton
157	Allington
158	Berwick St. Leonard
159	Potterne
160	Crudwell
161	Christian Malford
V 162	Figheldean
163	Wootton Rivers
V 164	Codford St. Mary
165	Sherston Parva
166	Britford
V 167	Downton (Wick)
V 168	Littleton Drew
V 169	West Dean
V 170	Idmiston (Porton)
171	Winterbourne Dauntsey
172	Ludgershall
L 173	Maddington
L 174	Bradford on Avon (Trowle Common)
175	Winterbourne Gunner
176	Maddington (Homanton Fields)
177	Enford (East Chisenbury)
178	Shorncote (in Glos. since 1896)
V 179	Wilton, Burcombe, Fugglestone, and Netherhampton
180	Landford (1860)

W.R.O.	
181	Bower Chalke (1860)
L 182	Landford (1861)
183	Edington
184	Marston Maysey
185	Boscombe
L 186	Steeple Langford
V 187	Wylye
V 188	Broad Chalke and Chilmark
189	Bradford on Avon (Holt)
190	Donhead St. Mary
191	East Knoyle (1867)
192	Chippenham and Langley Burrell
193	Seagry and Christian Malford

Q.S. enrolled deeds 60–61
Purton (Momes Lease)

Acc 7/22	Highworth (Eastrop, Westrop, and Hampton)
Acc 154/2 & 3	Ramsbury
Acc 154/5	Aldbourne
Acc 248/159	Market Lavington (Easterton) map
Acc 304/1	Chute
Acc 359/21	Ashton Keynes (Leigh)
Acc 374/5	Ashton Keynes
Acc 374/16	Minety
Acc 402/3	Chirton (Conock)
Acc 425/1	Wilcot
Acc 490/1019	Stanton St. Quintin
Acc 542	Chippenham (Tytherton Lucas and Langley Burrell)
Acc 551/114	Wroughton
Acc 551/115	Wroughton (Elcombe and Uffcott)
Acc 735/43	Chilton Foliat
Acc 748/5	Bradford on Avon (Bradford Leigh Common, Forwards Common)
Acc 836	Market Lavington map
Acc 845	Longbridge Deverill map

Sav.	Great Bedwyn (Crofton Fields)
	Little Bedwyn
	Collingbourne Ducis
	Collingbourne Kingston (Aughton)
	Collingbourne Kingston (Collingbourne Vallance)
	Mildenhall

APPENDIX II

SELECT LIST OF PRINCIPAL ALLOTTEES

WITH ACREAGES ALLOTTED

The following list indicates the totals of allotments, in all the awards and agreements extracted above, to peers, dignitaries of the church, ecclesiastical and other foundations, and families of gentry to whom, in most instances, allotments were made under more than one award or agreement.

	acres
Earl of Pembroke	24,260
Bishop of Salisbury	11,135
Marquess of Bath	8,830
Dean and chapter of Salisbury, and prebends	8,121
Marquess of Ailesbury	6,901
Wyndham family	5,848
Earl of Radnor	5,819
Hicks Beach family	5,691
Alexander Baring	3,411
Paul Cobb Methuen	3,401
Duke of Marlborough	3,217
Ashe (*later* Holmes) à Court family	3,021
Dugdale Astley	2,979
Winchester College	2,417
Earl of Malmesbury	1,964
Dean and chapter of Winchester	1,897
Nicholas Nicholas	1,788
Lord Chedworth	1,692
Prince of Wales	1,587
Harry Biggs	1,555
Eleanor Sutton	1,400
Bishop of Winchester	1,398
Lord Churchill	1,352
Heytesbury almshouse	1,276
John Benett	1,275
Duke of Somerset	1,232
Marquess of Lansdowne	1,191
King's College, Cambridge	1,181
William Temple	1,036
Earl of Ilchester	1,026
Charterhouse hospital	975
Earl Nugent	953
Lord Ashburton	862
Lord Rivers	759
Earl of Suffolk	716
Adam Williamson	714
Dowager Lady Nelson	689
Long family	652
Ewelme almshouse	633
George Matcham	555
Somerset hospital	513
Earl de Grey	513
Merton College, Oxford	482
Chafyn Grove family	473
New College, Oxford	423
Earl of Abingdon	364
Eton College	357
Corpus Christi College, Oxford	348
Duke of Montagu	347
Earl Grosvenor	343
St. Nicholas's Hospital, Salisbury	329
Dean of Salisbury	292
Bishop of Oxford	283
Earl of Shaftesbury	278
Magdalen College, Oxford	265
Dean and chapter of Gloucester	242
Sir A. Bayntun-Rolt	218
Joshua Smith	154
Lord Holland	142
Duke of Beaufort	134
Fulwar Craven	133
Joseph Neeld	124
Dean and canons of Windsor	116
Earl Manvers	111

GENERAL INDEX

References are to the numbers of the abstracts, not to pages, except for a few references to the Introduction which are preceded by 'p.'

The following groups of references to place-names are not included in the index: field-names and other minor local names; places named only to indicate direction or location (e.g. Calne in no. 34); places named only as being excluded (e.g. Pitton in no. 2); places named only as subject to an inclosure Act (e.g. Winterbourne Earls in no. 4). Subheadings are given under place-names only where the references for the subheadings are different from those for the main name (e.g., there is no subheading for vicar under Aldbourne, but there is one under Chiseldon); similarly, cross-reference is not made from the name of a parish to that of a hamlet unless there are references for the hamlet that are not given for the parish. The county in which a place outside Wiltshire lies is given after the name where it appears in its alphabetical position, and not elsewhere.

Under a surname, all the references to the same forename have been grouped together, except that references to the name modified in the abstracts by the addition of an address, office, etc., or by seniority have been separately indexed. Therefore it does not follow that all the references grouped after a name are to a single person, or that all the references to one man are in a single group: for example, the references that follow the first Thomas Davis of the four distinguished in the index may be—indeed probably are—to two different men, and there may be overlaps between that sub-entry and the three that follow it. The title 'Rev.' is omitted in the names of clerical incumbents; lay rectors are not indexed as such. A person other than a peer whose forename is not given in the abstract is indexed at the end of the entry for his surname, with a dash (——) in place of his forename, or, if he has one, a title. Peers are indexed under their surnames, whether or not the surnames are given in the abstracts. References to devisees, executors, feoffees, guardians, heirs, representatives, and trustees are not distinguished.

The Introduction has been indexed only selectively, the appendixes not at all.

The index does NOT indicate where a name occurs more than once in an abstract.

WILTSHIRE RECORD SOCIETY

(As at 31 December 1969)

PRIVATE MEMBERS

AILESBURY, The Marquess of, D.L., J.P., Sturmy House, Savernake Forest, Marlborough

ALLEN, N., 46 Westland Road, Faringdon, Berks.

APPLEBY, E. C., 1 Jacks Lane, Frome, Som.

ARCHER, P. J., Cotswold View, Old Station Road, Highworth

AUSTIN, Mrs. D. M., Woolcombe Farm, Toller Porcorum, Dorchester, Dorset

AWDRY, Mrs. R. W., M.B.E., Haven Court, Cary Park, Babbacombe, Devon

BADENI, The Countess, Norton Manor, Malmesbury

BARNES, C. Egbert, J.P., Hungerdown House, Seagry, Chippenham

BARRINGTON-BROWN, C., Tapshays, Marnhull, Dorset

BATTEN POOLL, Captain A. H., V.C., M.C., Ugborough House, Ivybridge, Devon

BEATTIE, J. M., Dept of History, University of Toronto, Canada

BERRETT, A. M., 65 Mandeville Road, Southgate, London N.14

BIRLEY, N. P., D.S.O., M.C., Hyde Leaze, Hyde Lane, Marlborough

BLADON, Major F. McK., Middledean, Swallowcliffe, Salisbury

BLAKE, T. N., Glebe Farm, Tilshead, Salisbury

BLEASE, H. F., 5 Victoria Road, Trowbridge

BONNEY, Mrs. H. M., Flint Cottage, Netton, Salisbury

BRICE, G. R., Branchways, Willett Way, Petts Wood, Kent

BROOKE, Mrs. T. C., Sandfield, Potterne, Devizes

BROOKE-LITTLE, J. P., M.V.O., Richmond Herald of Arms, College of Arms, Queen Victoria Street, London E.C.4

BROWN, W. E., The Firs, Beckhampton, Marlborough

BUCKERIDGE, J. M., 104 Beacon Road, Loughborough, Leics.

BUCKLAND, L. J., Twelvetrees, Amesbury, Salisbury

BURGE, Miss H. M., The Old Rectory, Huish, Marlborough

BURGE, S. F. M., The Old Rectory, Huish, Marlborough

BURNETT BROWN, Miss Janet M., Lacock Abbey, Chippenham

BUXTON, E. J. M., Cole Park, Malmesbury

CAREW-HUNT, Miss P. H., Cowleaze, Edington, Westbury

CARTER, Miss N. M. G., Gatehouse, Cricklade

CARTWRIGHT, Miss Elizabeth, Iford Manor, Bradford on Avon

CLANCHY, M. T., Dept. of History, The University, Glasgow W.2

CLARK, Miss G. F., 38 Ormonde Terrace, London N.W.8

CLAY, Dr. R. C. C., Manor House, Fovant, Salisbury

CODRINGTON, Miss Nancy E., Wroughton House, Swindon

COKER, John, 64 Warwick Crest, Arthur Road, Edgbaston, Birmingham 15

CRITTALL, Miss Elizabeth, 16 Downside Crescent, London N.W.3

DANIELS, C. G., 81 Goffenton Drive, Oldbury Court, Fishponds, Bristol

DIBBEN, A. A., 222 King Street, Hammersmith, London W.6

DOYLE, Leslie, Cheviot, Clay Lane, Wythenshawe, Manchester 23

DUGDALE, H. J., Apple Tree Cottage, Wilton, Grafton, Marlborough

DYKE, P. J., 35 Buckleigh Avenue, Merton Park, London S.W.20

ECCLES, The Viscount, K.C.V.O., P.C., Dean Farm, Chute, Andover, Hants

EDWARDS, W. A., Long Acres, Everleigh, Marlborough

ELLIS, R. L., 5 Avebury Park, Lovelace Gardens, Surbiton, Surrey

ELRINGTON, C. R., Institute of Historical Research, University of London, Senate House, London W.C.1

FANE, Mrs. Edmund, Boyton Manor, Warminster

FILBY, P. W., Librarian, Maryland Historical Society, 201 West Monument Street, Baltimore, Md. 21201, U.S.A.

FLOYD, Lt.-Col. Charles, O.B.E., Great Chalfield Manor, Melksham

FORBES, Miss Katherine G., Bury House, Codford, Warminster

FRY, Mrs. P. M., 18 Pulteney Street, Bath

FULLER, Major Sir Gerard, Bt., Neston Park, Corsham

GIBBON, Canon Geoffrey, The Vicarage, Somerford Keynes, Cirencester, Glos.

GIMSON, H. M., Grey Wethers, Stanton St. Bernard, Marlborough

GODDARD, Mrs. G. H., The Boot, Scholard's Lane, Ramsbury, Marlborough

GOULD, C. P., 1200 Old Mill Road, San Marino, California, U.S.A.

HALCOMB, R. F., 75 High Street, Market Lavington, Devizes

HALLWORTH, Frederick, Northcote, Westbury Road, Bratton, Westbury

HAM, Chester W., Jr., 187 Rounds Avenue, Providence, Rhode Island 02907, U.S.A.

HARFIELD, Capt. A. G., 19th Signal Regt., R.A.F. Changi, c/o G.P.O. Singapore

HARFIELD, Mrs. A. G., 19th Signal Regt., R.A.F. Changi, c/o G.P.O., Singapore

HATCHWELL, R. C., The Old Rectory, Little Somerford, Chippenham

HAWKINS, M. J., 121 High Street, Lewes, Sussex

HAYMAN, The Revd. P. E. C., The Vicarage, Rogate, Petersfield, Hants

HEDGES, R. K., Charlton House, Shaftesbury, Dorset

HOARE, H. P. R., Gasper House, Stourton, Warminster

HOBBS, Miss N., 140 Western Road, Sompting, Lancing, Sussex

HODGETT, G. A. J., King's College, London W.C.2

HUFFMAN, Mrs. Percival, Longbridge Deverill House, Warminster

HURSTFIELD, Prof. Joel, 7 Glenilla Road, London N.W.3

JACKSON, R. H., 17 Queens Road, Tisbury, Salisbury

JENNINGS, R. A. U., Newlands, 46 London Road, Salisbury

JEREMY, David J., Curator, Merrimack Valley Textile Museum, North Andover, Mass. 01845, U.S.A.

JOHN, D. Murray, O.B.E., Civic Offices, Swindon

JOLLIFFE, M., Fourah Bay College, Freetown, Sierra Leone

JONES, The Revd. Kingsley C., The Vicarage Flat, Cop Lane, Penwortham, Preston, Lancs.

KEATINGE, Lady Teffont, Salisbury
KEMPSON, E. G. H., Sun Cottage, Hyde Lane, Marlborough
KNIGHT, Eric R., 5 Linley Close, Swindon
KOMATSU, Prof. Y., Institute of European Economic History, Waseda University, Tokyo 160, Japan.

LANGTON, Sir Henry, D.S.O., D.F.C., D.L., Overtown House, Wroughton, Swindon
LANSDOWN, Michael J., 37 Hilperton Road, Trowbridge
LATHAM, Mrs. W. J., Dark Lane House, Marlborough
LEVER, R. E., Reads Close, Teffont Magna, Salisbury
LITTLE, J. E., The Pantiles, Chapel Lane, Uffington, Berks.
LONDON, Miss V. C. M., Underholt, Westwood Road, Bidston, Birkenhead

MACKINTOSH, Duncan, C.B.E., Etchilhampton House, Etchilhampton, Devizes
MANN, Miss Julia de L., The Cottage, Bowerhill, Melksham
MARGADALE, The Lord, Fonthill House, Tisbury
MASTERS, H. A. C., Hossil Lane, Stanton Fitzwarren, Swindon
METHUEN, The Lord, Corsham Court, Corsham
METHUEN, The Hon. Mrs. Anthony, J.P., Ivy House, Corsham
MILLBOURN, Sir Eric, C.M.G., Conkwell Grange, Limpley Stoke, Bath
MITTON, A. W. D., The Dungeon, 239 Earl's Court Road, London S.W.5.
MOODY, G. C., Montrose, Shaftesbury Road, Wilton, Salisbury
MORRIS, Miss Bronwen E., 9 Cleveland Gardens, Trowbridge
MORRISON, The Hon. Charles, M.P., Fyfield Manor, Marlborough
MOULTON, Alexander E., The Hall, Bradford on Avon

NAN KIVELL, R. de C., 20 Cork Street, London W.1
NEWALL, R. S., Avon Cottage, Lower Woodford, Salisbury
NORTHAMPTON, Emma, Marchioness of, O.B.E., The Curatage, Horningsham, Warminster

PAFFORD, J. H. P., Hillside, Allington Park, Bridport, Dorset
PASKIN, Lady, Wishford, Salisbury
PERRY, Simon H., 117 London Road, Kettering, Northants.
PETO, Brig. C. H. M., D.S.O., D.L., Lockeridge House, Marlborough
PETO, Lt.-Col. Sir Michael, Bt., Manor House, Yatton Keynell, Chippenham
PONTING, K. G., Becketts House, Edington, Westbury
POTHECARY, S. G., 41 Australian Avenue, Salisbury
POWELL, W. R., 2 Glenmead, Shenfield, Romford
PUGH, Prof. Ralph B., 67 Southwood Park, London N.6

RAMSAY, G. D., St. Edmund Hall, Oxford
RATHBONE, Maurice G., Craigleith, Snarlton Lane, Melksham Forest
RAYBOULD, Miss Frances, 20 Radnor Road, Salisbury
REEVES, Dr. Marjorie E., 38 Norham Road, Oxford
REYNOLDS, A., The White House, Riverfield Road, Staines, Middlesex
ROGERS, K. H., Silverthorne Cottage, Erlestoke, Devizes
ROOKE, Mrs. R. E. P., The Ivy, Chippenham
ROOKE, Miss Susan F., The Ivy, Chippenham
ROSS, Harry, Leighton Villa, Wellhead Lane, Westbury
ROWE, Mrs. H. M., 85 Charnhill Drive, Mangotsfield, Bristol
RUNDLE, Miss Penelope, 11 West Street, Wilton, Salisbury

SANDELL, Richard E., Hillside, 64 Devizes Road, Potterne
SAWYER, L. F. T., 51 Sandridge Road, Melksham
SHADBOLT, Mrs. L. G., Birkhall House, High Kelling, Holt, Norfolk
SHEWRING, Dennis S., 4 Clifton Street, Treorchy, Rhondda, Glam.
SOMERSET, The Duke of, D.L., Bradley House, Maiden Bradley, Warminster
STEDMAN, A. R., 9 The Green, Aldbourne, Marlborough
STEELE, Mrs. N. D., 41 Castle Road, Salisbury
STEVENSON, Miss J. H., Institute of Historical Research, University of London, Senate House, London W.C.1
STEWART, Miss K. Pamela, Moxham Villa, 57 Lower Road, Bemerton, Salisbury

STRATTON, J. M., Manor House Farm, Stockton, Warminster

STYLES, Philip, 21 Castle Lane, Warwick

TANNER, Miss J. M., 155 Shrivenham Road, Swindon

TAYLOR, Christopher C., Royal Commission on Historical Monuments (England), The Lodge, Anstey Hall, Trumpington, Cambridge

THOMPSON, Mrs. M. W., Box Cottage, Wilcot, Pewsey

TILLEY, Edward William, 23 Wardwick, Derby

TWINE, S. W., 2 Elgin Road, Wood Green, London N.22

TWISS, J. C., 9 Oak Lane, Easterton, Devizes

VERNON, Mrs. B., Keevil Manor, Trowbridge

VERNON, Miss Thelma E., Dyer's Leaze, Lacock, Chippenham

VINER, Brig. G. A., O.B.E., Anchor Cottage, Chidham, Chichester, Sussex

WADE, Miss Elmira M., O.B.E., Bridge Cottage, Lacock, Chippenham

WALKER, Revd. J. G., Buttermere Hill, Churt, Farnham, Surrey

WATKINS, W. T., Carn Ingli, 16 Westbury Road, Warminster

WEINSTOCK, Arnold, Bowden Park, Lacock, Chippenham

WIGAN, Mrs. D., Fifteenth Century Cottage, Etchilhampton, Devizes

WILLAN, Group Capt. F. A., D.L., Bridges, Teffont, Salisbury

WILLIAMS, Neville J., 57 Rotherwick Road, Hampstead Garden Suburb, London N.W.11

WILLIAMS, Major R. S. A., Little Bridge House, Chinnock, Crewkerne, Som.

WILLOUGHBY, R. W. H., Langford Way, Berwick St. James, Salisbury

WILTSHIRE, Julian M., Ashlyns Cottage, Lybury Lane, Redbourn, Herts.

WIMHURST, N. E. P., The Villas, Etchilhampton, Devizes

WORTHINGTON, B. S., Vale Lodge, Colnbrook, Bucks.

YOUNG, C. L. R., 25 Staveley Road, Chiswick, London W.4

YOUNG, W. E. V., Gawens, Ebbesborne Wake, Salisbury

UNITED KINGDOM INSTITUTIONS

Aberdeen. King's College Library
Aberystwyth. National Library of Wales
,, University College General Library
Bangor. University College of North Wales
Bath. General Reference Library
Birmingham. Central Public Library
,, University Library, Edgbaston
Bridgwater. Somerset County Library
Brighton. University of Sussex Library, Falmer
Bristol. City of Bristol Library
,, University Library
Cambridge. University Library
Devizes. Wiltshire Archaeological and Natural History Society
Dorchester. County of Dorset Library
Edinburgh. National Library of Scotland
,, University Library
Exeter. University Library
Glasgow. University Library
Gloucester. Bristol and Gloucestershire Archaeological Society
Hull. University of Kingston upon Hull Library
Leeds. University Library
Leicester. University Library
Liverpool. University Library
London. British Museum
,, College of Arms
,, Guildhall Library
,, Inner Temple Library
,, Institute of Historical Research
,, London Library
,, Public Record Office
,, Royal Historical Society
,, Society of Antiquaries
,, Society of Genealogists
,, University of London Library
,, City of Westminster Public Library
Manchester. John Rylands Library
Marlborough. Adderley Library, Marlborough College
Norwich. University of East Anglia Library
Nottingham. University Library

Oxford. Bodleian Library
„ New College Library
Reading. Central Library
„ University Library
St. Andrews. University Library
Salisbury. Bourne Valley Historical Society, Allington
„ History Dept., College of Sarum St. Michael
„ Diocesan Record Office
„ The Museum
„ City of New Sarum Public Library
„ Salisbury & South Wilts. College of Further Education
Sheffield. University Library
Southampton. University Library
Swansea. University College of Swansea Library
Swindon. Borough of Swindon Public Library
„ Swindon College Library
Taunton. Somerset Archaeological and Natural History Society
Trowbridge. The Tabard Press
„ Wiltshire County Library
„ Wiltshire Record Office, County Hall
The Wiltshire Times & News
York. University of York Library

OVERSEAS INSTITUTIONS

AUSTRALIA

Canberra. National Library of Australia
Melbourne. Victoria State Library
Sydney. Fisher Library, University of Sydney

CANADA

Downsview, Ontario. York Universities Libraries
Kingston, Ontario. The Douglas Library, Queen's University
London, Ontario. The Lawson Memorial Library, University of Western Ontario
Peterborough, Ontario. Dept. of History, Trent University
Toronto, Ontario. University of Toronto Library
Montreal, Quebec. Sir George Williams University Library
Ottawa. Carleton University Library

REPUBLIC OF IRELAND

Dublin. National Library of Ireland
„ Trinity College Library

JAPAN

Osaka. Institute of Economic History, Kansai University
Sendai. Institute of Economic History, Tohoku University

SWEDEN

Upsala. Kungl Universitetets Bibliotek (Royal University Library)

UNITED STATES OF AMERICA

Ann Arbor, Mich. General Library, University of Michigan
Baltimore, Md. Peabody Institute of the City of Baltimore
Bloomington, Ind. Indiana University Library
Boston, Mass. Public Library of the City of Boston
„ „ New England Historic Genealogical Society
Boulder, Col. University of Colorado Libraries
Buffalo, N.Y. The Lockwood Memorial Library, State University of New York at Buffalo
Cambridge, Mass. Harvard Law School Library
„ „ Harvard College Library
Chicago, Ill. University of Chicago Library
„ „ Newberry Library
Cleveland, Ohio. Public Library
De Kalb, Ill. Northern University of Illinois, Dept. of History
East Lansing, Mich. Michigan State University Library
Haverford, Pa. Haverford College
Iowa City. State University of Iowa Library
Ithaca, N.Y. Cornell University Library
Los Angeles, Cal. Public Library of Los Angeles
„ „ „ University Research Library, University of California
Minneapolis, Md. Dept. of History, Minnesota University.
Newark, Del. University of Delaware Library

New Haven, Conn. Yale University Library
New York. Columbia University of the City of New York
,, ,, Public Library, City of New York
Notre Dame, Ind. Notre Dame University Memorial Library
Philadelphia, Pa. Pennsylvania University Library
Princeton, N.J. Princeton University Library
Salt Lake City, Utah. Genealogical Society of Utah
San Marino, Cal. Henry E. Huntington Library
Stanford, Cal. Stanford University Library
Urbana, Ill. University of Illinois Library
Washington, D.C. Library of Congress
Winston-Salem, N.C. Wake Forest College Library

LIST OF PUBLICATIONS

The Wiltshire Record Society was founded in 1937, as the Records Branch of the Wiltshire Archaeological and Natural History Society, to promote the publication of the documentary sources for the history of Wiltshire. The annual subscription is £2. In return, a member receives a volume each year. Prospective members should apply to Miss Thelma E. Vernon, Dyer's Leaze, Lacock, Chippenham, Wiltshire. Many more members are needed.

The following volumes have been published. Price to members £2 and to non-members £2 10s., postage extra. Available from the Hon. Treasurer, Mr. M. J. Lansdown, 37 Hilperton Road, Trowbridge, Wiltshire.

I *Abstract of Feet of Fines relating to Wiltshire for the reigns of Edward I and Edward II.* Edited by R. B. Pugh (1939)

II *Accounts of the Parliamentary Garrisons of Great Chalfield and Malmesbury, 1645–6.* Edited by J. H. P. Pafford (1940). Illustrated

III *Calendar of Antrobus Deeds before 1625.* Edited by R. B. Pugh (1947)

IV *Minutes of Proceedings in Sessions, 1563, 1574–92.* Edited by H. C. Johnson (1949)

V *List of Records of Wiltshire Boroughs before 1836.* Edited by M. G. Rathbone (1951)

VI *The Trowbridge Woollen Industry as illustrated by the Stock Books of John and Thomas Clark, 1804–24.* Edited by R. F. Beckingsale (1951). Illustrated

VII *Guild Stewards' Book of the Borough of Calne, 1561–1688.* Edited by A. W. Mabbs (1953)

VIII *Andrews and Dury's Map of Wiltshire, 1773.* A reduced facsimile in 'atlas' form, with an introduction by Elizabeth Crittall (1952)

IX *Surveys of the Manors of Philip, First Earl of Pembroke and Montgomery, 1631–2.* Edited by E. Kerridge (1953)

X *Two Sixteenth Century Taxation Lists, 1545 and 1576.* Edited by G. D. Ramsay (1954)

XI *Wiltshire Quarter Sessions and Assizes, 1736.* Edited by J. P. M. Fowle (1955)

XII *Collectanea.* Edited by N. J. Williams, with a foreword by T. F. T. Plucknett (1956)

XIII *Progress Notes of Warden Woodward for the Wiltshire Estates of New College, 1659–75.* Edited by R. L. Rickard (1957). Illustrated

XIV *Accounts and Surveys of the Wiltshire Lands of Adam de Stratton, 1268–86.* Edited by M. W. Farr (1959)

XV *Tradesmen in Early-Stuart Wiltshire: A Miscellany.* Edited by N. J. Williams (1960)

XVI *Crown Pleas of the Wiltshire Eyre, 1249.* Edited by C. A. F. Meekings (1961)

XVII *Wiltshire Apprentices and their Masters, 1710–60.* Edited by Christabel Dale (1961)

XVIII *Hemingby's Register.* Edited by Helena M. Chew (1963)

XIX *Documents Illustrating the Wiltshire Textile Trades in the Eighteenth Century.* Edited by Julia de L. Mann (1964)

XX *The Diary of Thomas Naish.* Edited by Doreen Slatter (1965). Illustrated

XXI, XXII *The Rolls of Highworth Hundred, 1275–87.* Edited by Brenda Farr (1966, 1968). Map

XXIII *The Earl of Hertford's Lieutenancy Papers, 1603–12.* Edited by W. P. D. Murphy (1969). Illustrated

XXIV *Court Rolls of the Wiltshire Manors of Adam de Stratton.* Edited by R. B. Pugh (1970)

VOLUMES IN PREPARATION

Civil Pleas of the Wiltshire Eyre, 1249, edited by M. T. Clanchy; *Wiltshire Extents for Debts*, edited by Angela Conyers; *Wiltshire Returns to the Bishop's Visitation Queries, 1783*, edited by Mary Ransome; *Salisbury General Entry Books*, edited by Alan Crossley; *The Wiltshire Forest Eyre, 1257*, edited by N. J. Williams; *The Charters of Lacock Abbey*, edited by K. H. Rogers; *Abstract of Feet of Fines relating to Wiltshire for the reign of Edward III*, edited by C. R. Elrington; *The Edington Cartulary*, edited by Janet Stevenson.

A leaflet giving fuller details may be obtained from Miss Vernon.